40TH ANNIVERSARY

Chord Systems

Sound and Structure

For Guitar

LEON WHITE

© 1979 - 2019 Leon R. White · All Rights Reserved · info@sixstringlogic.com

Version 4.01

Acknowledgments

DEDICATED TO JUDY WHITE

Graphic Guidance and Cover Design: Jeffrey D. Brown

Musical Inspiration - Ted Greene, Mike Warren, George Van Eps

Proof Reading - Tony Mandracchia, Robert S. Anderson, David Godfrey, and Judy White

Special thanks to my students and readers for inspiration and advice, and to John Pisano for his kind words that inspired this edition.

Contents

Acknowledgments — 2
Preface — 7
   Introduction — 7
   Overview of the Book — 7
Getting Started — 9
   Where Musical Styles Can Be Found In This Book — 9
   About the Diagrams — 10
   Rhythm Notation — 10
   Chord Terminology — 11
   Our First Technique -"Double Stops" — 12
The Stringset - Simplifying Everything — 14
   Musical, Visual, and Physical — 14
   Musical Intervals and Stringsets — 15

Section 1 - Six Note and Five Note Chords — 16

Open Chords Reviewed — 16
   Basic Open Chords — 16
   Open Chords from Each Root and Family — 17
Chord Names for Advanced Chords — 18
   Chord Families — 19
   Minor Chord Family — 19
   Major Chord Family — 19
   Dominant Chord Family — 20
   Roman Numeral Introduction — 20
More Advanced Open Chords — 21
   Examples — 21
   Sample Rock Progressions — 23
Barre Chords: The First Movable Fingerings — 24
   Open Chords Re-Fingered To Be Movable — 24
   The Dreaded "C" Shape Barre Chord — 26
   Movable 9th Chords — 26
   Additional Barre Chords — 27
   Progression Examples for Barre Chords — 28

Section 2 - Four Note Chords — 30

Four Note Movable Fingerings — 30

Overview and Logic	30
The Theory of Four Note Seventh Chords	31
Systematic Inversions	32

Seventh Chord Inversions - 4321 Stringset — 33

Introductory Examples	33
The First Systematic Inversions	34
Progression Examples	36
Comparing the 4321 Systematic Inversions	40
4321 Chord Licks	41

Essential Chord Fingerings on 4321 — 43

Comparing the mi7 and mi7♭5	43
Using the Progressions with the Essential Fingerings	44
The Major Chord Family	45
The Minor Chord Family	47
Minor Chord Family Examples	50
The Dominant Chord Family	51

The 6432 Stringset — 53

Introductory Examples	53
Systematic Inversions	54
Progression Examples	55
Comparing the 4321 and 6432 Stringsets	58

Essential Chord Fingerings on 6432 — 59

The Major Chord Family	59
The Minor Chord Family	61
The Dominant Chord Family	64

The 5432 Stringset — 66

Introductory Examples	66
Systematic Inversions	67
Progression Examples	68
Comparing the 5432 Stringset and Barre Chords	70
Comparing the 5432 and 4321 Fingerings	71

Essential Fingerings on 5432 — 73

The Major Chord Family	73
The Minor Chord Family	75
The Dominant Chord Family	77

The 5321 Stringset — 80

Introductory Examples	80

Systematic Inversions	81
Progression Examples	82
Comparing 5321 and 6432 Fingerings	84

Essential Chord Fingerings on 5321 — 85

The Major Chord Family	85
The Minor Chord Family	87
The Dominant Chord Family	89

Strummable Altered Chord Fingerings — 91

The Major Chord Family	91
The Minor Chord Family	92
The Dominant Chord Family	93
Playing ii - V - I Progressions	96

Ambiguous Chords — 97

Fourths, Ninths, and Elevenths	97
Minor Seventh #5 Chords	98
Diminished Seventh Chord	99

Section 3 - Four Note Chords in Action — 100

Inversion Scales — 100

Major Seventh Chord Scale Examples	101
Chord Scales on Mixed Stringsets	102
Minor Seventh Chord Scale Examples	103
Chord Scale Progressions by Stringset	104

Inversion Scales in the Bass — 105

Walking Bass Lines	105
Mixed Stringset and Bass Lines	108
12 Bar Blues in G - Chord Bass Style	109

Section 4 - Three Note Chords: Triads — 111

Introductory Examples	111
Triad Rules	112
Adjacent String Triad Fingerings on the 321 Stringset	113
Triads on the 432 Stringset	114
Triads on the 543 Stringset	115
Triads on the 654 Stringset	116
Triad Licks	117
Triads in the Major Scale	119

Section 5 - Chord Substitution ... 121

   Overview of This Approach ... 121
   Enrichment Examples ... 122
   Chromatic Enrichment ... 123

Common Tone Chord Substitution ... 124

   Common Tone Chords from the Same Scale ... 124
   Chord Comparisons in the Major Scale ... 125

Common Tone Chord Substitution in Minor Scales ... 127

   The Melodic Minor Scale Common Tone Chords ... 129

Chromatic Common Tone Chord Substitution ... 130

   Common Tone Minor Seventh Flat Five Chords ... 131
   ♭5 Chromatic Common Tone Substitution ... 132
   Diminished Sevenths and the 7♭9 Chord ... 133
   Augmented Chord Substitution ... 135

Cycles in Chord Substitution ... 136

   Introduction ... 136
   Back Cycling Within a Major Key ... 139
   ♭5 Substitution and Half Steps ... 140
   Back Cycling Substitution Review ... 142
   Changing Tonality ... 151

Section 6 - References ... 154

Technique ... 154

   Left Hand Techniques ... 154
   Right Hand Techniques ... 154

Harmony Quick Reference ... 156

   The Chromatic Scale ... 156
   Major Scale Spellings and Seventh Chords ... 156
      Using the Table ... 156
   Spelling Triads and Seventh Chords ... 157
   Interval Names ... 158

Other Stringsets ... 159

Other Reference Materials ... 160

Preface

This book was first written in 1978 and published by Professional Music Products with the subtitle "Structure and Application." Several years later the original book was broken up into three volumes and a massive 288 page dictionary (Chord Systems Volumes One through Four).

I've decided to take advantage of all the great new technology for printing and publishing and re-release all that material as a single volume. More than that, however, I've clarified it substantially. The majority of topics in the original editions are included here along with most of the examples. However, the explanation and order of presentation have been revised to make the book easier to use, and the dictionary is not included because of size limitations.

The explanations continue to show

- how chords are *played*.
- how the chords are *learned*, and
- how the chords *relate to each other*.

There are now several different ways to use the book:

- Front to Back
- By Level
- By Musical Style
- By areas of interest. The table of contents is very detailed to help you find what you're interested in.

Introduction

The purpose of this book is to provide a consistent and cohesive method for learning about chords. The approach is intended to *cross levels, topics, and musical styles.* My goal is to show you a map of how all chords relate to each other - by sound, fingering, harmony, fingerboard location, and musical style. And then, to help you navigate through what interests you.

What has been lacking for many players is the discussion of the most fundamental musical components that should guide a player in learning chords. Two of these components are the sounds chords can provide, and the functional structure of chords, musically, and physically.

There are different paths through the book, so don't be afraid to make your own trail. You can work front to back, or jump into a topic. As you do, you'll begin to see new connections that accelerate your learning.

Overview of the Book

Essential ideas include chord families, stringsets, overlapping and related chords, passing tones, and right hand technique.

Chords can be thought to have three basic families of chord sounds:

- Major
- Minor
- Dominant

That is a good outline of all the thousands of sounds chords can make. Each of these three "chord families" contains a large group of chords that basically sound and function in similar ways.

Using a categorization like this allows us to break the seemingly massive topic of chords into smaller bites. Techniques discuss methods to finger and sound chords to get the most out of your music, and to show you what benefits a particular technique can provide.

One technique might help in one situation, while another fingering or technique might help play the same chord in a different situation.

Techniques for learning include mental and physical models that guitar players can use to learn, remember, and play chords. Recognizing similar visual shapes and their corresponding sounds is another way to remember chords. I've also tried to include all of those types of techniques. Some are specific to the type of guitar being played, and I've noted that where necessary.

Following is a graphic showing the various concepts together, and how they're delivered in the book.

As you'll see there are essential themes that travel through all sections of the book:
- The chords are organized from six string fingerings to four string and three string chords.
- The complexity starts with familiar diatonic sounds and progresses to more chromatic sounds.
- The techniques move from basic strumming to advanced right hand techniques.
- The musical application moves from basic accompaniment to solo guitar playing.

The "high leverage" ideas include
1. Using chord families to help learn sounds
2. Using the stringset idea to organize inversions, voicings, and right hand playing style
3. The application of basic harmony to link chords, fingerings, progressions and notes together in a simple manner.

The book is divided into six sections (including a reference section). The topics for each section are outlined below: The fundamental tools are shown *across* the sections.

Introduction

Section 1	Section 2	Section 3	Section 4	Section 5	Section 6
OPEN POSITIONS	Four Note Chords	Four Note Chords in Action	Triads	Chord Substitution	REFERENCES
Six String Chords	Four *String* Chords	Inversion Scales -Top Voice	Five Types Triads on Adjacent Strings	Common Tone Chord Substitution	Technique Chord Names Chord Spelling
Five String Chords	The Stringset Systematic Inversions	-Bass Voice (Walking Bass) Advanced Comping	Diatonic Triads Crossing Stringsets	Chromatic Common Tone Substitution	Major Scales Other Stringsets
Movable Open chords	Diatonic Seventh Chords			Cycles In Progressions for Substitution	External References
BARRE CHORDS	Diatonic and Chromatic Chords				
Advanced Barre Chords	Chord Streams				

		Musical Sounds (and Styles)			
		Harmonic Structures			
		Physical Structures and Techniques			

Getting Started

Where Musical Styles Can Be Found In This Book

The listing below is a general idea of where you can find chords for a certain style of music. I think any chord can be used in any style, but the more commonly heard sounds have been identified to help point out items of initial interest. Don't hold me to it . . .

Traditional, Campfire, Worship, School Songs, "Beginner" music - **Beginning Chords**:

    Section 1 - Open and then Barre Chords

Rock, Blues, Pop, Country, Bluegrass, Celtic, Spanish and Flamenco - **Beginning and Intermediate:**
    Section 1 - Barre Chords

Pop, Country - **Intermediate**:

    Section 1 - Advanced Open Chords

    Section 1 - Advanced Barre Chords

Rock, Blues, Pop, Smooth Jazz, Euro Dance - **Intermediate, and Advanced**:

    Section 2 - Four Note Chords on the 4321 Stringset

Big Band and Standards Comping - **Intermediate Jazz**:

    Section 2 - Four Note Chords on the 6432 Stringset

    Section 2 - Strummable Chromatic Chords

Jazz - **Intermediate and Advanced**:

    Section 2 - Four Note Chords on the 6432, 5432, 4321, and 5321 Stringsets

    Section 3 - Four Note Chords in Action

Rock, Pop, Country, Blues and - **Advanced:**

    Section 4 - Triads

Chord Substitution, Re-harmonization, Preparing for Solo Chord Melody - **Advanced Harmony**:

    Section 5 - Chord Substitution

References on Scale and Chord Spelling, Chord Names, and Keys

    Section 6 - References

NOTE: Classical guitar instruction typically integrates music notation, chords, harmony, and performance into a single stepped method. Chords are not studied separately, and only classical music styles are part of the focus. As guitarist Ted Greene has demonstrated, even classical music can be included in a "popular" teaching method, but classical harmony as such, is not specifically identified within this book. The conventional classical guitar, with its wider and flat fingerboard will also require some adjustments to some of the more advanced chords because some techniques are not easily used on that instrument (double stops being the most obvious). That being said, classical guitarists will find lots of opportunities for learning within the book.

About the Diagrams

Shown below are examples of various chord fingering diagrams used in the book.

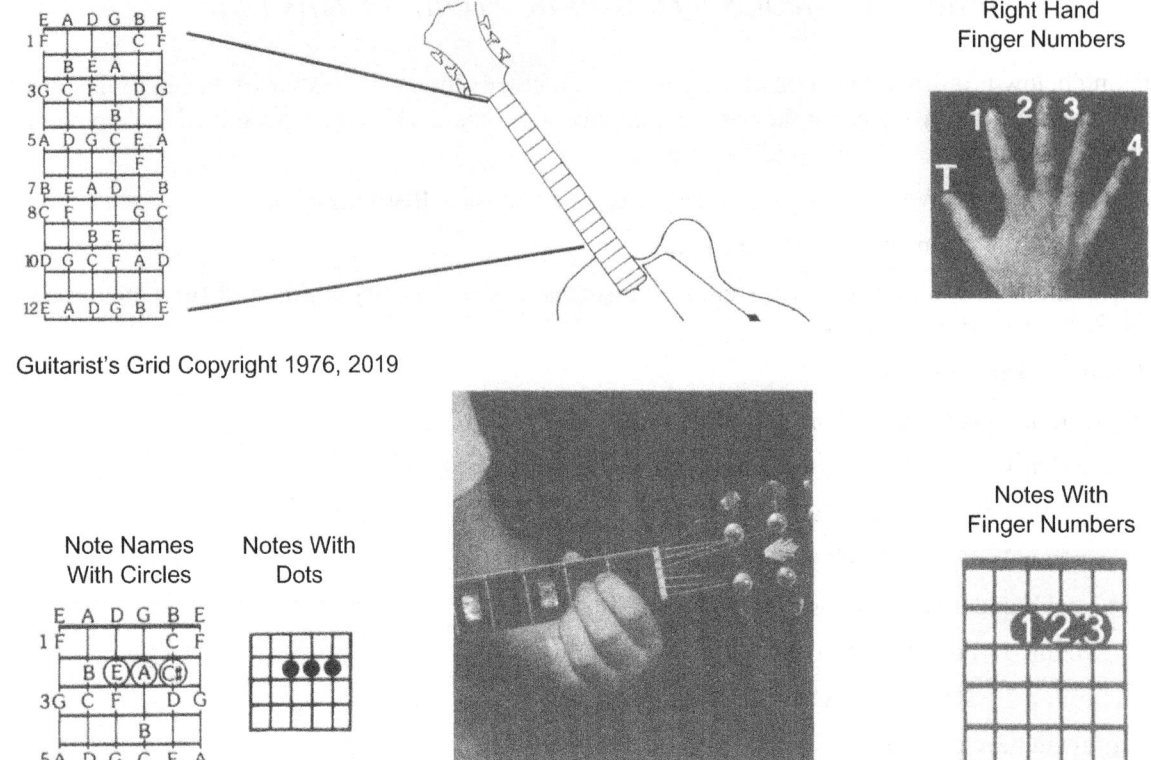

Guitarist's Grid Copyright 1976, 2019

The Guitarist's Grid illustrates the 'natural' notes found on the fingerboard. Seeing the grid repeatedly will help you learn the location of notes. The grid is also used to show the names of the notes that appear in the chord.

If left hand fingerings need explanation, the fingers will be numbered in the circles on a standard grid.

When the chord is familiar, or there are multiple ways to finger the chord, black dots will be used to show the location of the notes to be played. The fingering is your choice.

As a result, I switch back and forth between diagram styles depending upon what I want to emphasize.

Rhythm Notation

Throughout the book this symbol / is used to indicate one *beat* of music. That does *not* mean one strum (although it could be played with one strum).

/ / means 2 beats. ‖: is the start of a section that will be repeated when you see the other symbol :‖

The strumming and fingerpicking patterns you choose are up to you.

26. ⟵ Example numbers are shown on the left side in gray type - good for reference, but not too distracting.

Chord Terminology

Arpeggiate	To arpeggiate a chord is to play the notes in the chord one at a time instead of together.
Arpeggio	Typically an arpeggio is a melodic line composed of chord tones played sequentially.
Barre	A technique to fret three or more strings with a single left hand finger.
Chord	
Color	"Color" is commonly used to refer to the sound quality of a chord - dark, open, and bright are some of the colloquial terms used to refer to chords. The description is an attempt to describe how a chord sounds.
Density	"Density" is another colloquial term referring to how close together the notes of a chord are located. A chord with small intervals is "small" or "tight" or "close."
Extension	When adding a 9th, 11th or 13th to a chord you are adding "extensions" - notes that extend the chord beyond a seventh. There are diatonic extensions and chromatic extensions.
Family	"Family" is used to describe a group of chords that share a common note, like a third or seventh. Traditionally there are three chord families - major, minor and dominant.
Inversion	Inversion describes the order of notes in a chord (from low to high, or high to low).
Root	The root of a chord is the alphabetical letter at the beginning of the name. The root of A7#9♭5 is "A." The root of B♭13#11 is "B♭."
Stream	"Chord Stream" is a colloquial term, coined by Ted Greene I think, that refers to a group of chords. Each chord in the stream is played one after the other, and sometimes with melody notes played in between. The grouping could be by chord type, or scale, or other criteria, but they are presented as a *set of chords,* which is a "stream of chords."
Scale	A "chord scale" is a group of chords, often inversions of the same chord, that includes a scale-like melody.
Shape	"Shape" refers to the physical shape of your left hand as you play a chord.
Stringset	"Stringset" is the term I use to identify the strings that are played as part of the chord.
Voicing	"Voicing" is a term similar to inversion, but can refer to a particular location on the guitar.

Our First Technique - "Double Stops"

A "double stop" is a technique where you play (or "stop") two strings with *one finger*. You'll do this in more advanced chords, and also to keep some fingers available for adding notes in chord licks and playing solo guitar.

Play the examples below:

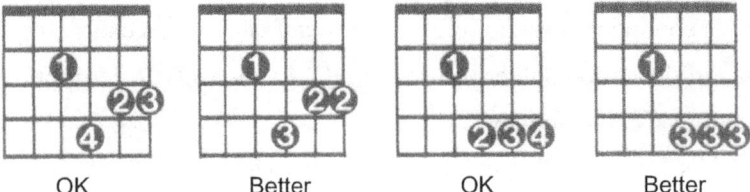

       OK   Better   OK   Better

In both examples the 4th finger is freed up to play other notes.

In four note chords double stops are less an option than a necessity to play changes quickly or to play a chord and add or remove an additional note. If you don't use double stops at all, now is a good time to begin.

NOTE: If you play rock guitar licks you may already use one finger to play two strings - don't forget about that! If you have a classical guitar background, or are playing a nylon string guitar exclusively, you may find some of the double stops difficult because the strings are located farther apart. I'm afraid you'll have to "make do." I've noticed a number of my European students seem to have learned a rather strict "one-finger-per-string" rule when fingering chords. If you have that background I hope you'll give double stops a try. Many chord licks and chord melody arrangements require double stops to help you get a good legato sound.

How to Practice Double Stops

1. Double stops can be played using *any left hand finger*. This sometimes shocks new students, but try it anyway. The basic practice movement is to play the two top strings with one finger.

I often play two notes with the index finger and hold them there. Then I play two strings with the second finger, followed by the third finger and then the fourth finger. You can sound the two strings together. Keep all fingers down as you add a finger, and play the example both ascending and descending.

The best way to start is to try to aim you finger for the space in between the two strings, but land toward the second string a bit. We all say "my fingers are too small" at first. Both Ted Greene and I came up with the explanation that your fingers seem to grow into the needed size, and that seems to be what happens. Repetition will conquer all.

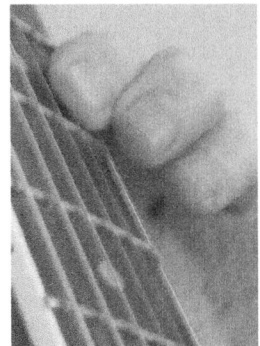 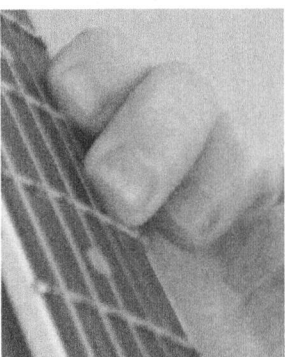 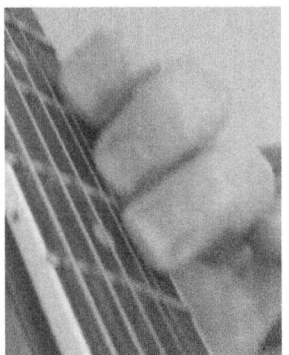 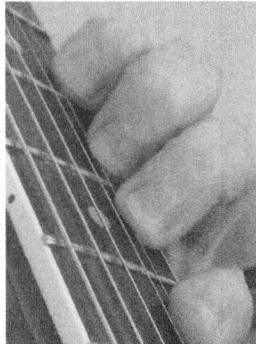

1st finger down on two strings . . . then the second finger . . . .   then place the third finger down . . . and finally the fourth finger.

If you are very young (and haven't finished growing yet) or have very small hands you may have difficulty with double stops. A teacher can tell you. Don't persist in practicing if you experience pain.

Important Note: A single chord fingering can often be played with several different fingerings. If this is a new idea, now is a good time to get used to knowing multiple ways to play the same box with black dots. Cultivate that skill, look for opportunities, and use barres and double stops to find new finger assignments.

How to Look for Double Stops

I'll try to point out opportunities for trying double stops as you continue through the book. The key things to do are

1. Remember to *look* for double stops when you see new chords (they'll be two notes on adjacent strings on the same fret)
2. Decide which chord fingerings might benefit
3. Practice the new chord with and without double stops.

Please note that a small barre, say covering three strings, functions the same as a double stop. Keep an eye out for places to use that technique as well.

"Back in the day . . ." Anything for a buck. Bacon Silver Bell tenor banjo, tired Les Paul Special, Martin D12-20, original "Black Beauty" Les Paul Custom, Martin 00-18, Ode 5 string banjo, Fender P-Bass, *circa early 1970's.*

* "Back in the day" instruments were ones I played and that have since found new homes.

The Stringset - Simplifying Everything

Musical, Visual, and Physical

"STRINGSET" is defined as a group of strings that a chord *fingering* occupies. The first stringset most guitarists play is "all the strings" - open chords, or "the top five strings" for five string open chords. However when we get to four note chords stringsets become more subtle, and more powerful. For instance:

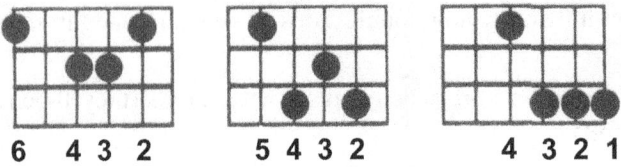

Sound only the numbered strings

I've named the stringsets by the strings used in the fingering. In the diagram above the first stringset is called the "6432" stringset. The second grid shows the "5432" stringset. The top four strings are referred to as the "4321" stringset.

There can be any number of strings in a stringset, and a stringset can contain any combination of strings.

There are five reasons that the stringset is a powerful organizational tool for learning chords:

Stringsets influence chord *sounds* because they

1. Organize chord sounds and *harmonic structure*
2. Determine right hand techniques
3. Influence tone (boy do they do that!)

Stringsets organize chord structure and *harmonic logic* because they

4. Display connections between chord fingerings across the fingerboard
5. Simplify and accelerate the learning of chords because
    a. They provide sonic connections between voicings and fingerings.
    b. They enable the player and teacher to connect chord concepts like chord scales, inversions, walking bass, and chord melody together.
    c. The visual shape re-enforces chord fingerings by harmonic spelling ("3rd in the bass").

Stringsets connect the sound, visual shape, and harmonic structure into a single visible model.

George Van Eps was the first guitarist to identify chords in this manner (although he applied the idea a bit differently).

I use stringsets throughout this book, so you'll get a chance to see them in action in a variety of situations.

NOTE: The group of strings to be played is a consideration for BOTH HANDS.

For the left hand, the fingering shows the notes to be fretted (and sometimes the fingers to be used).

There are two basic right-hand techniques that a guitarist may use to play chords:

- Strumming the strings, and
- Plucking the strings, which is commonly known as "fingerstyle," "fingerpicking," "classical," or even "Chet Atkins Style" (among others).

A third technique combines holding a flatpick while picking strings with fingers 2, 3, and 4.

Strumming and fingerstyle are two different techniques. Strumming is best used for playing chords located on adjacent strings. Fingerstyle playing is adaptable to most strum-able chord formations, and it can also sound chords lying on NON- ADJACENT strings.

3.

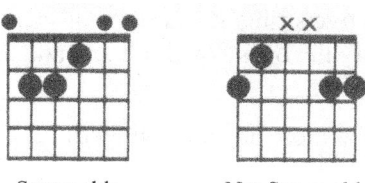

x = a string that should not be sounded

Strum-able   Not Strum-able

A guitarist should learn chords that he can play, i.e., chords compatible with the right hand technique(s) used.

Musical Intervals and Stringsets

Shown below are two chords on adjacent strings, and two chords with the "three and one" stringset (one muted string between the bass and the three adjacent strings). The two chords on the left side have the interval of a third and a 5th between the two lowest notes.

The two chords on the right have the interval of a sixth and seventh respectively.

4.

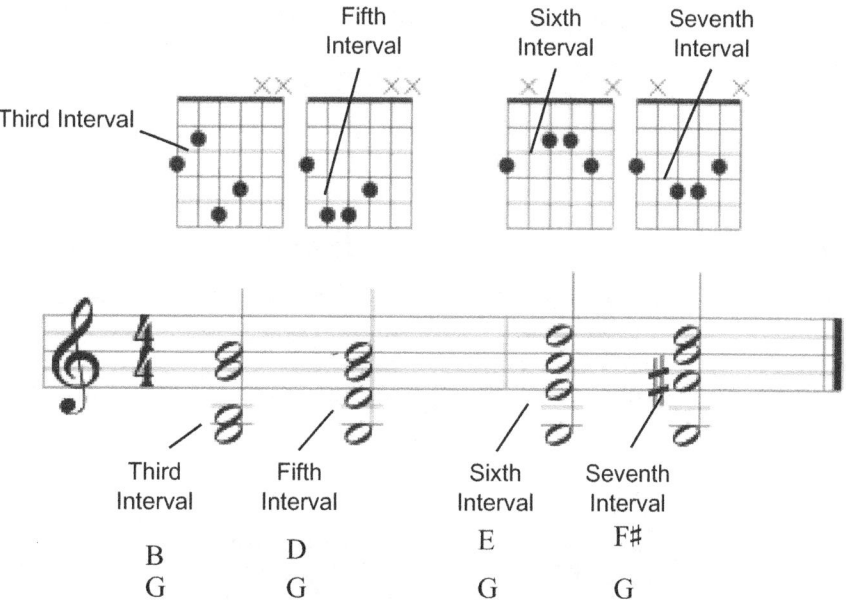

In general, the adjacent string chords have closer intervals between notes in the bass then the "three and one" stringsets. The distance between bass notes may seem like a small difference, but it actually changes the sound of the chords significantly as it also pushes the other notes higher.

In short, the stringset concept is both a physical *and* a musical structure. It isn't just about chord fingerings. Even though you may not be able to play all the chords above, you can understand where they sit and how they work if you understand the simple stringset idea.

With stringsets you learn the sounds of similar groups by the density of the chords. ("Density" meaning how close together the notes are.) The sounds will become part of your vocabulary in an orderly and repeatable process. The sound and fingerings of guitar chords is not a random collection of dots on the page. *The sounds have a reason.*

Section 1 - Six Note and Five Note Chords
Open Chords Reviewed

Here are the basic open chords (on six and five strings), and some of their more advanced fingerings. You may know most of these chords, but identify the ones you don't and add them to your palette of available fingerings.

All these chord fingerings will be used in the more advanced fingerings as we progress to four note chords or even three note chords.

Basic Open Chords

Play the notes indicated by a black dot (with or without a numeral in it). The numbered circles show recommended left hand fingerings for fretted notes. The black dots *behind* the nut indicate open strings to be sounded with the fretted notes. An 'x' would indicate a note that should NOT be played. To begin with, play each chord once. This table is a quick reference only.

5.

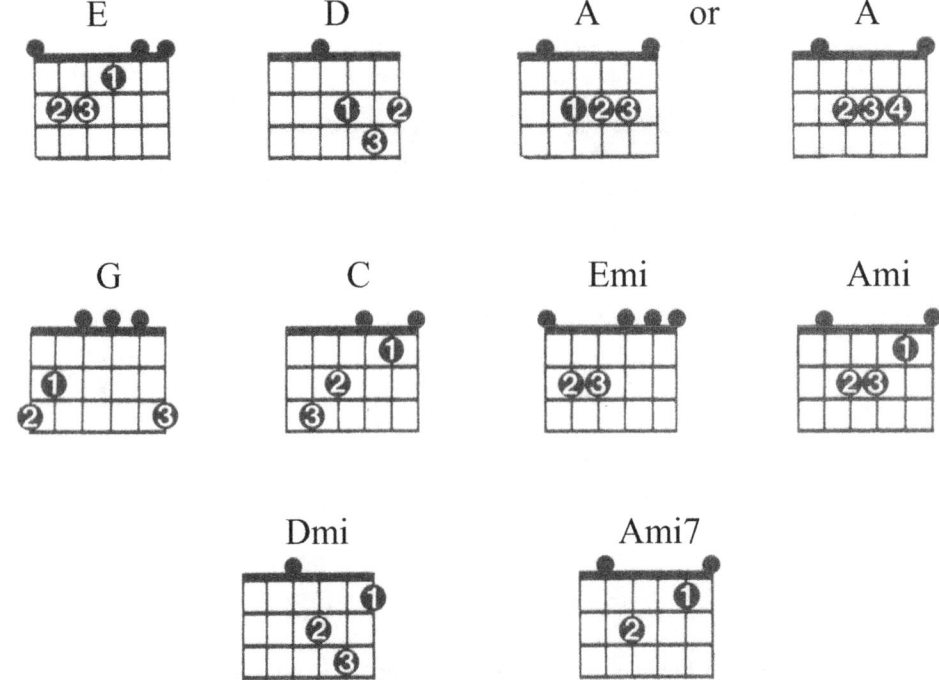

Play these chords as you normally finger them. Then try to use different fingers for the same notes. The G chord could be played using fingers 2, 3, and 4. The Emi chord might be played with a double stop with the second finger. Just notice the differences now, but know that you're going to use a lot of those other fingerings going forward.

Practice Note: When learning new chords in progressions you need to start at a slow tempo and check each string to see if you can hear the note being fretted. You'll often have to "tune up" your left hand to get all the fingers pressing down the notes cleanly. As you improve the tempos can increase.

Open Chords from Each Root and Family

Play the notes indicated by a black dot (with or without a numeral in it). An 'x' would indicate a note that should NOT be played. To begin with, play each chord once. This table is a reference only.

6.

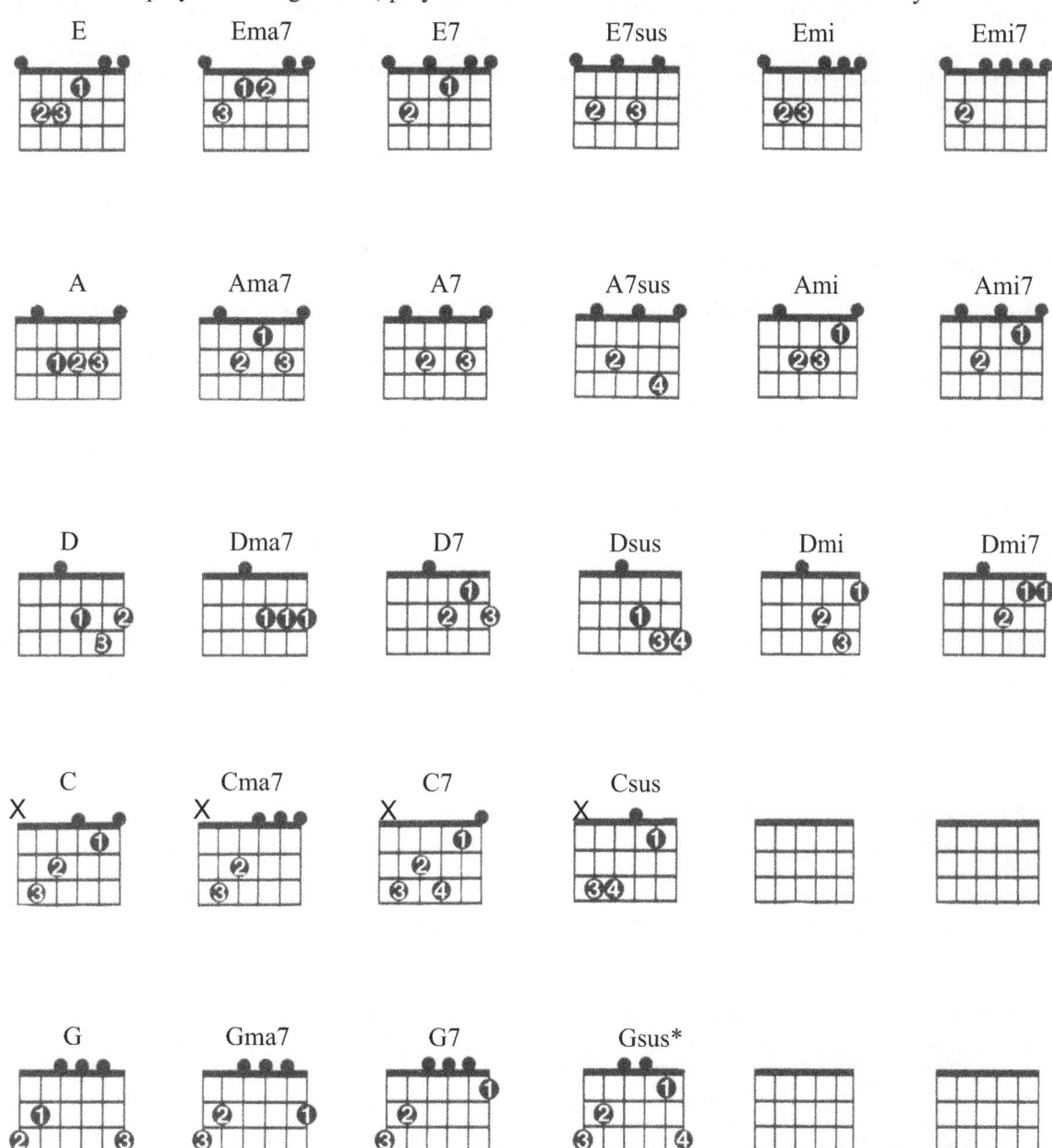

You'll notice that both "7sus" and "sus" chords appear in the table if you look down the "sus" column. *The "Gsus" chord in the bottom row also has a B note (5th string). Technically a sus chord moves the third up to the 4th, but this fingering has become common because it fits with other open G chords - you can hammer the C note (first finger) on or off to make a small chord lick.

The examples above illustrate the one note difference between various chords. But, they have another benefit. Many of these pairs of chords can be used as small chord 'licks' you can use when you're given one of the chords, and want to add some color. You'll probably recognize a few. Listen to the examples as possible chord fills.

Chord Names for Advanced Chords

Shown below are the common names for some of the advanced open chord fingerings we'll be using. This discussion is to help you to say the name out loud, and understand the notes included. It is common for one fingering to have several different names or symbols because of the regional and stylistic habits musicians have. We'll try to include the different names along with the actual scale degrees (in numbers) for notes theoretically included in the chord.

Some of this may be a bit confusing if you're new to it. That's because it can be confusing if you're new to it.

Understanding the "Formulas"

Chords can be defined by the notes they contain. Often that definition is also the chord's name. But, what are the numbers that appear in a formula?

The numbers indicate the note of the major scale that matches the root of the chord.

In a C chord of any kind "C" is the root (indicated by the "1" or an "R").

E is the "third" of a C major chord as indicated by a "3."

G is the "fifth" of a C major chord and is indicated by a "5."

Watch:

C Major Scale	C	D	E	F	G	A	B	C	D	E	F	G A ...
Formula Numbers	1	2	3	4	5	6	7	(8)	9	(10)	11	(12) 13
C Major Chord	C		E		G							
	1		3		5							
C "Add 9" Chord	C		E		G				D			
	1		3		5				9			

There is much more to this discussion, but remember that each type of chord has a formula. The following table uses "C" as the root for all the chord name samples.

Chord Name	Chord Symbol(s)	Chord Formula
C Major Seventh	Cma7, Cmaj7, C7, C△7, CM7	R 3 5 7
C Major Ninth	Cma9, Cmaj9, C9, C△9	R 3 5 7 9
C Add Nine	Cadd9, C/9	R 3 5 9
C Minor Ninth	Cmi9, Cmin9, C-9	R ♭3 5 ♭7 9
C Minor Add 9	Cmi/9, Cmin/9	R ♭3 5 9
C Suspended	Csus, Csus4	R 4 5
C7 Suspended	C7sus	R 4 5 ♭7
C Minor Major 7th	Cmi/ma7, Cmi△7	R ♭3 5 7

Chord Families

The tricky part of chord formulas is that all the notes included in the formula may not always appear in a guitar chord *fingering*. We'll discuss this more as we progress.

Major Chord Family

major:	1	3		5				
ma6:	1	3		5	6			
ma7:	1	3		5		7		
ma/add 9; /9	1	3		5			9	
ma9:	1	3		5		7	9	
ma6/9:	1	3		5	6		9	
ma13:	1	3		5		7	9	(11)	13(6)
ma6/9#11 :	1	3		5	6		9	#11
ma9#11 :	1	3		5		7	9	#11
ma#11:	1	3		5				#11
sus or sus4:	1	4		5				
ma7#5:	1	3		#5		7		
ma9#5:	1	3		#5		7	9	

Minor Chord Family

minor:	1	b3		5				
mi6:	1	b3		5	6			
mi6/9:	1	b3		5	6		9	
mi6/ma7:	1	b3		5	6	7		
mi6/9/ma7:	1	b3		5	6	7	9	
mi6/9/#11 :	1	b3		5	6		9	#11
mi6/11 :	1	b3		5	6		9	11
mi7:	1	b3		5		b7		
mi7/11 :	1	b3		5		b7		11
mi9:	1	b3		5		b7	9	
mi11:	1	b3		5		b7	9	11
mi/add9:	1	b3		5			9	
mi7b5:	1	b3	b5			b7		
min7b5/11:	1	b3	b5			b7		11
mi7#5:	1	b3		#5		b7		
mi/ma7:	1	b3		5		7		
mi/ma9:	1	b3		5		7	9	
mi13	1	b3		5		b7	9	(11)	13

Dominant Chord Family

dom 7:	1	3			5		b7					
dom 7/6:	1	3			5	6	b7					
dom 9:	1	3			5		b7	9				
dom 13:	1	3			5		b7	9		11		13
dom 7 sus:	1		4		5		b7					
dom 7/6 sus:	1		4		5	6	b7					
dom 11:	1	3			5		b7	9		11		
dom 13 sus:	1		4		5		b7	9		11		13
dom 7b5:	1	3	b5				b7					
dom 7#5:	1	3		#5			b7					
dom 7b9:	1	3			5		b7	b9				
dom 7#9:	1	3			5		b7		#9			
dom 9b5:	1	3	b5				b7	9				
dom 9#5:	1	3		#5			b7	9				
dom 7b9b5:	1	3	b5				b7	b9				
dom 7b9#5:	1	3		#5			b7	b9				
dom 7#9b5:	1	3	b5				b7		#9			
dom 7#9#5:	1	3		#5			b7		#9			
dom 13b9:	1	3			5		b7	b9		11		13
dom 13#9:	1	3			5		b7		#9	11		13
dom 13b9b5:	1	3	b5				b7	b9				13
dom 13#11:	1	3			5		b7	9			#11	13
dom 9#11:	1	3			5		b7	9			#11	
dom 11b9:	1	3			5		b7	b9		11		
dom 11b9#5:	1	3		#5			b7	b9		11		
dom 7/11:	1	3			5		b7			11		
dom 7/6/11:	1	3			5	6	b7			11		
diminished 7:	1	b3	b5				bb7					
augmented:	1	3		#5								

Roman Numeral Introduction

Roman numerals are often used to identify specific chord progressions. Each chord built from a note in the major scale is given a Roman numeral. In certain regions the Roman numerals are all capital letters. Another approach, which I use, is to use capital letters for major chords, and lower case letters for minor chords. Shown below are the triads and seventh chords below the C major scale. I, IV, and V receive capital letters while the rest receive lowercase letters

C major scale	C	D	E	F	G	A	B	C
Triad chords	Cma	Dmi	Emi	Fma	Gma	Ami	Bdim	
Seventh chords	Cma7	Dmi7	Emi7	Fma7	G7	Ami7	Bmi7b5	
	I	ii	iii	IV	V	vi	vii	

More Advanced Open Chords

The chords in this section include more colorful sounds, and in some cases may be a little more difficult to play.

By "more colorful" I'm referring to chords with additional notes to a plain major, minor or dominant type. (A major is the basic chord, A major 7th or A add 9 are more colorful because they add one or more tones to the basic A major chord.)

More difficult fingerings often provide new sounds so repetition will help.

A good example is a blues progression. In jazz, blues progressions can begin on a *major 7th* chord, where rock and blues will use a major chord (or even a dominant 7th chord). The major seventh is sometimes heard to "soften" the sound of a progression. It isn't good or bad, just different.

I raise this point only to encourage you to be aware of new chords as you first introduce them into progressions. As mentioned elsewhere, the sound and your usage should govern your choices, not a book.

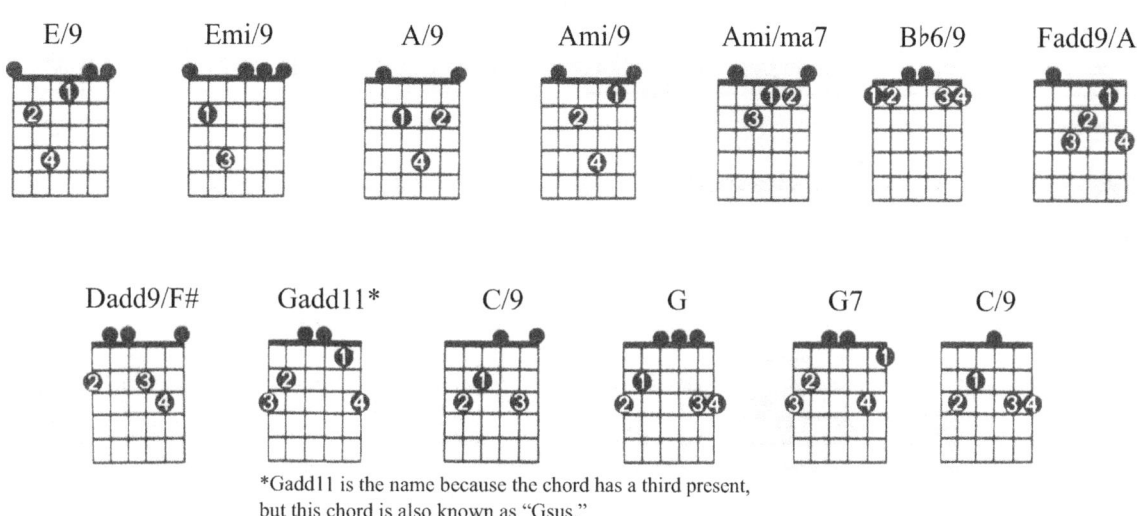

*Gadd11 is the name because the chord has a third present, but this chord is also known as "Gsus."

Examples

Play each chord for four beats.

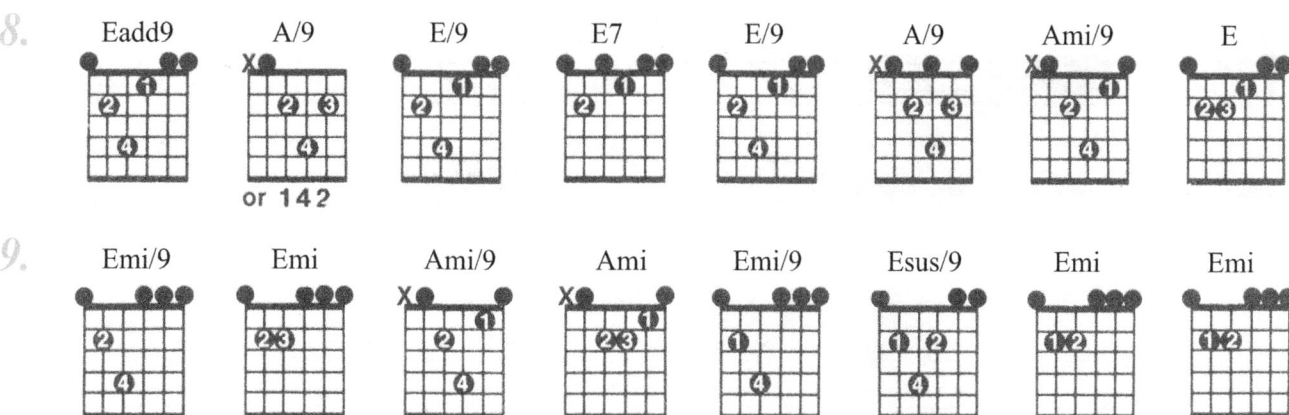

As illustrated above, both "add9" and "/9" refer to the same chord: R 3 5 9.

Play each chord for four beats. These examples demonstrate the suspended and minor sounds together.

10. Cadd9 C Cadd9 C Asus Ami Asus Ami

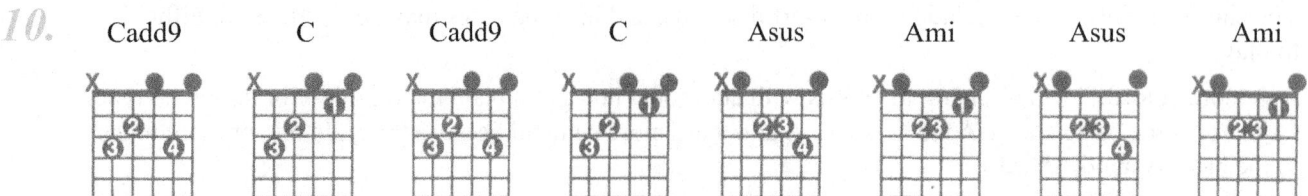

11. D/F# D7/F# D/F# D7/F# G Gadd11 G

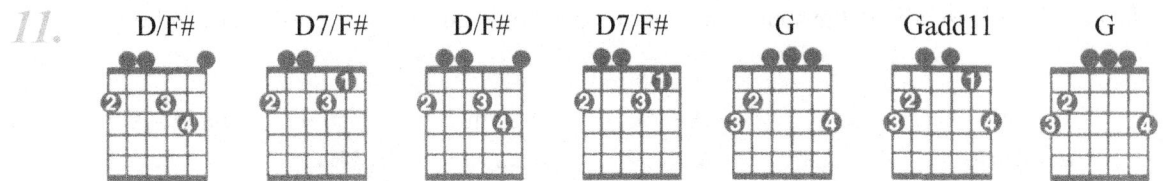

12. Esus E Asus A Dsus D Gadd11 G

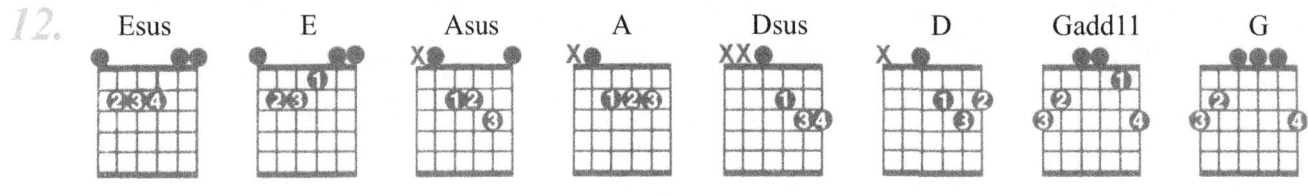

13. Csus C Cadd9 C Fma7 Fma9* Fma13 C

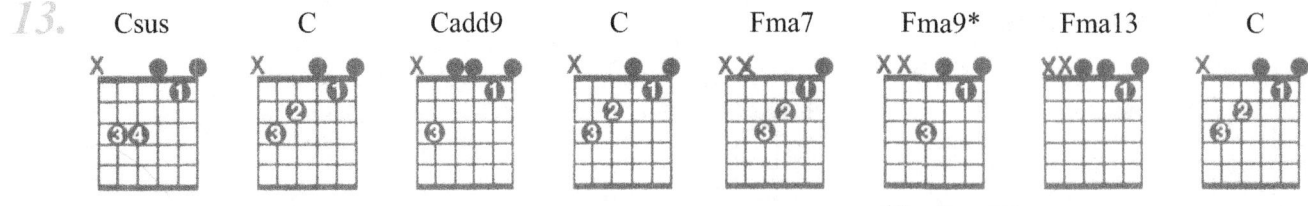

*Fma9 could be
Cadd11 too: CEGF

Sample Rock Progressions

These examples demonstrate new fingerings for open chords. The fingerings are illustrating the use of chords "up a fourth" to create chord fills and licks. (D major is a fourth above A major. C major is a fourth above G major.) Use the left hand fingering indicated. The *right hand* should be on the middle four strings.

14.

In all these examples you should try to play the bass string before you play the rest of the chord, whether you play with pick, pick-and-fingers (hybrid picking), or fingerstyle. It will sound much more familiar.

The open high E string is optional.

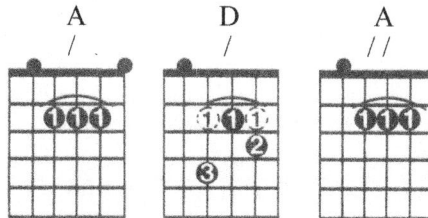

15.

This is a two bar figure.

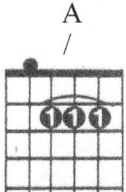 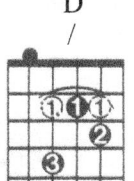  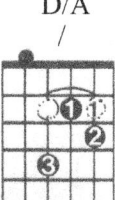   

16.

Mute the 5th string if possible. The 1st string is optional.

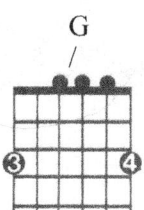 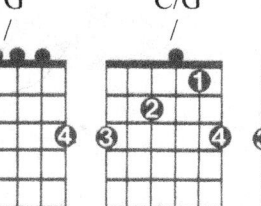  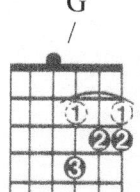 

Compare the first four boxes below (a minor sound) to the second four boxes (a major sound).

17.

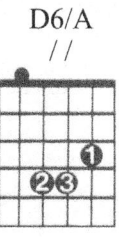 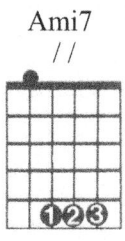 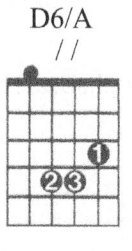 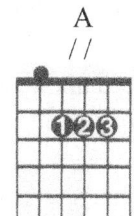 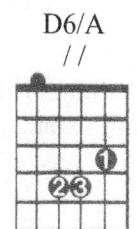 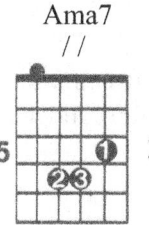

You'll find examples of progression licks "up a fourth" in all styles of music, and throughout this book. Become familiar with the idea, and maybe the roots of chords that appear "up a fourth."

Barre Chords: The First Movable Fingerings

Open Chords Re-Fingered To Be Movable

We're still looking at "big" chords of five and six string fingerings. These chords are based upon the open chords, but use a barre to make the notes originally sounded by the nut in the open position.

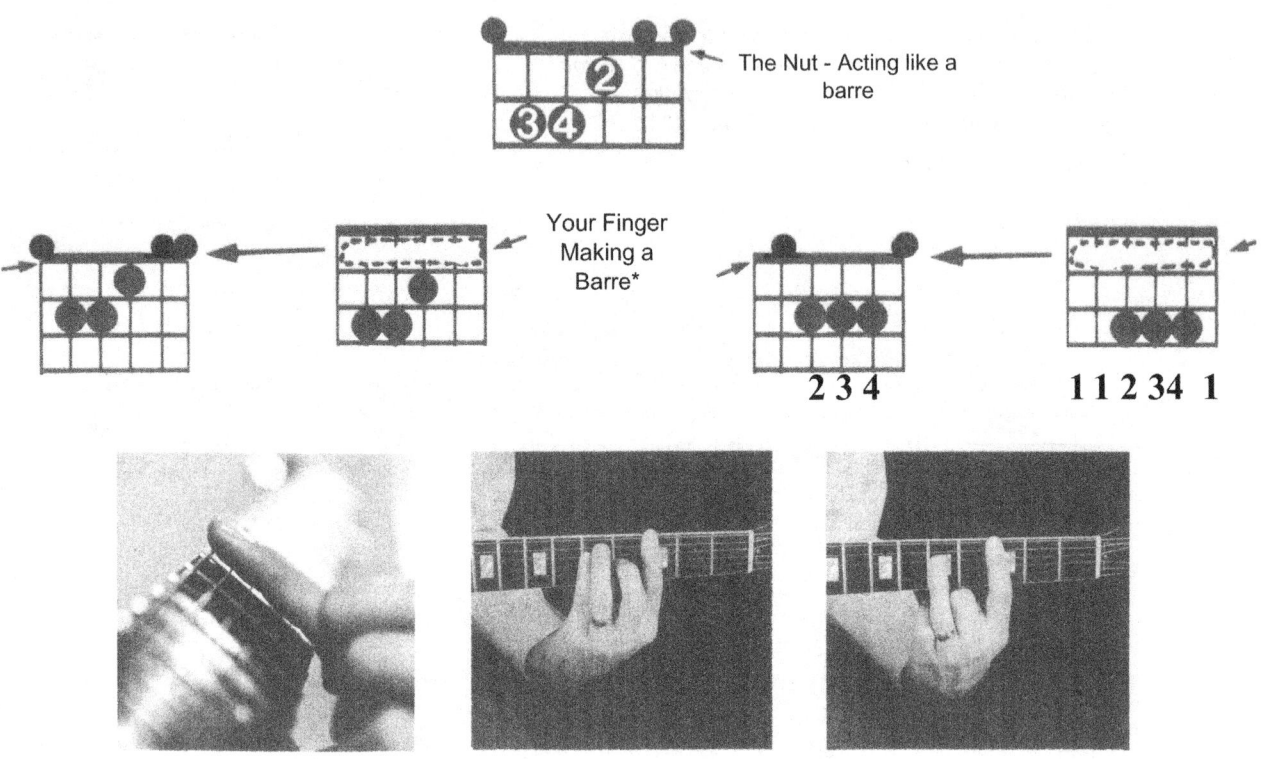

Naming Barre Chords

How can you remember the names of all the new chords you can make with the barre? There are two parts to each chord name: 1) The root of the chord -A, B, C, F# and so on, and 2) the color of the chord - major, minor, dominant seventh and so on. The color of the chord will become easier to hear as you practice.
But how can you remember the root of the chord? Below is a diagram showing the natural notes of the C major scale on the fingerboard. I use the natural notes as "sign posts" so that notes like A♭ can be found by reference (down one fret from A).

REMEMBER-Our system of notes is based upon an alphabet. The positions of the notes are fixed. G is always two frets above F and so on.

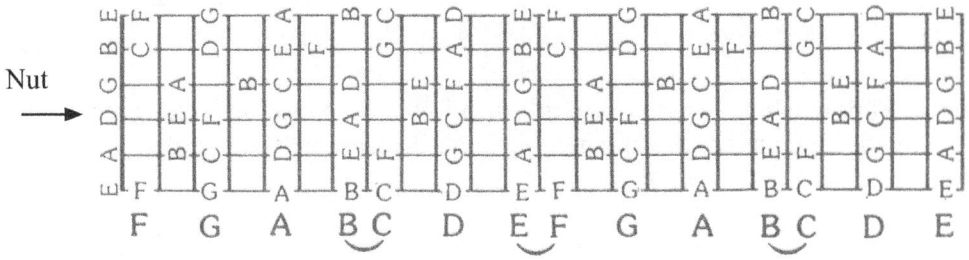

Review the chords below. Note that the first chord in each row is an open chord, and is followed by two "Barre" versions of the chord.

18.

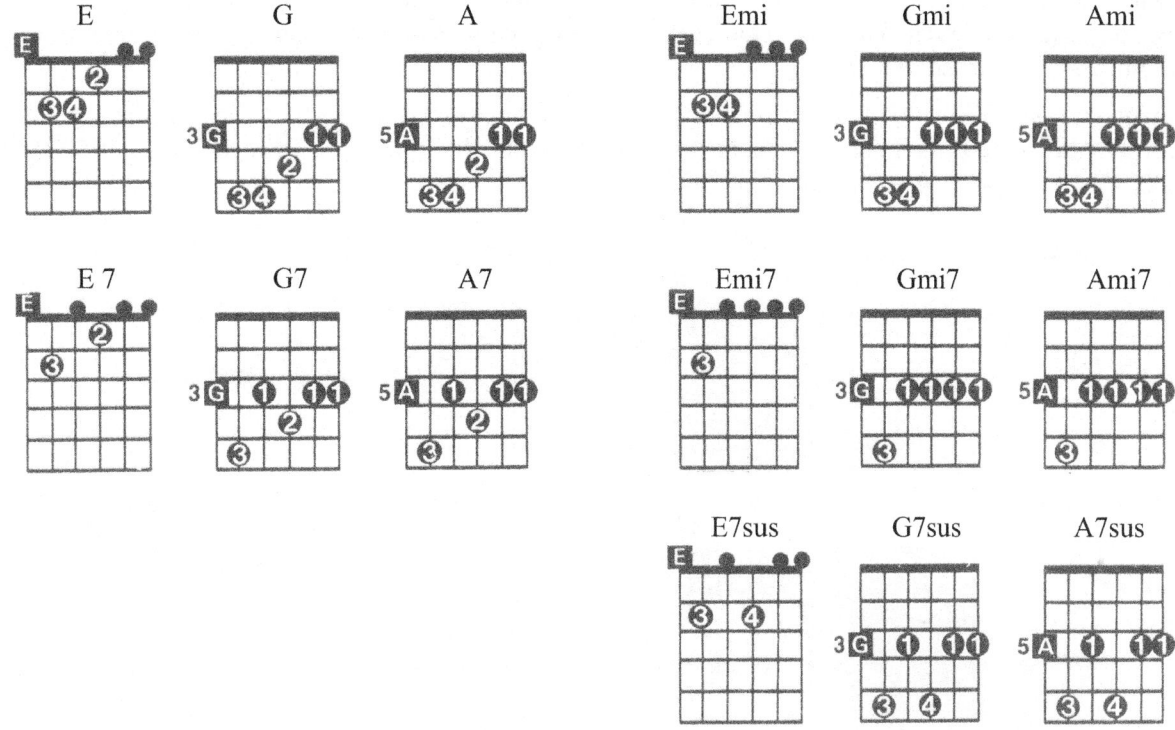

Please note: In the fingerings below the root is shown on the *5th* string. By happy coincidence, you can barre the 6th string in the same place. The fifth of the chord will become the lowest note. Easier to strum but a different sound.

19.

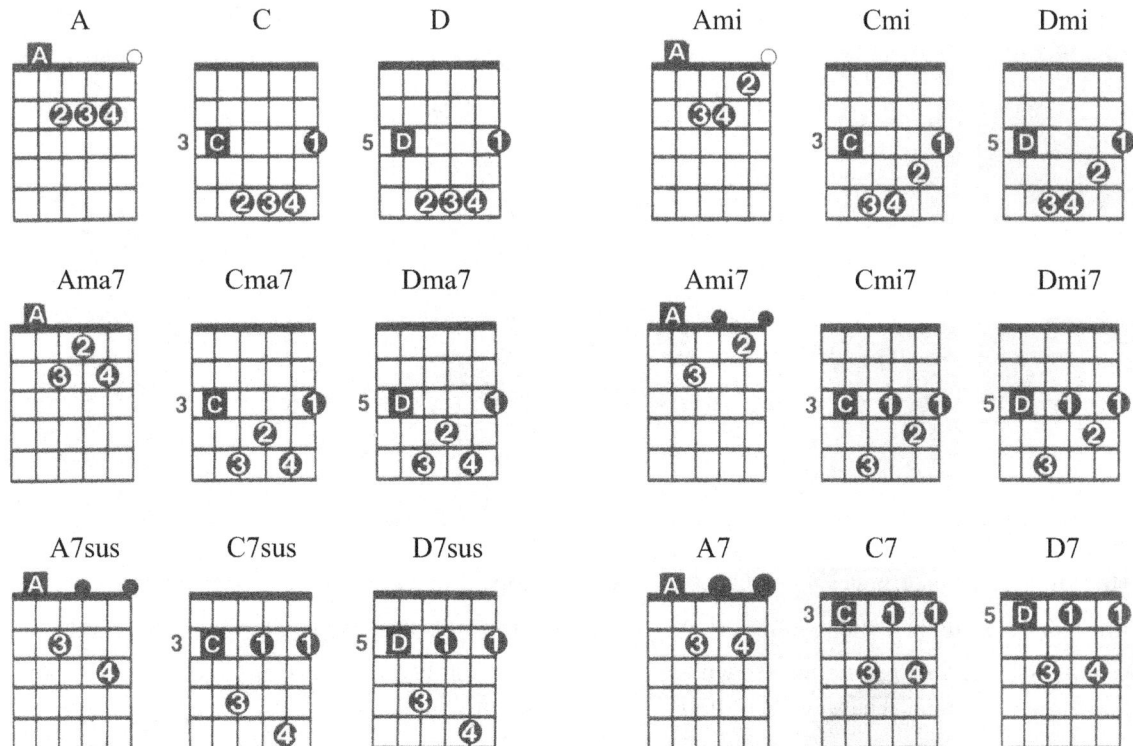

Chord Systems 40th Anniversary Edition - by Leon White

The Dreaded "C" Shape Barre Chord

Shown below is the basic open C major chord, followed by *barred* versions of that fingering to make chords from the root D. The barred version of this fingering requires the 4th finger to be placed above the other fingers to cover the root D.

Many players have difficulty with this fingering because of the position of the 4th finger, but place your fingers like the barre B minor seventh shape (same shape but no 4th finger) and then add the pinky. That usually solves the problem with a little repetition.

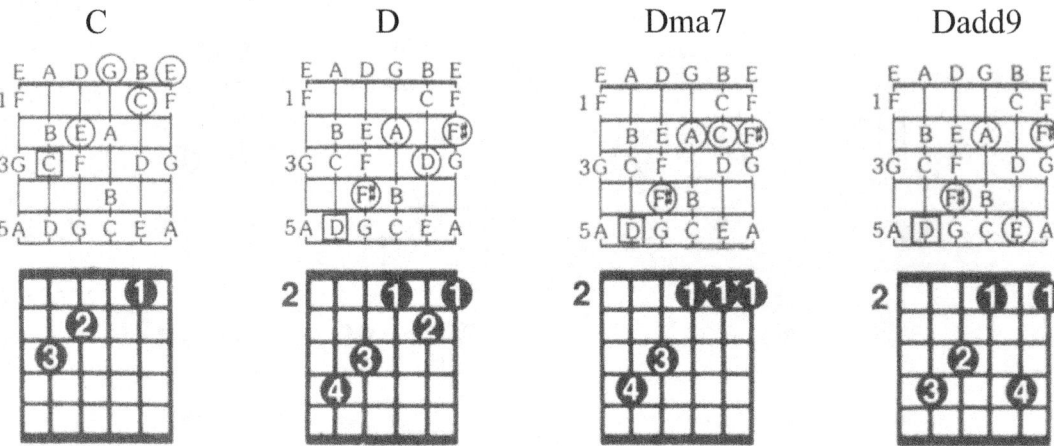

Movable 9th Chords

Shown below is the basic open B7 chord, followed by modified version to make the dominant 9th chord, and a movable fingering. If you're not comfortable with this fingering shape, take time now to practice it as this shape (with the 2nd finger on the bass notes) is essential. The chord is a go-to chord for blues progressions.

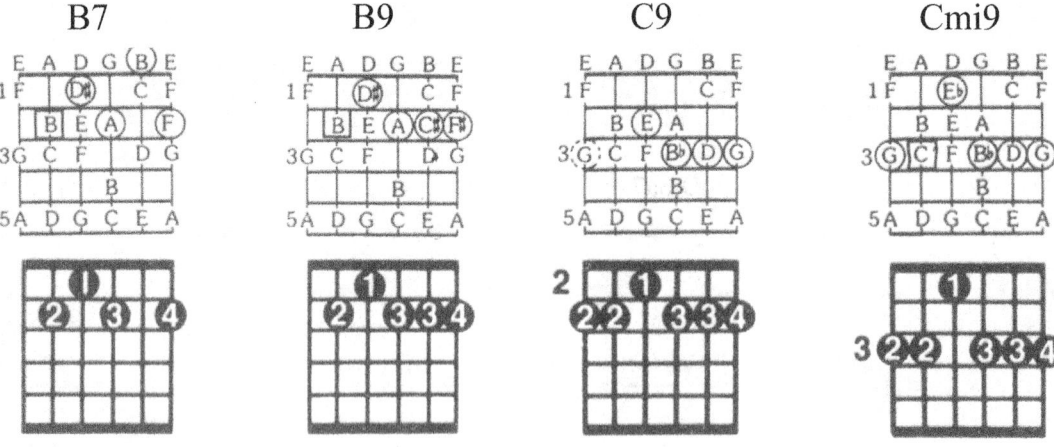

Note the suggested fingerings show a number of double stops. Finger as you feel comfortable.

The third chord could be called Gmi6 *or* C9. This association is discussed later in four note chords.

Please note that the Cmi9 fingering shown above has the root on the 5th string, and includes a G note (the fifth) as the lowest note. That note is optional, but is commonly included in this voicing.

Additional Barre Chords

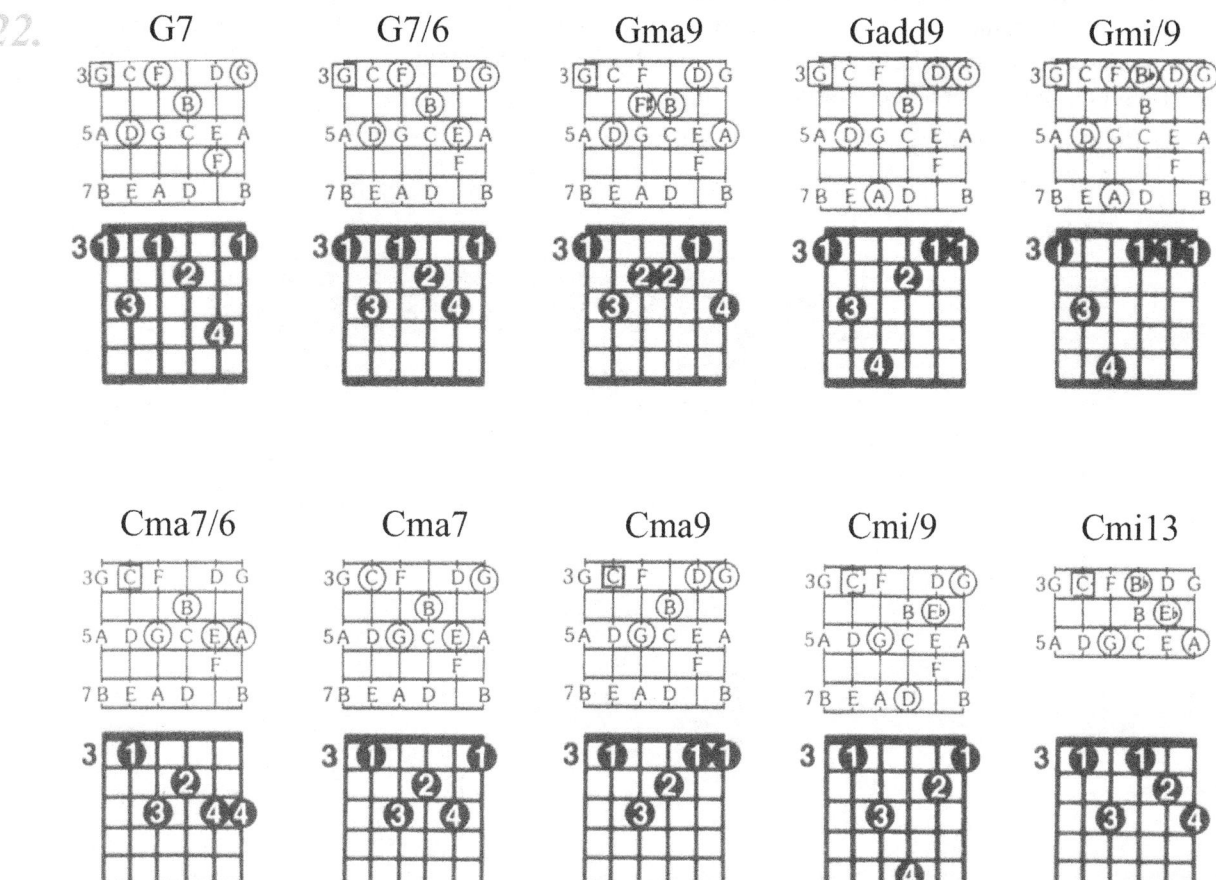

Shown above are two chords, the 1st and last, that are spelled R, 5, ♭7, 6 and some kind of third (Cma7/6 vs. Cmi13). In pure theory the 13th chord should have a 9th in the spelling. In practice people often describe these chords as 7/6 or 13 when there is NO 9th.

To learn more about this, see the reference sections for harmony and chord spelling.

Surprisingly perhaps, the Beatles frequently used the first two fingerings shown. "She's A Woman" uses one of these voicings as I recall. When you hear it that way it sounds less like a big band chord and more like a classic rock 'n roll chord.

*"Back in the day . . ."

My Gibson ES 150 - a blond 335 that was 3 inches deep and hollow. Note the orange label. It never sounded better then my 335.

Progression Examples for Barre Chords

Shown below are two very common barre chord licks. One is based on the 6th string (here with an A root), and one based on the 5th string (with a D root). This old fashioned lick, using two boxes, is the first example most of us see in licks that incorporate a chord and a companion chord up a 4th. (Think of "Johnny B Goode" and other Chuck Berry recordings.)

Emphasize the two lowest strings when strumming this.

23. **A7 Lick**

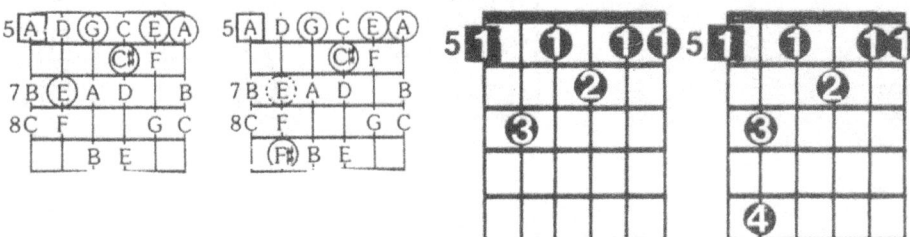

24. **D7 Lick**

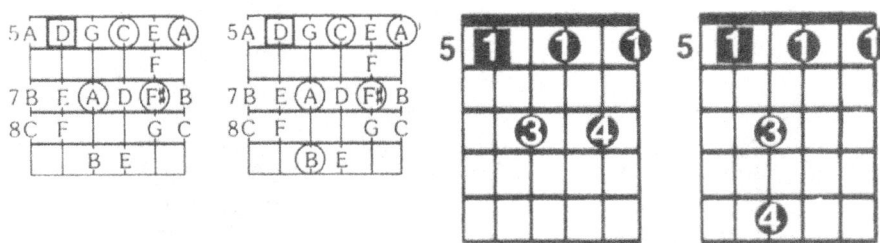

Each *row* below is a single example. Play each chord for four beats. The fingerings included here have some stretches and include new chord shapes, so give yourself some time and repetitions to get comfortable.

25.   Dma7   Gadd9   G   Dma7

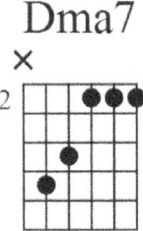 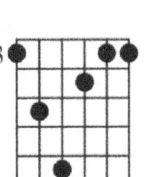 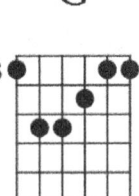 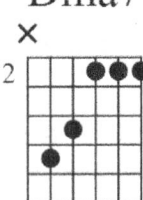

26.   G/A   A13   Dma7   G/C

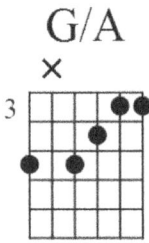 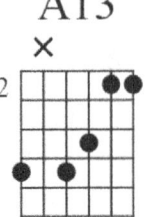 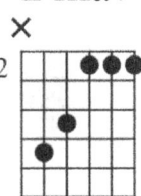 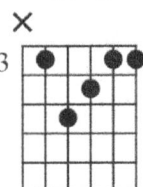

The examples below continue to focus on the mi/9 chords with big stretches. These add 9 chords are paired with plain minor or minor seventh chords to help you recognize and remember the sounds.

You might hear these sounds as "Johnny B Goode" goes minor.

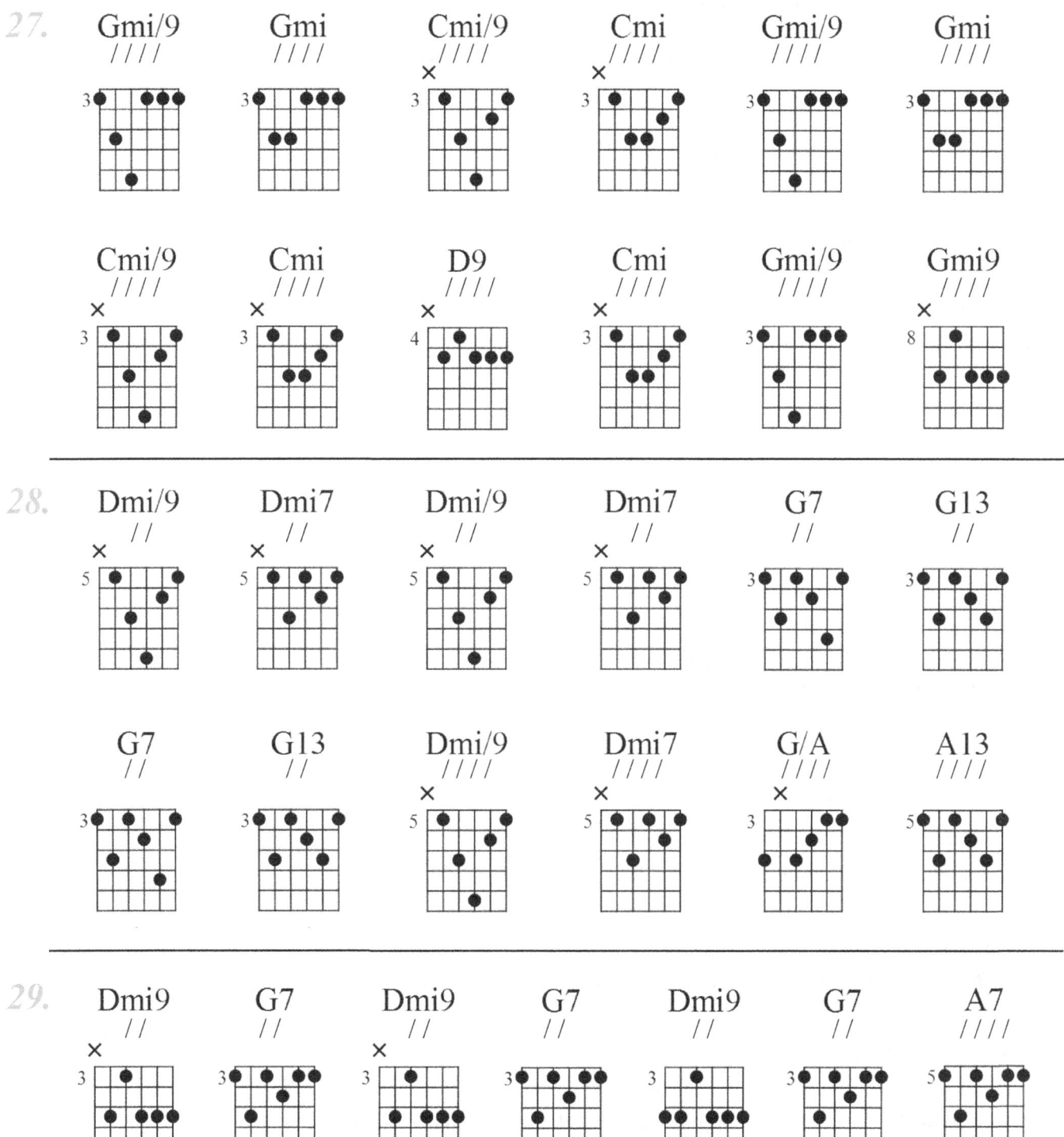

Section 2 - Four Note Chords

Four Note Movable Fingerings

Overview and Logic

So far the book has
- introduced the concept of the stringset,
- reviewed five and six string chords in the open position, and
- shown how to move those fingerings by using the barre.

We saw a few four note chords (like D major and F major) in the open position. However there is a whole blue print of movable four note chords, and that is the next piece of logic to add to our tool set.

We're going to focus on four stringsets in this section. The chords found here will get you through most rock, blues, country, jazz standards, and pop music.

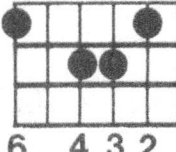 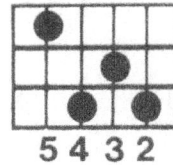 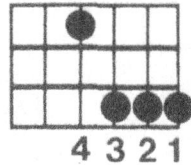

The topics in this section include the following:
1. Accompaniment fingerings for all styles
2. Common jazz chords and comping
3. Systematic inversions
4. Chord scales
5. Walking bass lines with chords
6. Moving lines inside chords
7. Common chromatic chord fingerings

That is a lot of material. This section is the largest part of the book.

The approach is outlined below:
1. Review seventh chords and the chord families
2. Introduce four note fingerings, with examples
3. Introduce the systematic inversion concept
4. Integrate the systematic inversion concept and
5. Expand the 7th chord fingerings to show the other chords in the families
6. Repeat for each of the major stringsets

The Theory of Four Note Seventh Chords

We've been playing seventh chords using the open and barre fingerings. It's time to look inside the chords and see why some of them sound different. Fundamental seventh chords are found inside a single major scale, as shown:

C major scale   C   D   E   F   G   A   B   C

Seventh chords   Cma7   Dmi7   Emi7   Fma7   G7   Ami7   Bmi7b5

These chords each have four different pitches - root, third, fifth, and seventh. One thing that can confuse some guitarists at first is that the number of *unique* pitches in chord spelling (for reference) doesn't always correspond with the number of notes played on the guitar. The open E7 chord below has six notes, of which there are two roots, E, two fifths, B, one third, G#, and one dominant seventh, D.

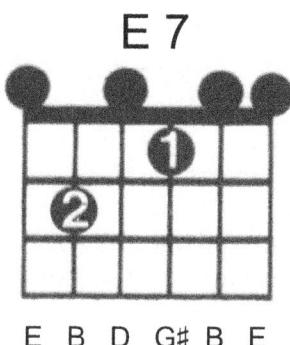

E7

E B D G# B E

While an E7 chord is typically **spelled** E G# B D, in a six note *fingering* there are doubled (or even tripled) notes. Note the difference between how we spell a chord in theory, and what we actually play.

Why the extra notes? The answers are loudness, ease of playing for the right hand, and sound.

The doubling of notes in a chord changes the sound of the chord, but not the name. That's why there are so many different E7 chord fingerings having 4, 5, or 6 notes. They all carry the same name in our shorthand naming system, but they sound different. (In more advanced playing we'll see partial chords of 3 notes or even two notes, but that's later.)

Since performing guitarists are often playing with keyboards and other instruments, playing all 6 strings can "get in the way" sound-wise. All we really need are a few of the notes. We're going to start with the 4 notes found in the seventh chords.

After learning the 'big' open and barre chords, we can begin to use smaller voicings. In this section we're going to work with four note fingerings. In certain styles of music the chords are sometimes voiced with only three notes ("Le Jazz Hot," or "Django" style is one example). We have lots of options and we're going to see them all laid out logically and connected together on the fingerboard.

This section is a big breakthrough if you haven't used these voicings before. You'll recognize that these voicings also overlap the open and barre chord fingerings we've already seen. That's why the open and barre chords were included at the beginning.

Everything is connected and consistent. (It isn't always taught that way though.) Many explanations are focused on musical style, and so selected chord fingerings are used and others omitted. Since we are NOT style driven, the fingerings will be laid out and you can choose which ones to use. The examples *will* illustrate various styles because you'll recognize the sounds, but you should do whatever you want.

Systematic Inversions

An "inversion" refers to a particular stacking order of notes in a chord from low to high (or high to low). In *systematic* inversions each of the notes in the chord moves up the neck to the next chord tone (hence "systematically"). If the lowest voice in the 1st chord is the 5th, then in the next inversion the lowest note will be the 7th. Moving higher on the neck the next fingering will have the root in the lowest voice. See the A major seventh chords below:

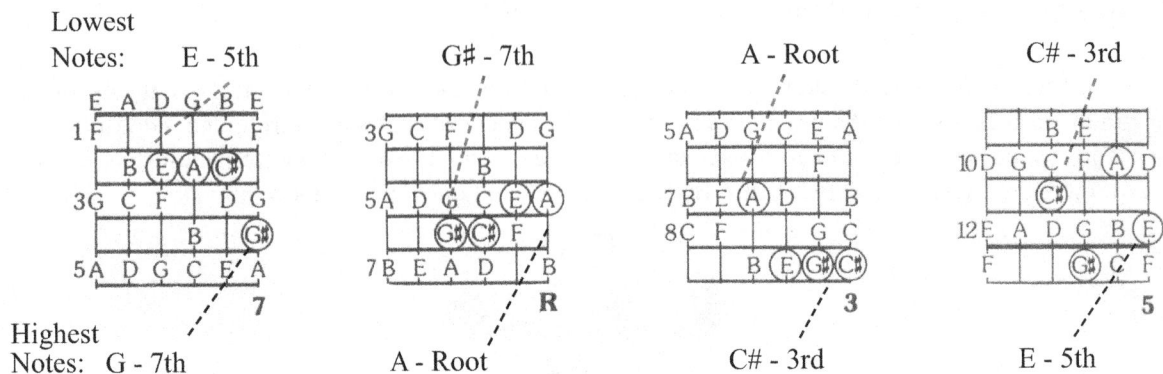

You'll see that the root note moves up to the 3rd; the 3rd moves up to the 5th; the 5th moves up to the 7th, and the 7th moves up to the root. There are always 4 inversions for these 4 note 7th chords on a stringset.

There are four musical ideas that intersect to power your playing these chords:

1. There are three basic chord families - major, minor and dominant.
2. Seventh chords (Root, third, fifth, and seventh) can be treated as the foundation chord fingerings for each family.
3. Seventh chords have four notes, and therefore have four inversions; each inversion has its own particular sound.
4. Stringsets will align the inversions and give great power in using the chords in songs.

We're going to learn the chords with this approach: seventh chords by family, with the four inversions, and by stringset.

All these ideas tie together in a simple structure of sounds. Chords with a third in the bass sound different from chords with a fifth in the bass, but sound the same on different stringsets.

Using the seventh chords, we'll then expand the chord colors by adding or changing notes to the basic seventh chord fingerings. This allows you to connect the more colorful chords back to the basic seventh chord inversion, so remembering and using chords becomes a cohesive, organized map.

The four inversions of a seventh chord will be the anchor points for adding all the other chords, like 9ths, 13ths, 13#11 and so on. You'll never get lost once you see the logic. You'll learn the sounds of the fingerings because you'll listen to them in an orderly way. I firmly believe this approach is the best way to organize and present chords. The examples are here to deliver the musical interest and cool sounds.

Seventh Chord Inversions - 4321 Stringset
Introductory Examples

The first chords we'll look at feature the 4321 stringset.

Shown below are some short progressions using these chords. You can strum these fingerings or play them fingerstyle. The following examples are a sort of a "meet 'n greet" with some 4321 fingerings. Just play them and enjoy them. (Each stringset will begin with a few examples to whet your appetite a bit.)

Medium slow ballad in the style of "Laura"

32.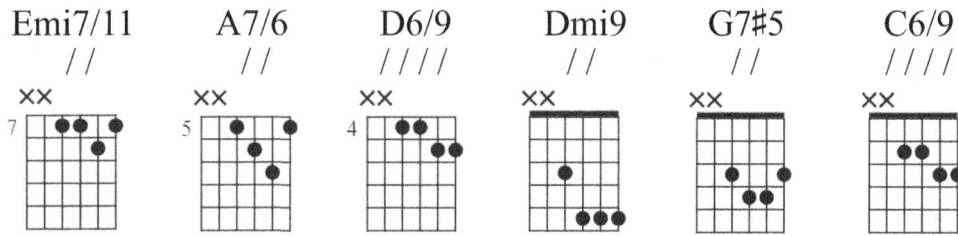

Up tempo rock or blues lick over an A7 chord

33.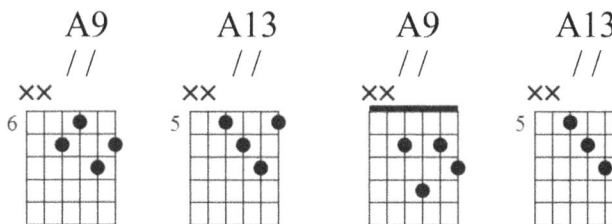

Up tempo swing comping style - starts on the '4' of the 1st bar. The second A13 should sound on the 'and' of 2. Try imitating the sounds of a small horn section (and no, I'm not kidding).

34.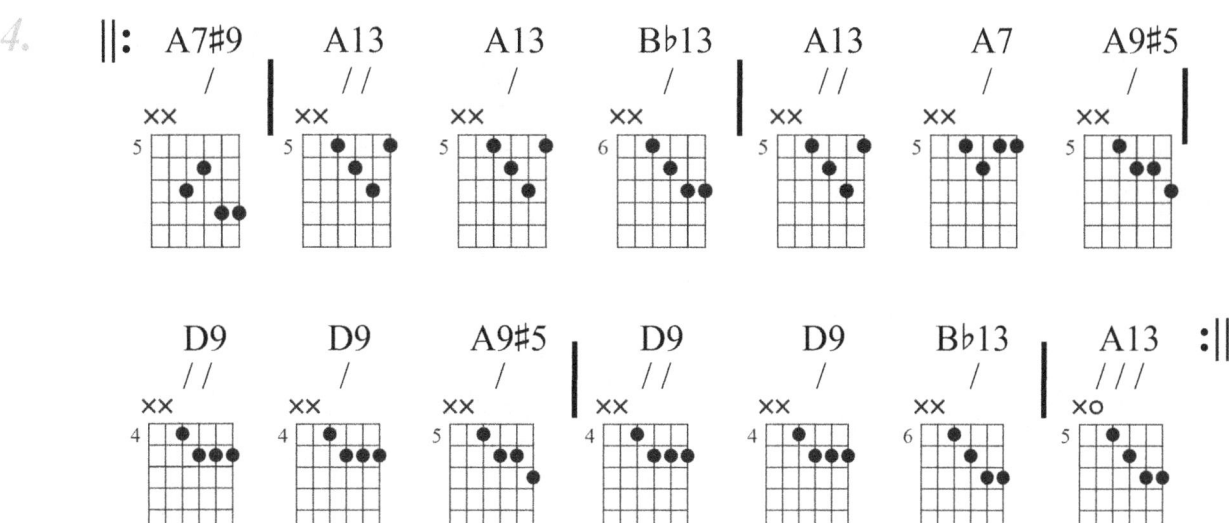

The First Systematic Inversions

NOTE: The next two pages are reference pages. That means you should look the inversions over, see which fingerings you recognize, and begin learning the fingerings in order, moving up and down the neck. Practice one chord family at a time. While you work on this page you can move on to the example pages that follow.

All three chord families - major, dominant, and minor - are shown. Play *across* a row to learn chords in the same family. Play *down* the columns to hear different chords in the same location (ma7, 7, and mi7 in the same place). Fingering is optional, but try to start using "double stops" if you they're new to you.

Remember to sound only the top four strings.

Ama7

A7

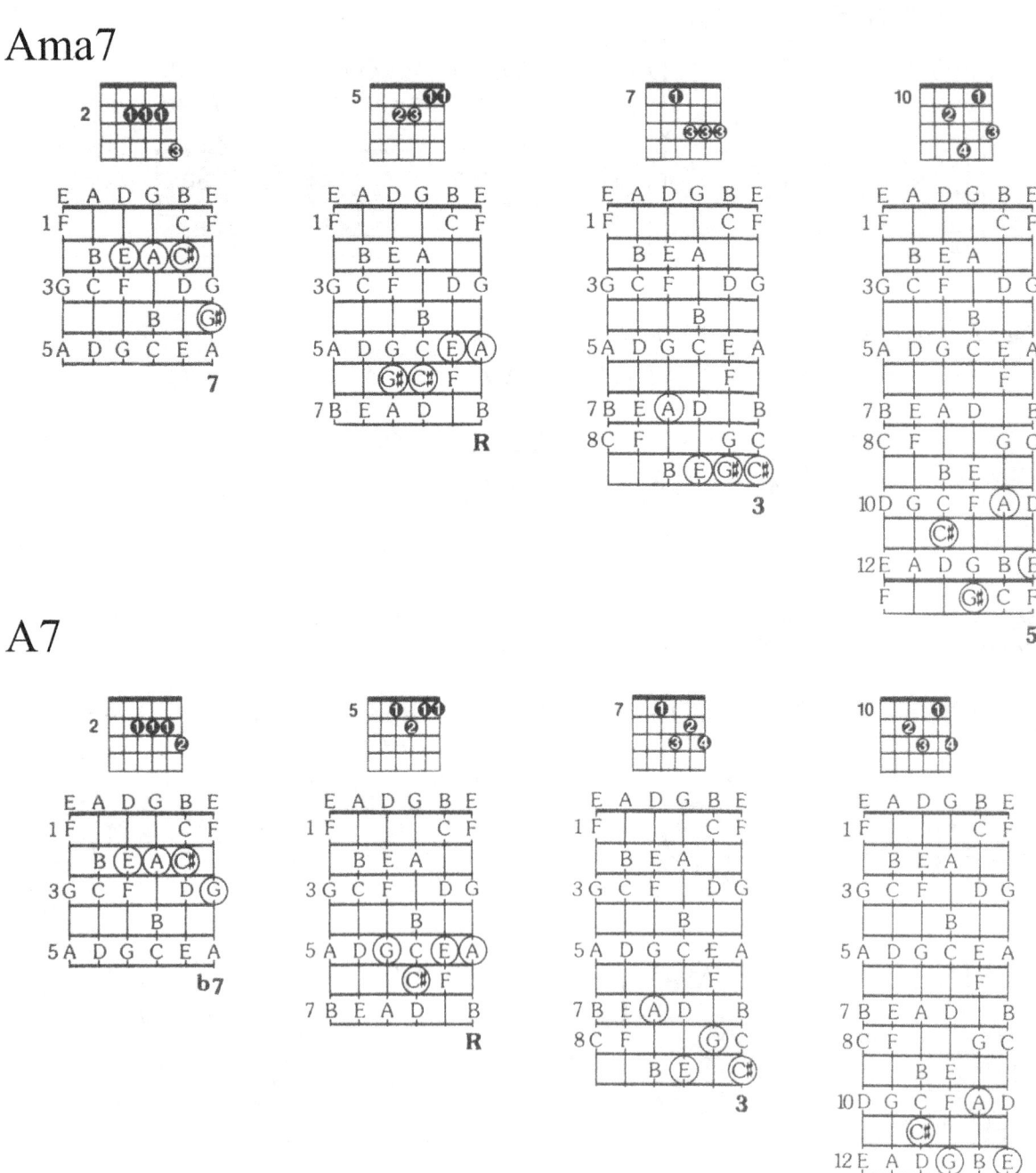

Ami7

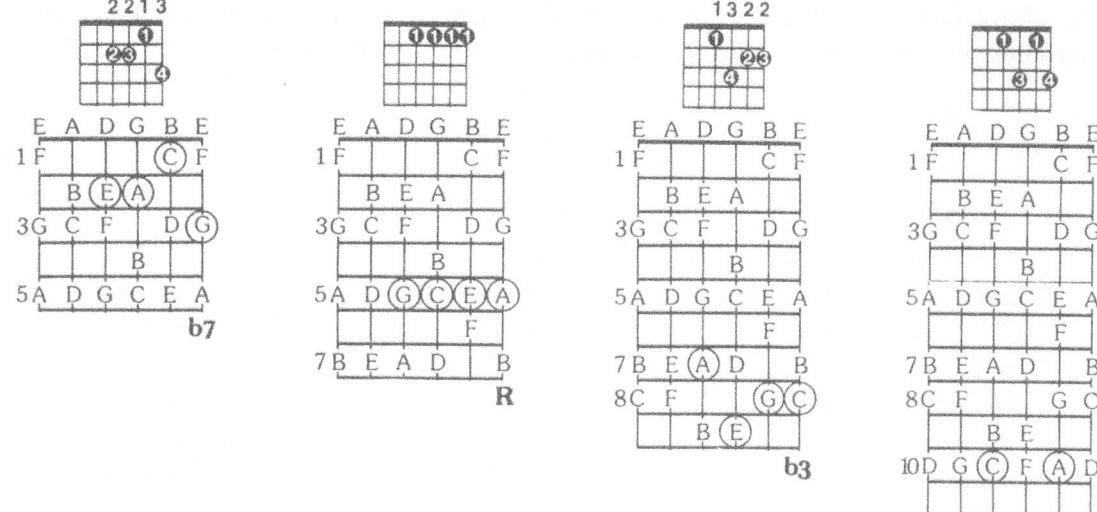

Learn these inversions one group at a time. For instance, work on the major seventh inversions first and then use the chords in the exercises. Then work on the dominant seventh and so on. Try to remember the root of the chord (is it a D, F, or an A chord?) in each fingering. Another way to keep track of the inversions is to try to remember which note is the highest (or lowest) note in the fingering, by DEGREE. For instance:

Is the "root," "third," "fifth," or "seventh" the highest note?

Remember:

When I use the grid with note names I'm trying to encourage you to see the notes by name. Take advantage of it if you wish. It won't hurt, but it is optional.

Shown below is an "Emi chord stream" - various Emi chords strung together, but without the note names shown. Seeing the note names can be helpful as you learn the fingerboard.

35.

Emi11	Emi11	Emi11	Emi11	Emi9	Em9
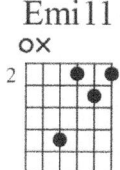	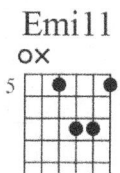	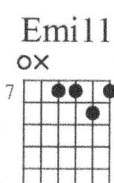	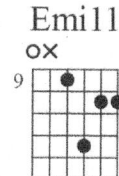	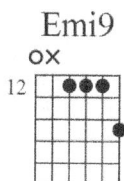	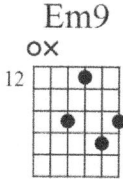

You may hit the low E string with each chord to keep the tonal center more obvious.

Progression Examples

Shown below are several examples that you can copy to help you remember the fingerings. Basically, play the chord stream (of four inversions) up the neck with one root, and down with a chord whose root is up the interval of a fourth. Here it's up Ama7 and down Dma7. You'll be comping that way, as well as playing chords and melodies that way. (And walking bass patterns also use this approach.)

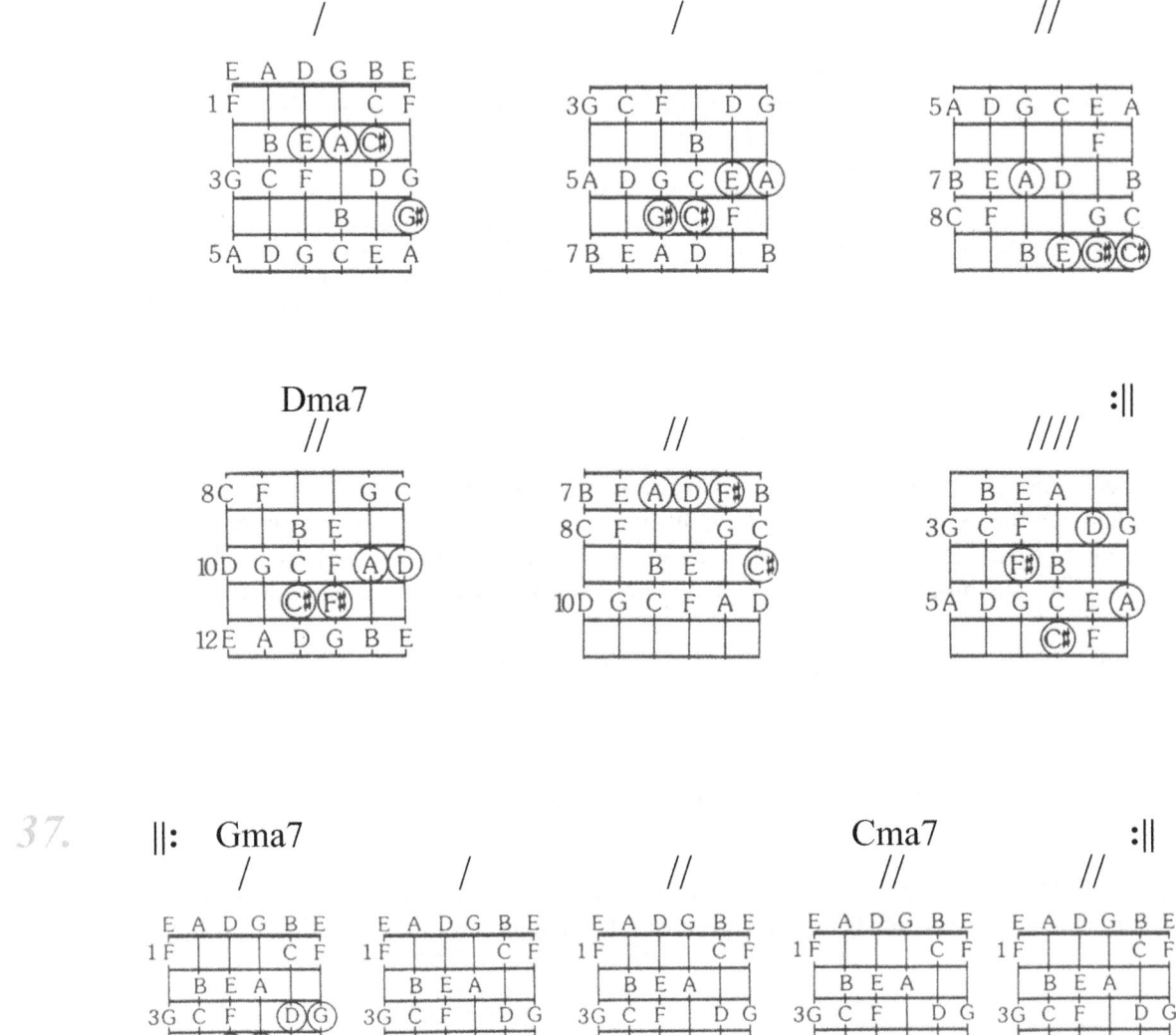

The example below uses dominant chords to walk around the cycle of fourths/fifths and ending with a Cmaj7. When you can play the example smoothly, with no halts or missed fingers, you're done with it.

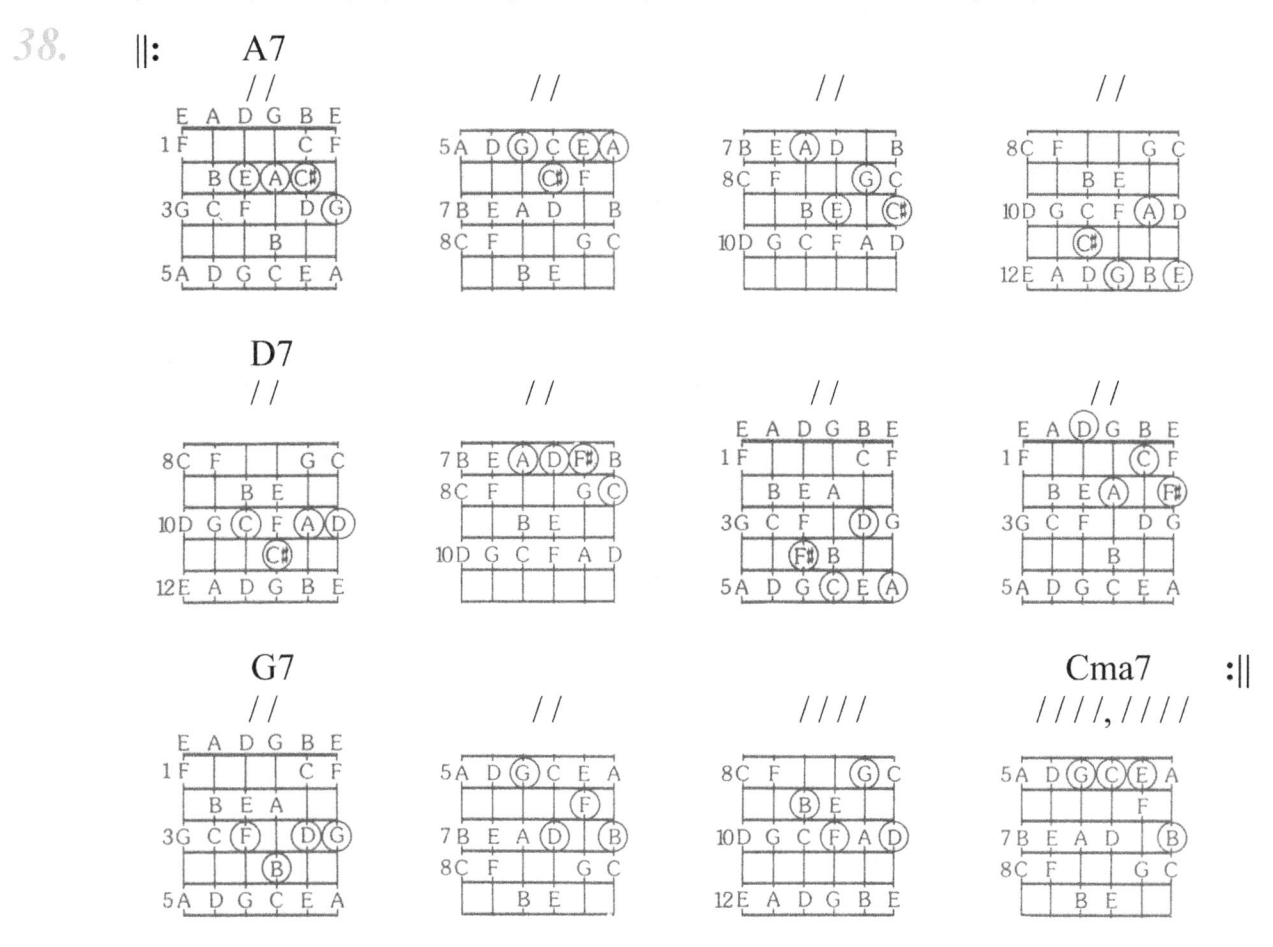

38. ||: A7 / /   / /   / /   / /

D7 / /   / /   / /   / /

G7 / /   / /   / / / /   Cma7 / / / / , / / / / :||

The next example emphasizes a descending bass line. You've probably heard this kind of progression played fingerstyle, at a medium (or slower) tempo.

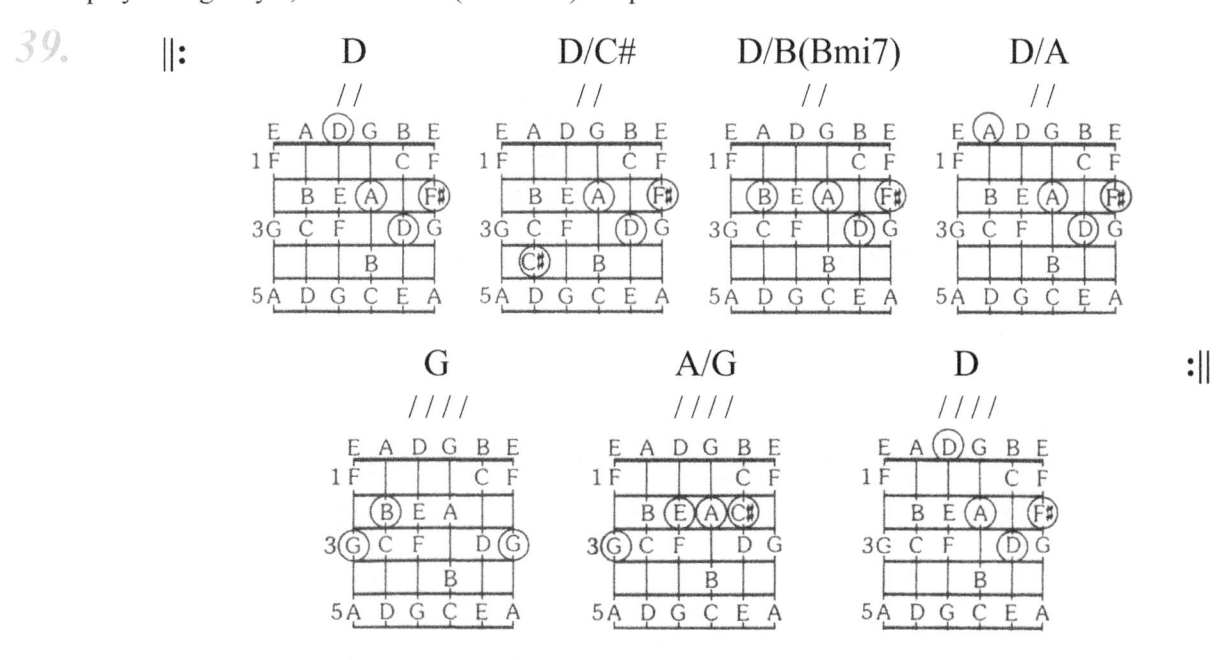

39. ||: D / /   D/C# / /   D/B(Bmi7) / /   D/A / /

G / / / /   A/G / / / /   D / / / /   :||

Moving around in 5ths using dominant chords - a country blues perhaps?

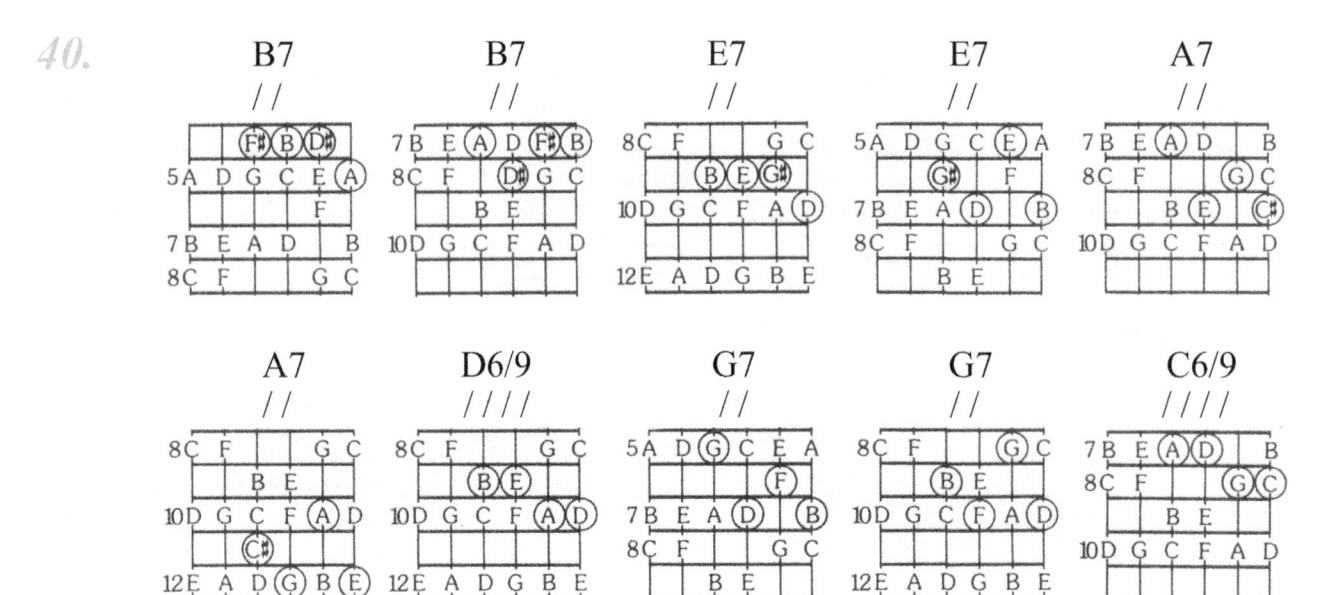

40.

B7 / / B7 / / E7 / / E7 / / A7 / /

A7 / / D6/9 / / / / G7 / / G7 / / C6/9 / / / /

Chords moving in ii-V-I progressions - a jazz standard perhaps, so easy swing?

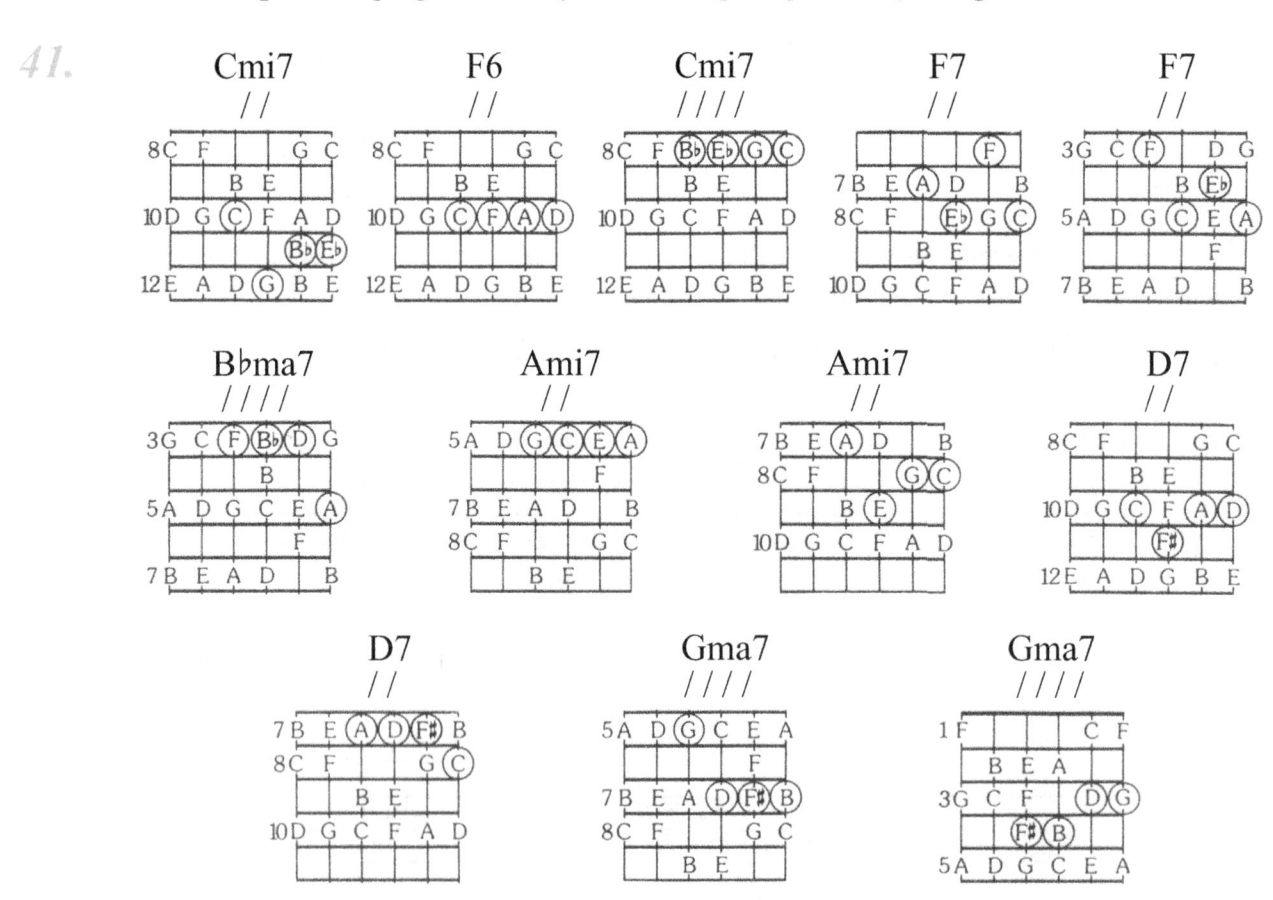

41.

Cmi7 / / F6 / / Cmi7 / / / / F7 / / F7 / /

B♭ma7 / / / / Ami7 / / Ami7 / / D7 / /

D7 / / Gma7 / / / / Gma7 / / / /

Play the following examples giving two beats for each chord fingering, except as noted.

42.

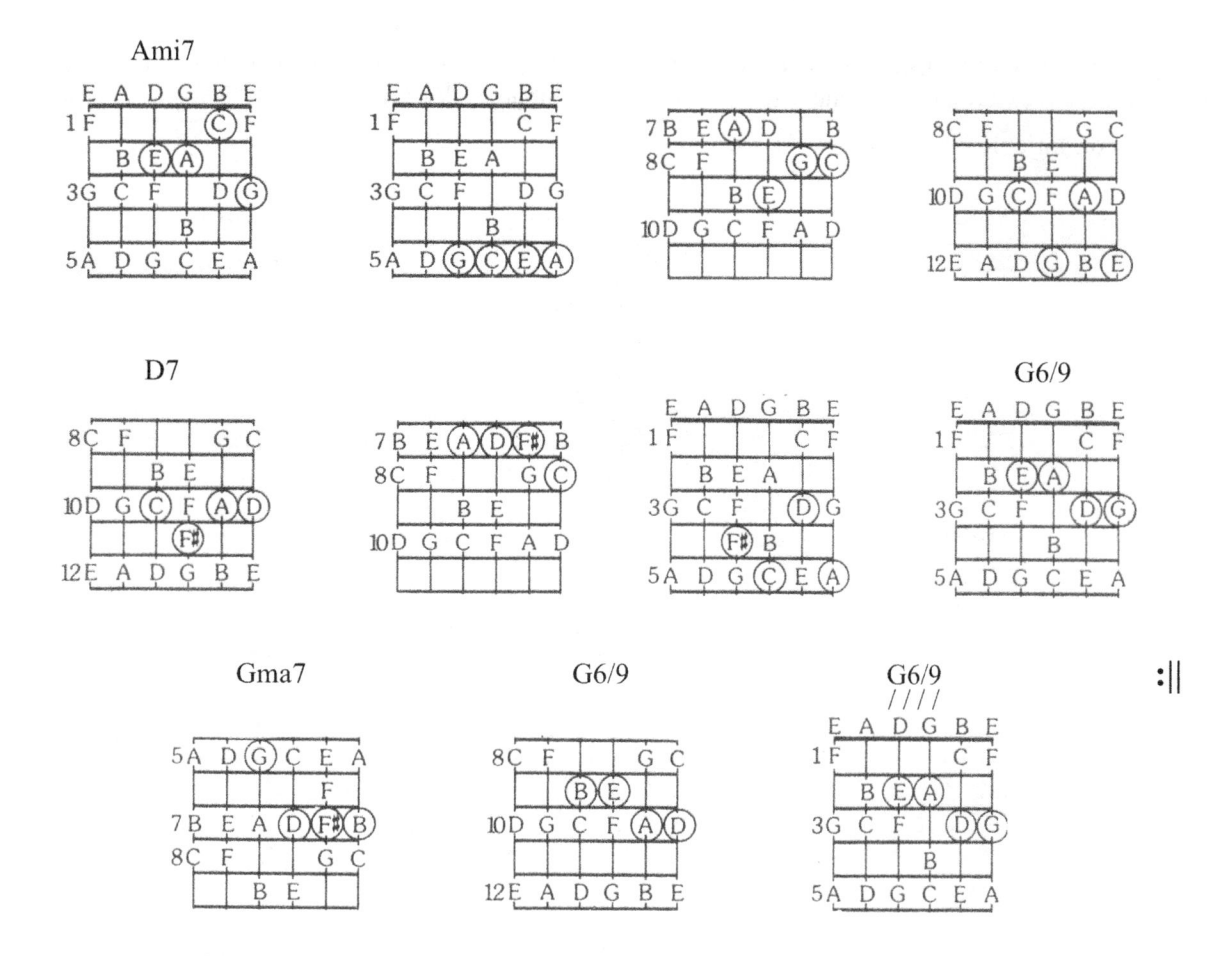

Ami7

D7

Gma7   G6/9   G6/9
                ////

:||

Below we move around the cycle of fourths with dominant chords.

43.

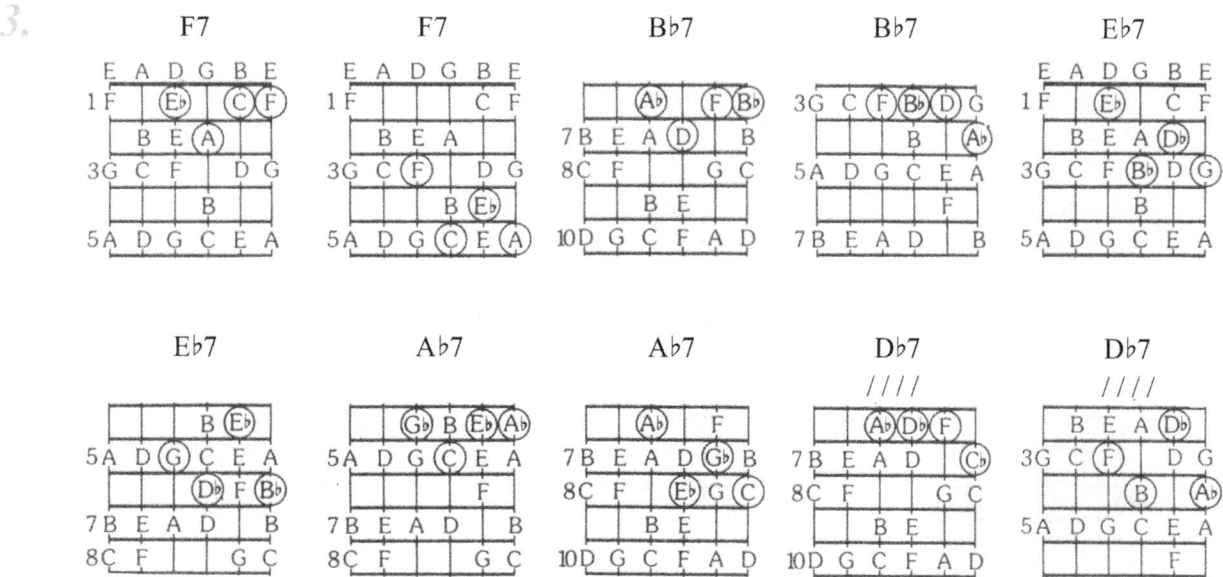

F7   F7   Bb7   Bb7   Eb7

Eb7   Ab7   Ab7   Db7   Db7
                     ////   ////

Comparing the 4321 Systematic Inversions

Compare the three families of chords in each position on the neck. Can you see the note that changes from column to column in the same row? Is it the same note in each position?

Are you comfortable playing across the rows?

44.

Everything is connected in both sound and structure. That's probably a good name for a book . . .

4321 Chord Licks

As noted before, chords up the interval of a 4th lend themselves to fills and licks in rock, blues, country and jazz. The following examples could be used over chords with a root of A. The roots in the licks are basically A - D - A in the first two examples. Some are dominant sounding, some major, and some minor. Play them all and learn to use them. The rhythm patterns are up to you. Start with two or four beats per chord. The arrow points to the C# note which can be hammered on from the C♮ for a more bluesy sound.

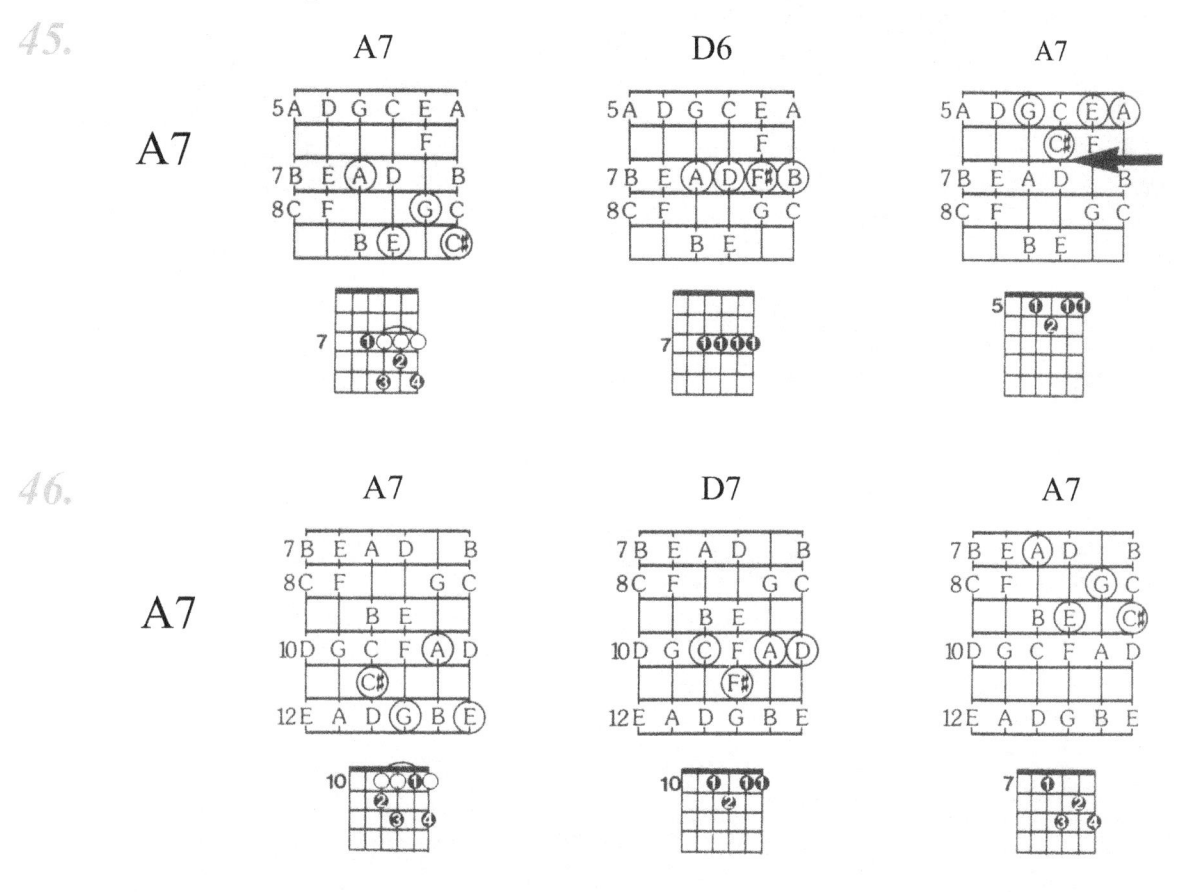

45. A7 / D6 / A7

46. A7 / D7 / A7

The lick below is a chord stream for use over an Amaj7. The two 6/9 chords were included because of their sound and easy fingering. You might hear this on a jazz ballad. Play up and down the neck.

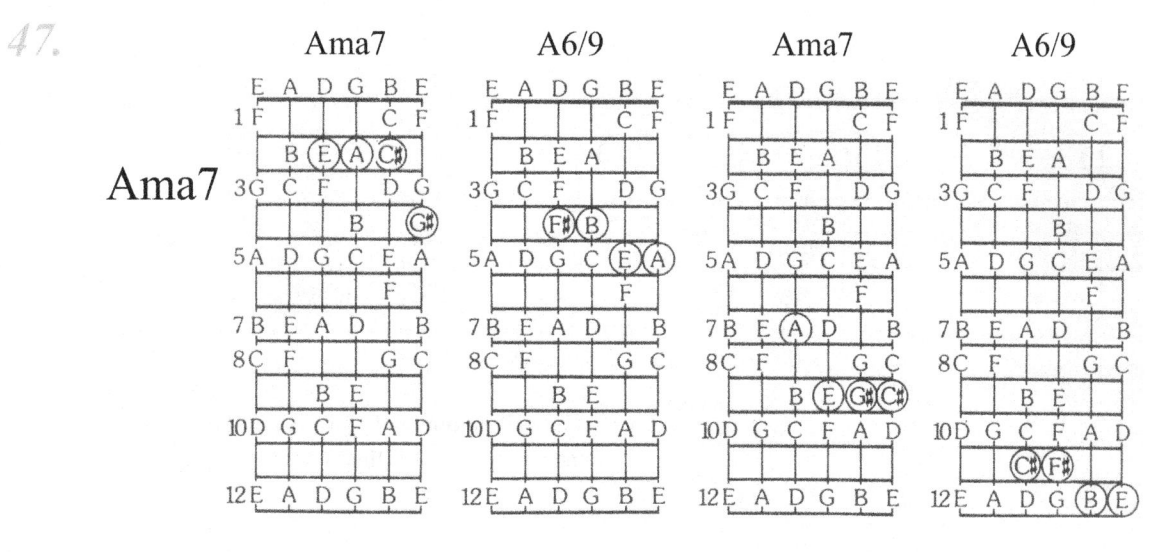

47. Ama7 / A6/9 / Ama7 / A6/9

The chord spellings are on the left hand diagrams while suggested fingerings are shown on the right. As before the rhythmic patterns are up to you. You can use two beats for the first two chords and four beats for the third chord, to start.

Try to use barres and double stops wherever you can. These are rock/blues sounds.

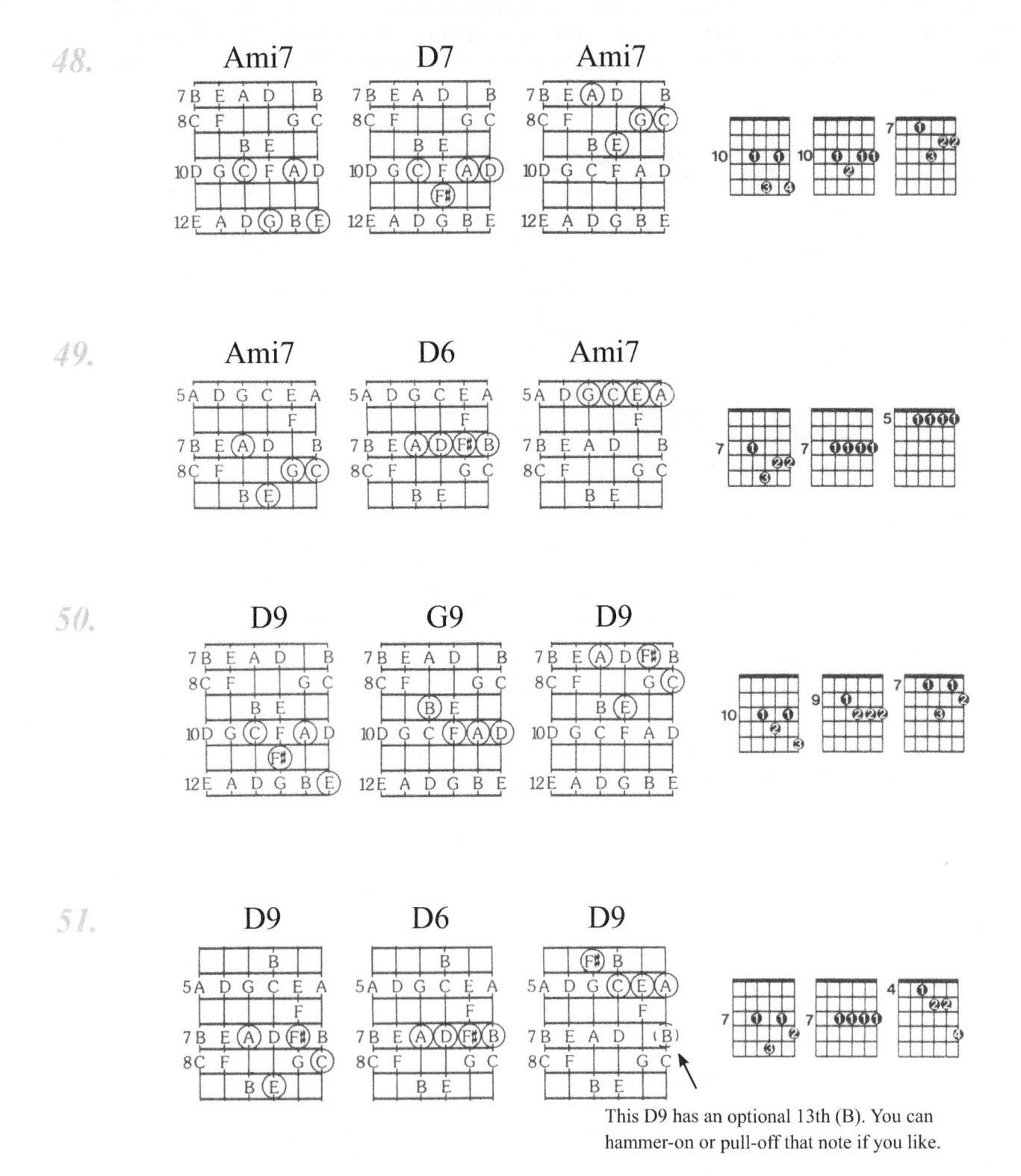

48. Ami7   D7   Ami7

49. Ami7   D6   Ami7

50. D9   G9   D9

51. D9   D6   D9

This D9 has an optional 13th (B). You can hammer-on or pull-off that note if you like.

Essential Chord Fingerings on 4321

We've focused on the principle seventh chords in each chord family - major, minor, and dominant. These basic seventh chords can be extended to include many of the other chords found in the family.

Following is a brief look at how the minor seventh fingerings can become fingerings for the minor seventh *flat five* chords. Review this material and become comfortable with the *process*.

Comparing the mi7 and mi7♭5

Shown below is the Ami7 chord we've already seen, and below that the A minor seven flat five chord. Note that the flatted fifth is E♭ (instead of E♮).

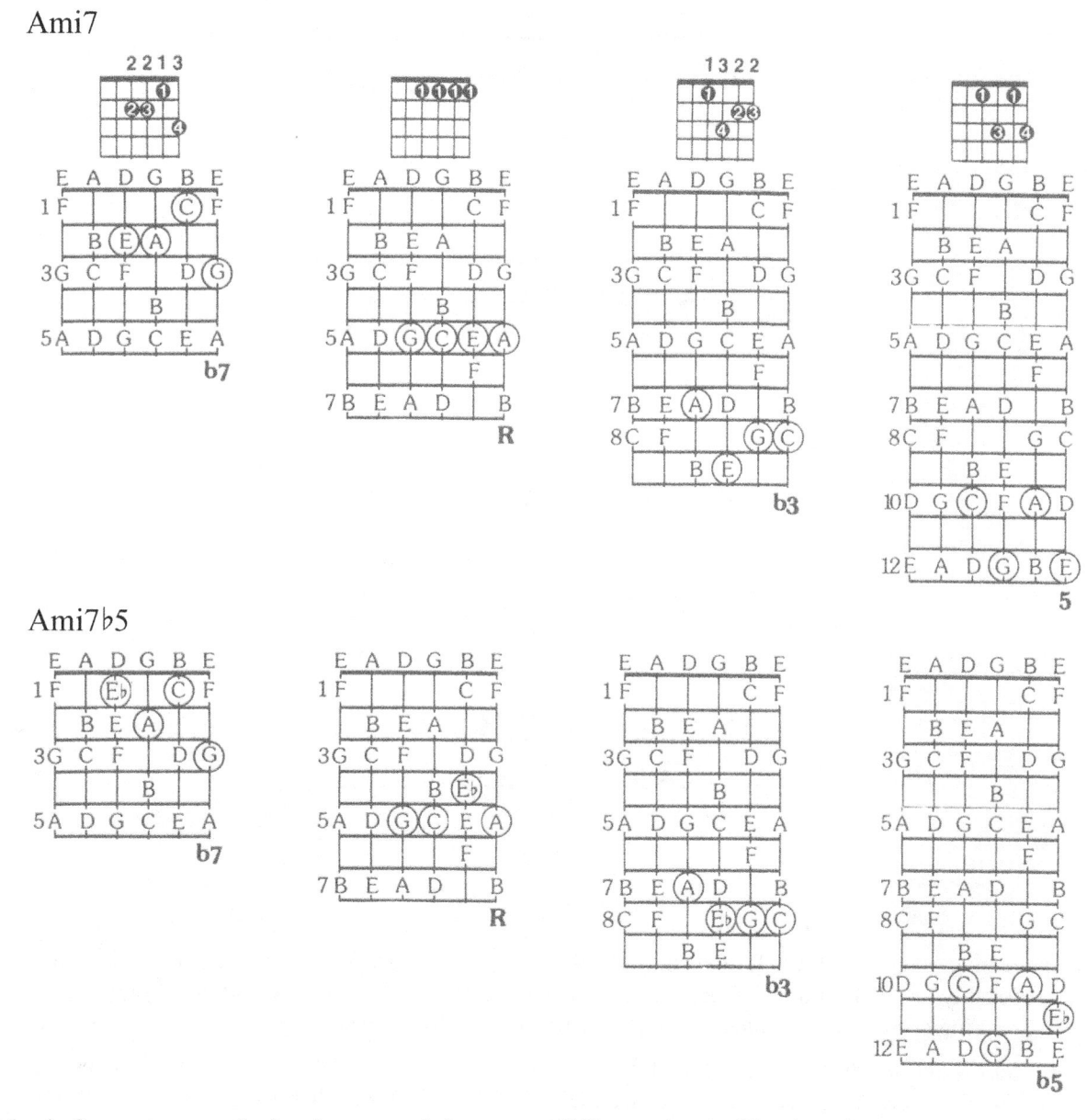

Ami7

Ami7♭5

A basic four note seventh chord can morph into many different chords (like the mi7 becoming a mi7♭5). The following pages explore many new chords derived from the basic seventh chords.

Chord Systems 40th Anniversary Edition - by Leon White

Using the Progressions with the Essential Fingerings

The essential fingerings show related chords together, and highlight the moving note (or "passing tone") that is within each chord.

As can be seen on the sample page below, there is an Emi7 and an arrow at the top left, and a Dma7 and an arrow on the bottom right of the diagram. In the center are the essential chords.

The progression being suggested is a ii - V - I of D major: Emi7 - A7(A9, A7#5 etc.) - Dma7. The "A7" refers to the group of A7 chords with their fingerings featured on the page.

These comparison pages of inversions are for browsing. There are hundreds of chords shown in this dictionary format. Explore and remember a chord if you have a use for it. Do NOT memorize all this!!!

52.

ii chord Emi7 → *The A7 chords to use as the V chord*

A7#5   A7   A7b5

↘ Dma7

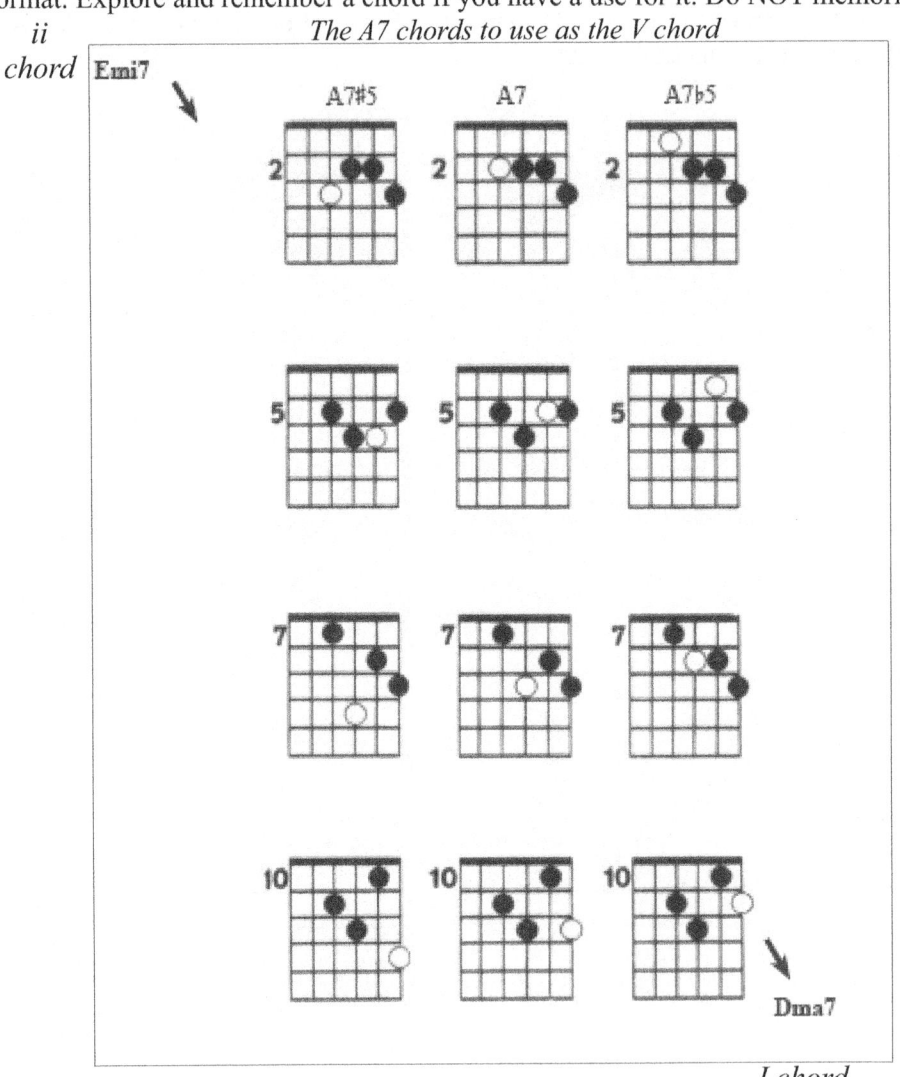

I chord

Each page gives suggested beats for the chords in the progression. The idea is that you select an Emi7 chord (probably on 4321) and play that. Then play one of the *rows* of A7 chords, and then finish with a Dma7 chord fingering of your choice (again probably on the 4321 stringset).

You'll hear the chords, the moving line, and the progression sounds in one step. Repeat this process for each row on the page. You'll also be able to see the note in the A7 chords that is moving to provide the melody and moving voice. *Huge mileage for one page*.

To get fancy, try *different* Emi7 chords on each *row*. Listen and mark the examples you'd like to use.

The Major Chord Family

These diagrams are systematic inversions aligned with each other to illustrate how the movement of one note effects each chord. Play down the 1st column to hear the reference chord (A major) and then *across the rows* to hear the various chords derived from it (Ama7, A7, A6). (The dominant 7 chord is here for reference only.) Each of these reference sections will include chords you can use to play a progression. Here it's a ii - V - I progression - Bmi7 to E7 to the A major chords shown. Play Bmi7 and E7 for four beats each, and then play a row, with *one beat for each chord* (ii - V - I).

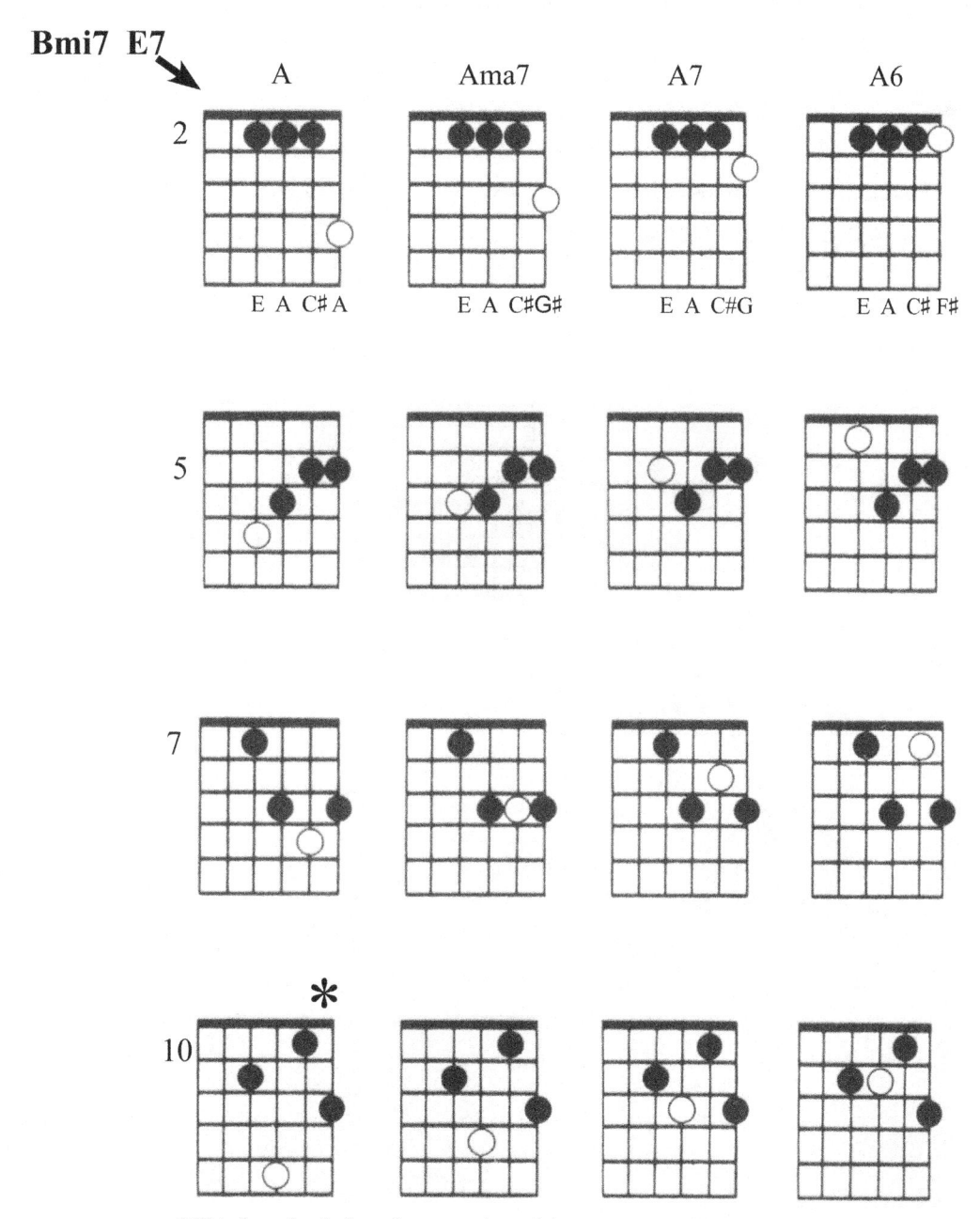

53. **Bmi7 E7**

* This fingering is for reference only, as it has two roots on the middle strings.

You've already seen the Ama7 and A7 chords so the only new chords are A major, the first column, and A6, the right-hand column. Can you see how chords relate to each other? Think on this a bit: moving a note or two around can get you a number of new chord sounds, but they're still related to what you know!

Chord Systems 40th Anniversary Edition - by Leon White

By now you should be getting comfortable playing chord inversions and you should be starting to use them in songs. Take your time here. And remember that you can use this section for reference.

Most of the chords in the major family might be played in place of a major 7th chord in songs. Experiment for yourself. This can really be a lot of fun, and there are many beautiful sounds waiting to be discovered here.   0 = the note changed to produce the new chord.

As before there is a ii - V - I progression you can use to play the A fingerings - Bmi7 to E7 to A major. Play each chord (Bmi7 E7) for four beats and then play four chords in a row with one beat for each A fingering (ii - V - I). Try to choose fingerings on the same stringset for Bmi7 and E7.

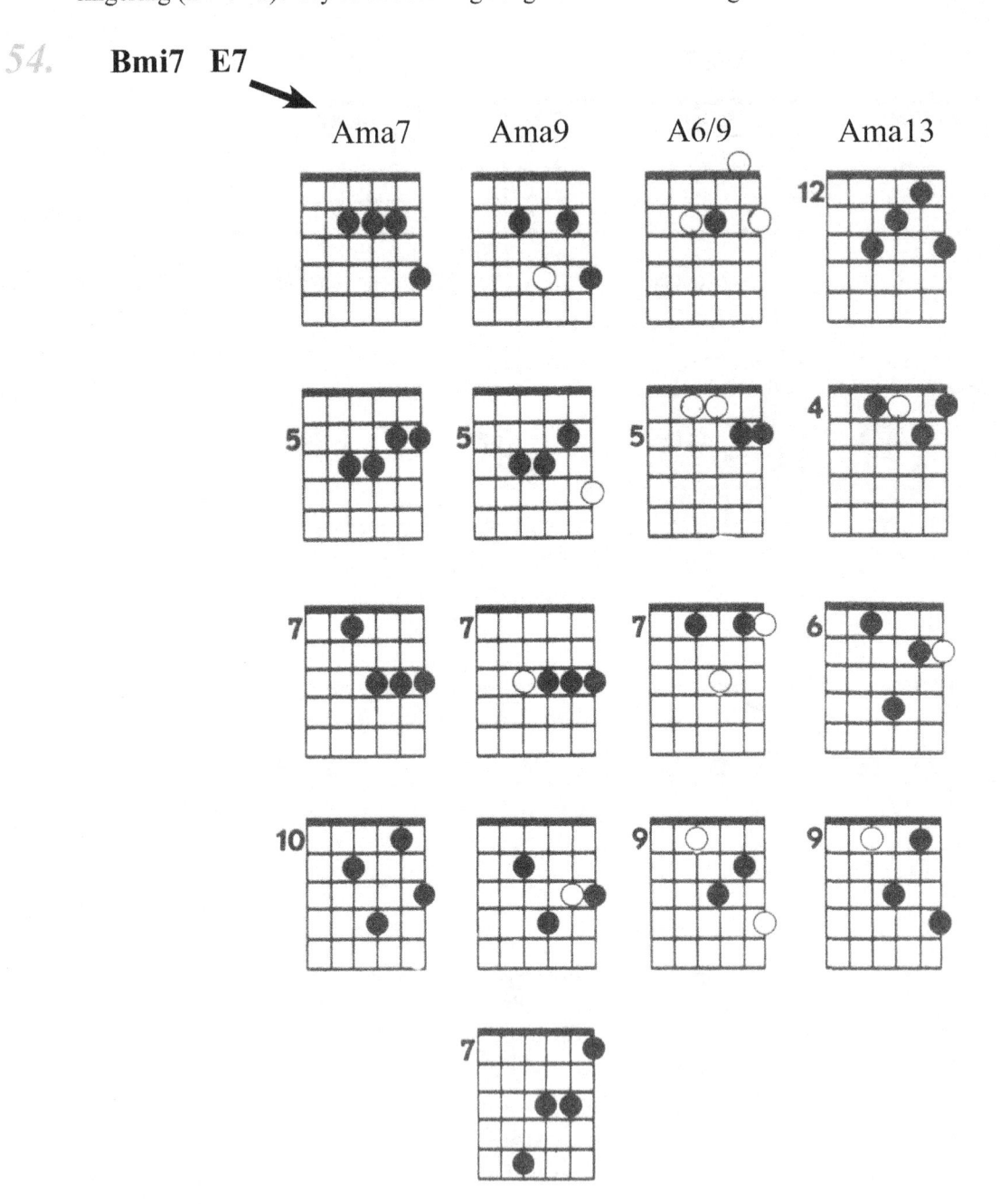

54.   **Bmi7   E7**

Ama7   Ama9   A6/9   Ama13

The chords "develop" from left to right on the page. For instance: The first column is Major 7th. What note changes to produce the chord to the right - Major 9th? Answer-the root moves" up" to the 9th.

Then . . . how does A Major 9 become A6/9? Look at the moving notes carefully.

The Minor Chord Family

In the next example the passing tone begins on the fifth and drops down to the ♭5 and then the 4th (often heard as the 11th). The three chords together might be used as a substitute for a plain Ami7.

For a progression sample consider these minor chords to be a ii chord. At the bottom are V and I chords. Use four beats for the minor chords, and four beats *each* for the V chord and the I chord (Dma7, G7).

55.

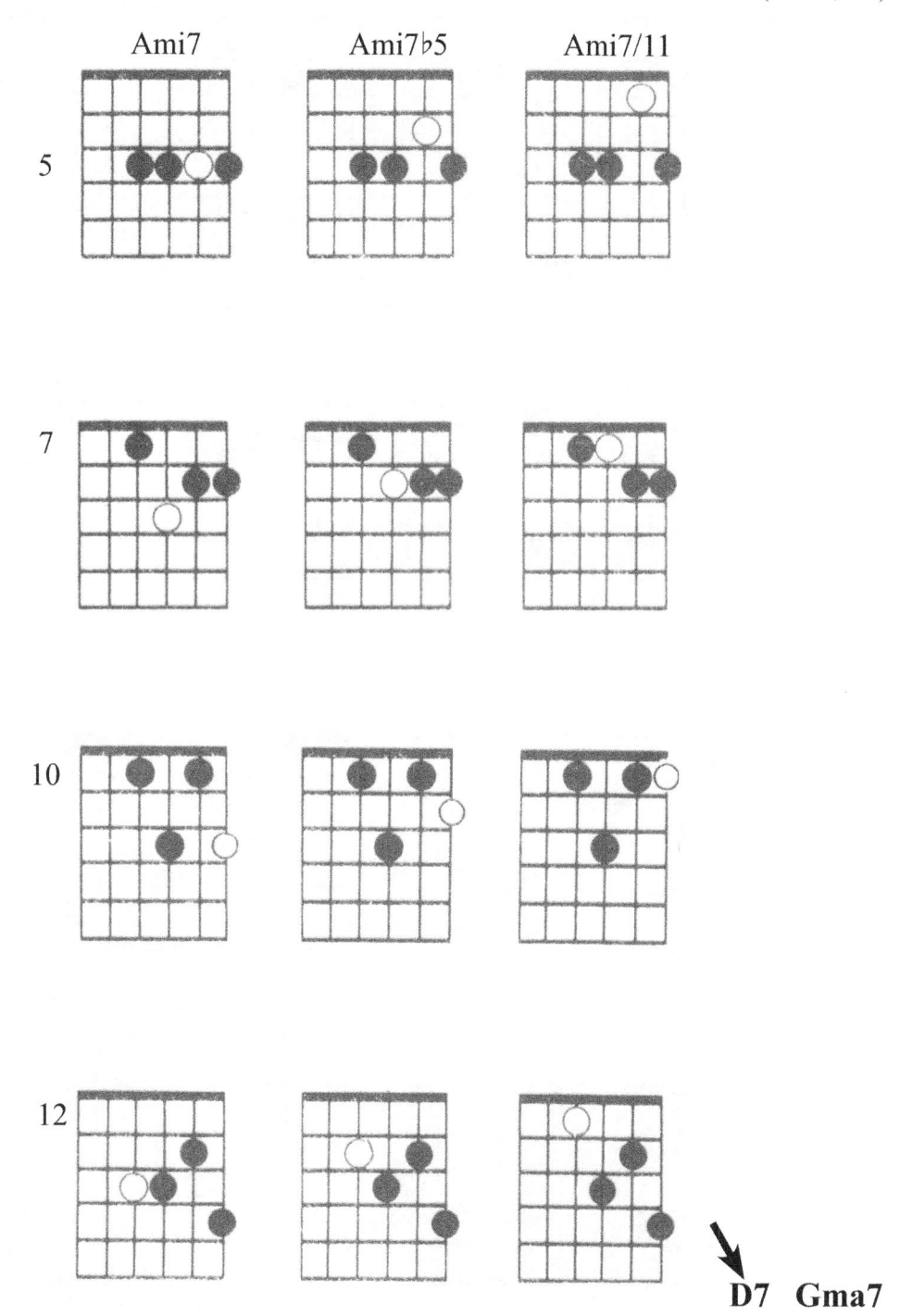

Ami7   Ami7♭5   Ami7/11

D7   Gma7

Repeat the rows across to make sure you can hear the moving voice. Each inversion has its own sound.

Chord Systems 40th Anniversary Edition - by Leon White • 47

In the example below, the moving voice is the root. It moves down to the ♮7, the ♭7, and finally the 6. As before, all or part of this phrase could be added to an arrangement asking only for "Ami7."

For a progression sample consider these minor chords to be a ii chord. At the bottom are the V and I chords. Use one beat for each minor chord, and four beats *each* for the V chord and the I chord.

56.

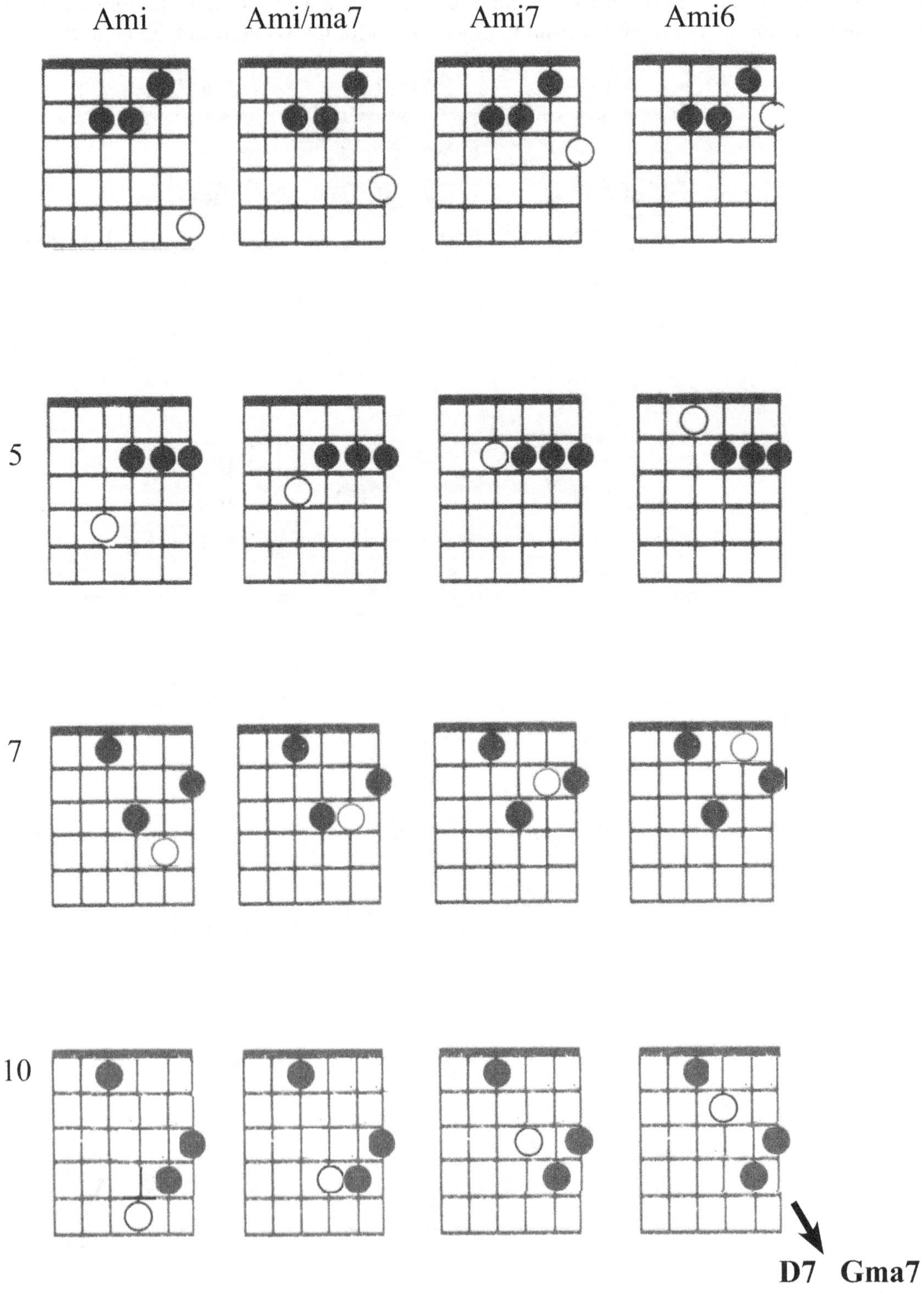

        Ami   Ami/ma7   Ami7   Ami6

5

7

10

                                                                                 D7 Gma7

Try to use the 4321 stringset for the D7 and Gma7 chords to have smoother voice leading.

In the example below, there are several moving voices. The seven moves to six, the five moves to flat five, and the root moves up to the ninth. As before, all or part of this phrase could be added to an arrangement asking only for "Ami7."

For a progression sample consider these minor chords to be a ii chord. At the bottom are the V and a I chords. Use one beat for each minor chord, and four beats each for the V chord and the I chord.

Ami7   Ami6   Ami7♭5   Ami9

D7   Gma7

The Ami9 shapes shown here look like major seventh fingerings, don't they? Ami9 and Cma7 inhabit the same notes: (A)   C   E   G   B   in 4 notes *could* be

C   E   G   B   in a Cma7 chord.

Play the open A string to hear the root more clearly.

Chord Systems 40th Anniversary Edition - by Leon White • 49

Minor Chord Family Examples

58. Ami7 Ami7♭5 D7 Gma7

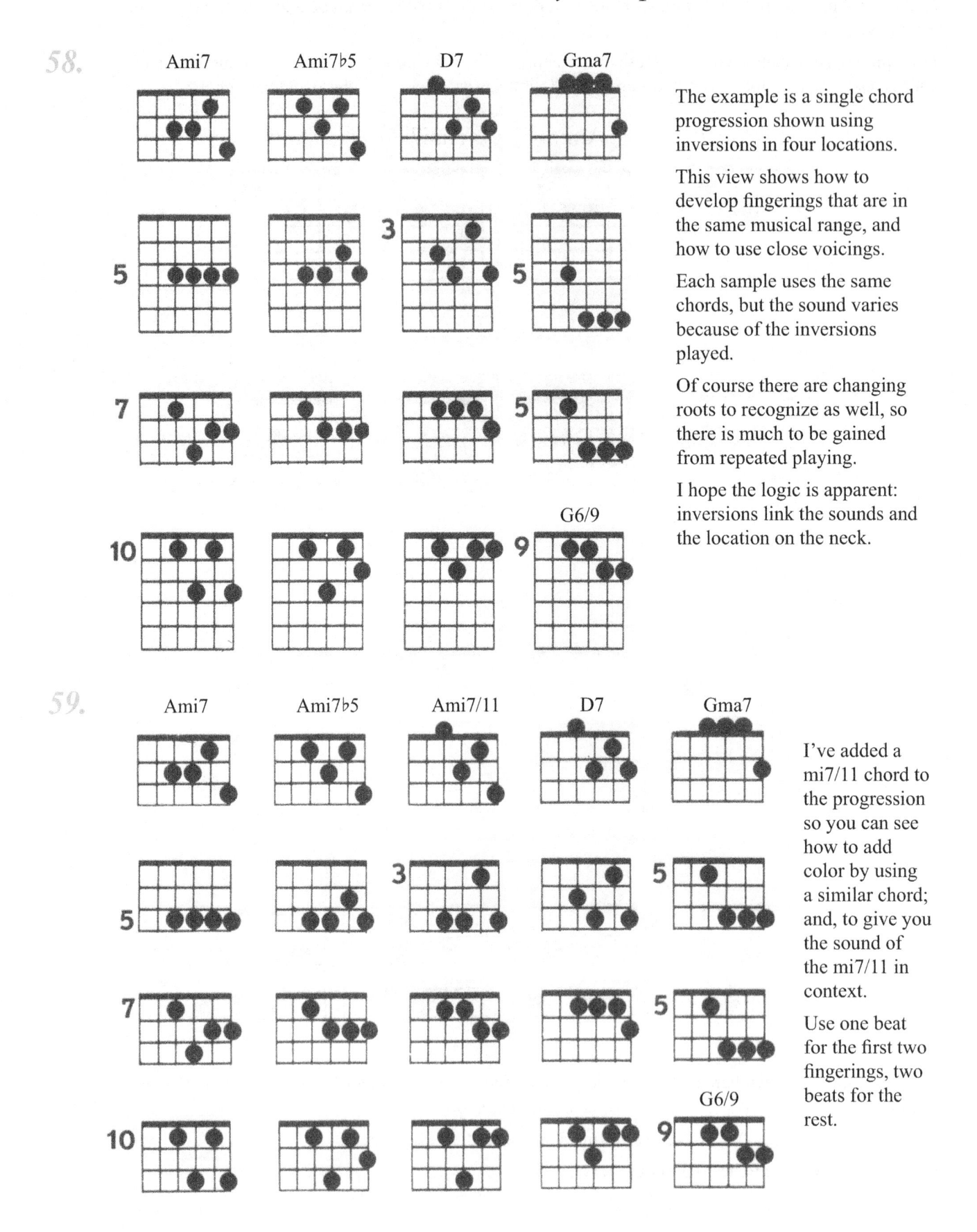

The example is a single chord progression shown using inversions in four locations.

This view shows how to develop fingerings that are in the same musical range, and how to use close voicings.

Each sample uses the same chords, but the sound varies because of the inversions played.

Of course there are changing roots to recognize as well, so there is much to be gained from repeated playing.

I hope the logic is apparent: inversions link the sounds and the location on the neck.

G6/9

59. Ami7 Ami7♭5 Ami7/11 D7 Gma7

I've added a mi7/11 chord to the progression so you can see how to add color by using a similar chord; and, to give you the sound of the mi7/11 in context.

Use one beat for the first two fingerings, two beats for the rest.

G6/9

The Dominant Chord Family

In these examples, the reference chord (A7) is placed in the center column so you can compare a raised 5th and a lowered fifth on either side. Play down each column and then play across the rows left to right.

For progression samples consider these dominant chords to be a V chord. At the top is a ii chord. At the bottom is a I chord. Give the Emi7 four beats. Use four beats for the *set* of dominant chords, and four beats for the I chord to produce a ii - V - I example.

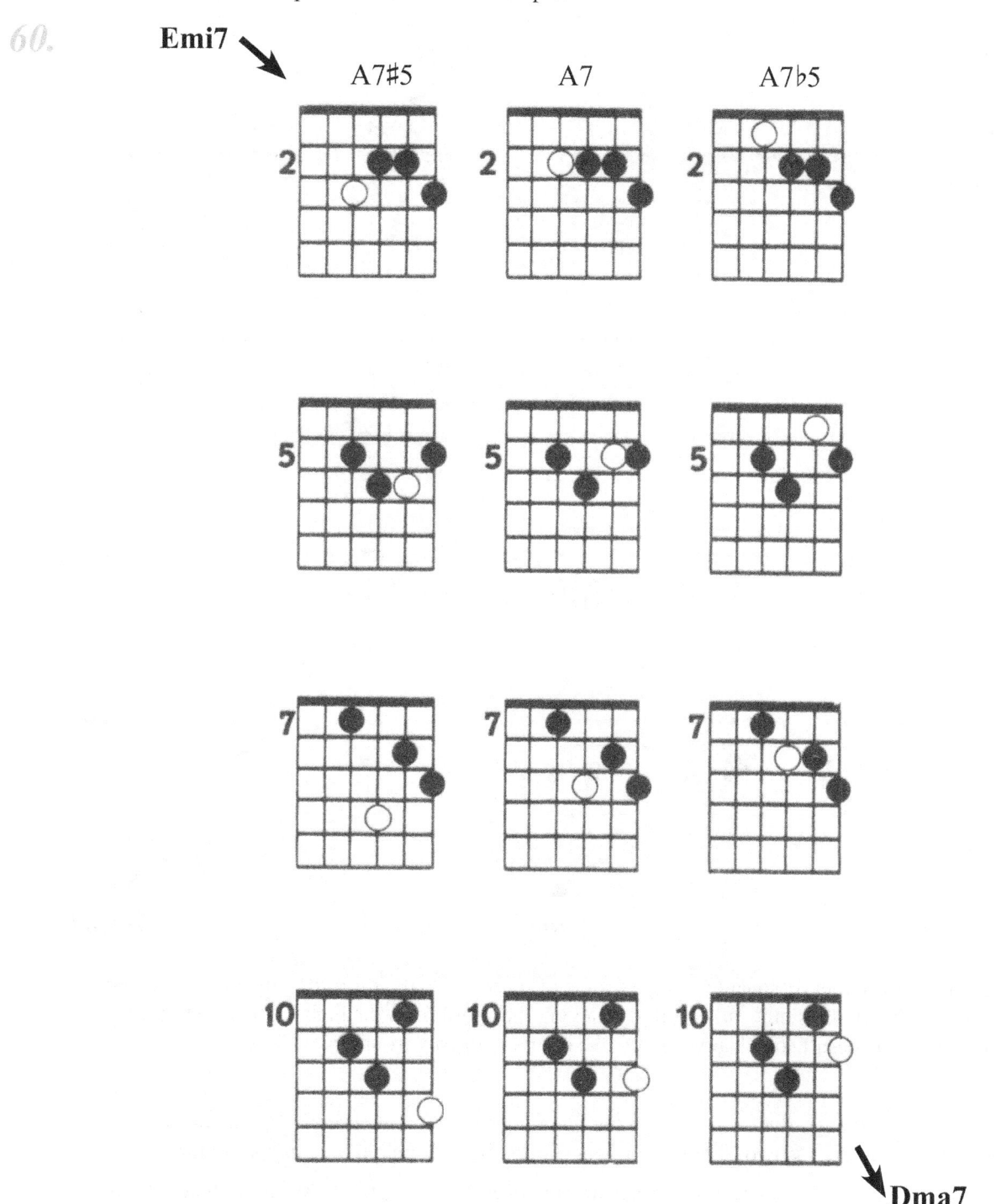

60.

Emi7 ↘

A7#5   A7   A7♭5

↘ **Dma7**

Chord Systems 40th Anniversary Edition - by Leon White • 51

The diagrams below depict two sets of moving voices. On the left side the voice is the #9 moving down. On the right side the moving voice is the fifth - starting with the #5 and ending with the flatted fifth. As before these passing tones can be used to construct short chord phrases. Each progression has four inversions. Listen to them, review the moving voices, and become comfortable with the altered sounds.

For progression samples consider these dominant chords to be a V chord. At the top is a ii chord. At the bottom is a I chord. Give the Emi7 four beats. Use four beats for your choice of A dominant chords, and four beats for the I chord (Dma7) to produce a ii - V - I progression.

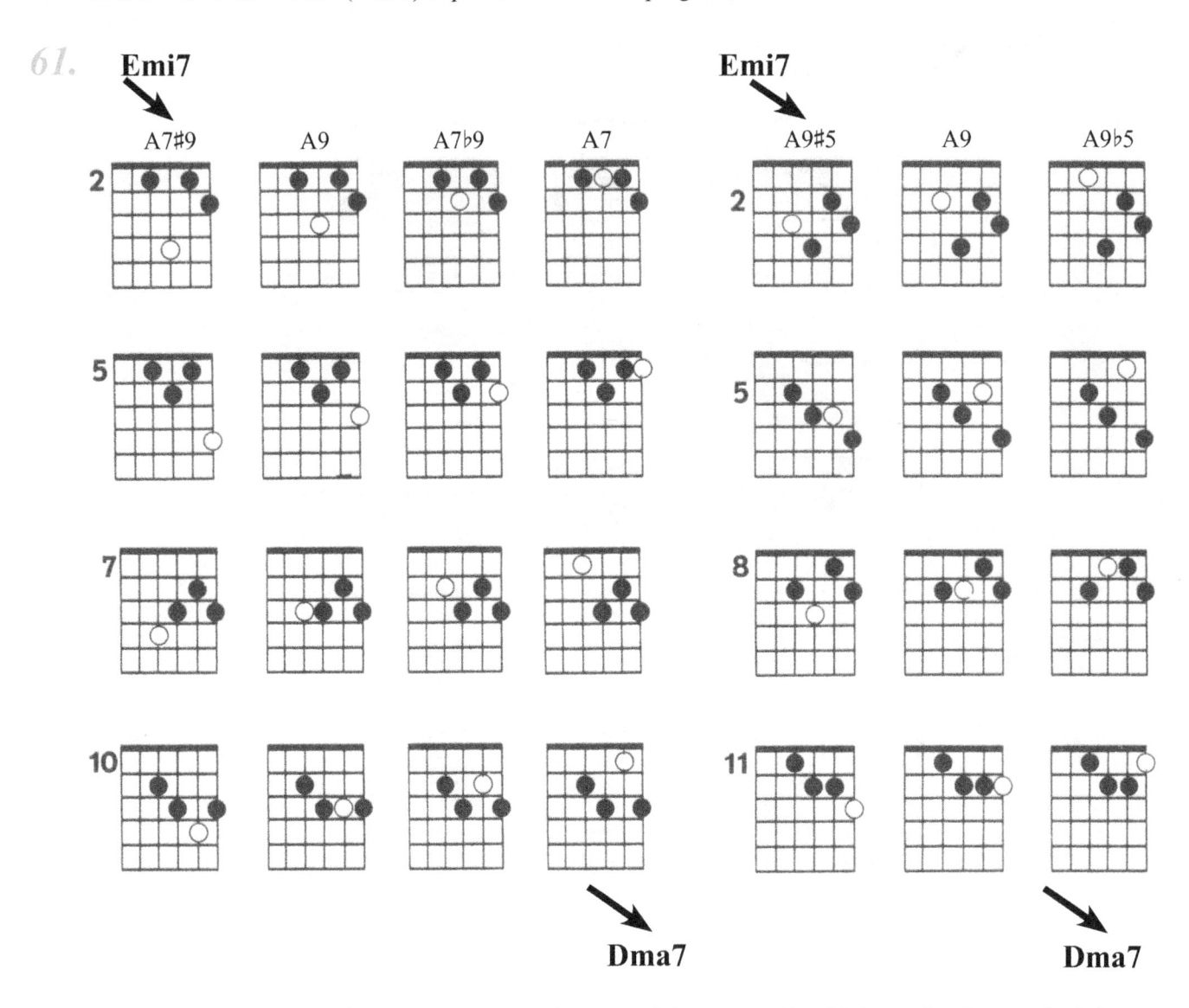

61.

Emi7 → A7#9　A9　A7♭9　A7　　　Emi7 → A9#5　A9　A9♭5

[Chord diagrams in rows at frets 2, 5, 7/8, 10/11]

↓ Dma7　　　　↓ Dma7

Note: There are some rather dissonant sounds in some of these rows (the third row first box on the left hand side). While that A7#9 is quite an earful, try playing the chord from the highest to lowest voice. And even if that one chord doesn't sound so welcome, the others in the row sound pretty good.

You may have noticed that you've seen some of the fingerings as different chords. That's not an error. Some fingerings can be used as two or more different chords. It is the magic of using only four notes.

I'm using chords from the root A because you can add the open 5th string (the A string) to these chords so you can clearly here the sound with the root. That will help keep the synonyms less confusing.

The 6432 Stringset

The 6432 stringset holds many popular chords, and provides many chords used in jazz accompaniment. In addition, we'll use it to demonstrate walking bass lines, and chords with melody lines.

Unlike the 4321 stringset, the 6432 stringset has one unplayed string.. That requires us to mute the fifth string with the left hand when strumming. While it may seem awkward at first if this is new to you, the muting will become second nature. Simply lean the finger on the sixth string over to block the fifth from ringing.

We'll begin like we did with the 4321 stringset, with a few examples to illustrate some of the sounds. Play the examples either by strumming or by fingerstyle (including pick-and-fingers). Each row is one example.

Introductory Examples

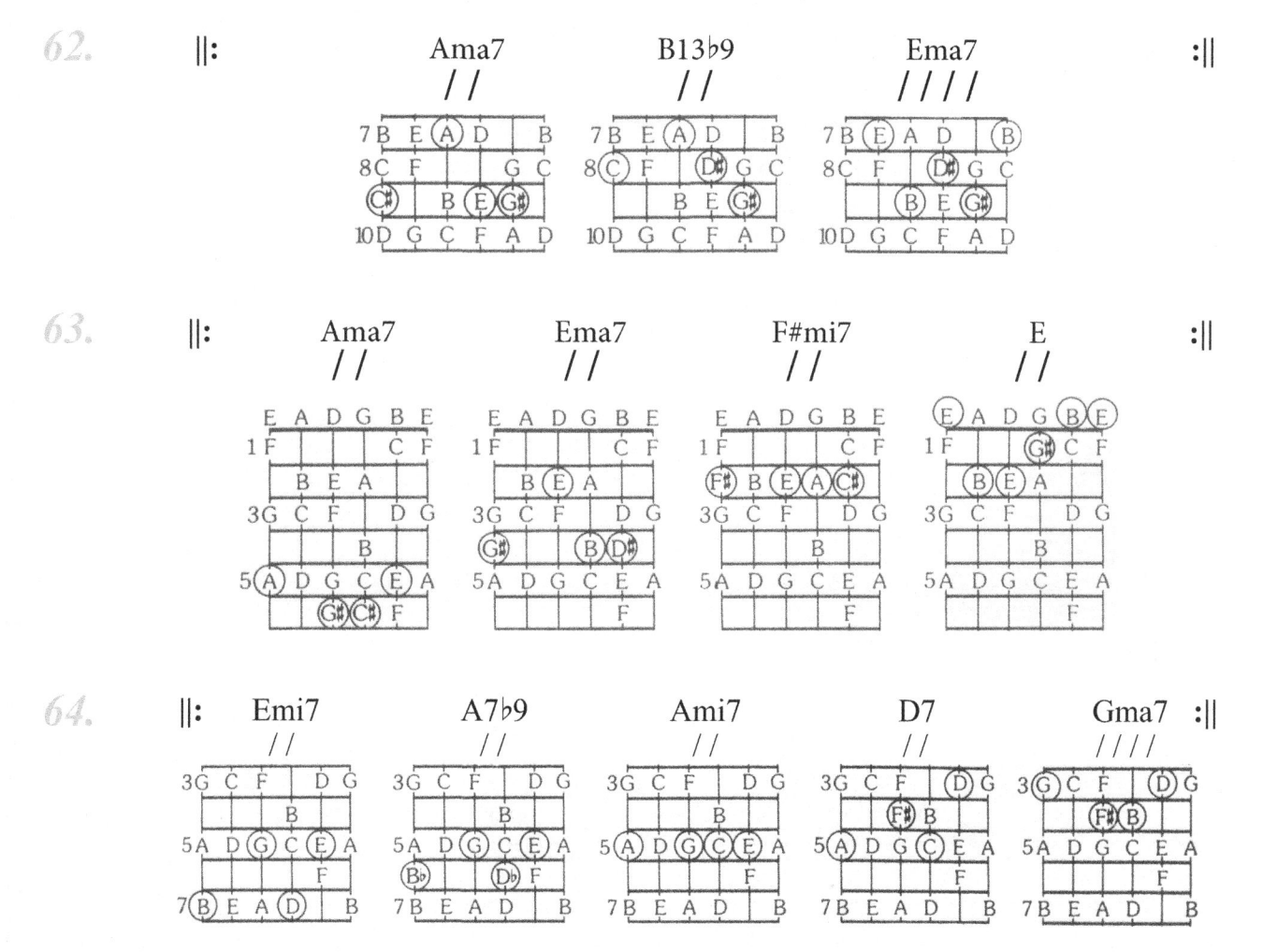

62. ||: Ama7 / /   B13♭9 / /   Ema7 / / / /   :||

63. ||: Ama7 / /   Ema7 / /   F#mi7 / /   E / /   :||

64. ||: Emi7 / /   A7♭9 / /   Ami7 / /   D7 / /   Gma7 / / / / :||

"Arpeggiating" a chord means to finger it with the left hand as normal, but play the notes *one string at a time* with the right hand. There are a variety of ways to do this, and the reference section has additional details on right hand techniques.

The point here is that you can "break-up" the chord by playing only one or two notes at a time. The 6432 stringset lends itself to these techniques because of the size of the voicings and the prominence of the bass voice. Use these techniques to make music out of the systematic inversions and the example progressions!

Systematic Inversions

Practice the inversions for each chord by playing across the rows shown, and playing up and then down the neck. Practice until you can play them smoothly without errors or pauses. These are absolutely essential!

Be sure to look at each fingering and identify possible double stop opportunities.

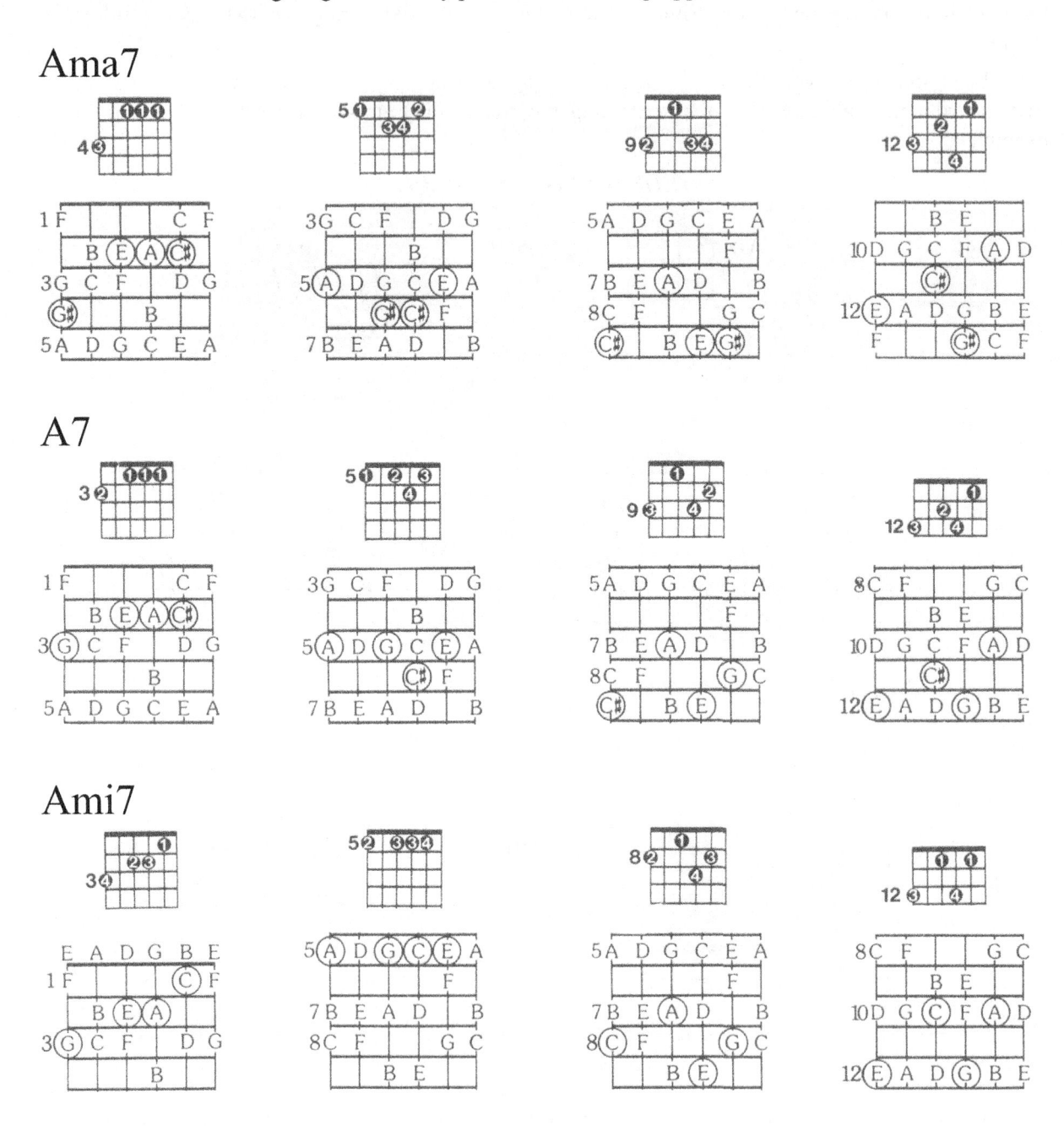

Ama7

A7

Ami7

Advanced Techniques - Special Note* This might be a good opportunity for you strummers to try playing fingerstyle if you haven't done so already. Just place your right hand fingers on the correct strings and pluck all the strings at the same time. Any awkwardness you may feel will soon disappear with a little repetition.

Progression Examples

Another benefit of learning chords by stringset is that once you've got your right hand working correctly, you can stop thinking of it and concentrate on the new chords. Fingerstyle players will notice that they can get different sounds by which strings they choose to sound first in a chord. The example in the middle of the page is intended to be three beats per chord, and takes up two lines. The rest are one row each.

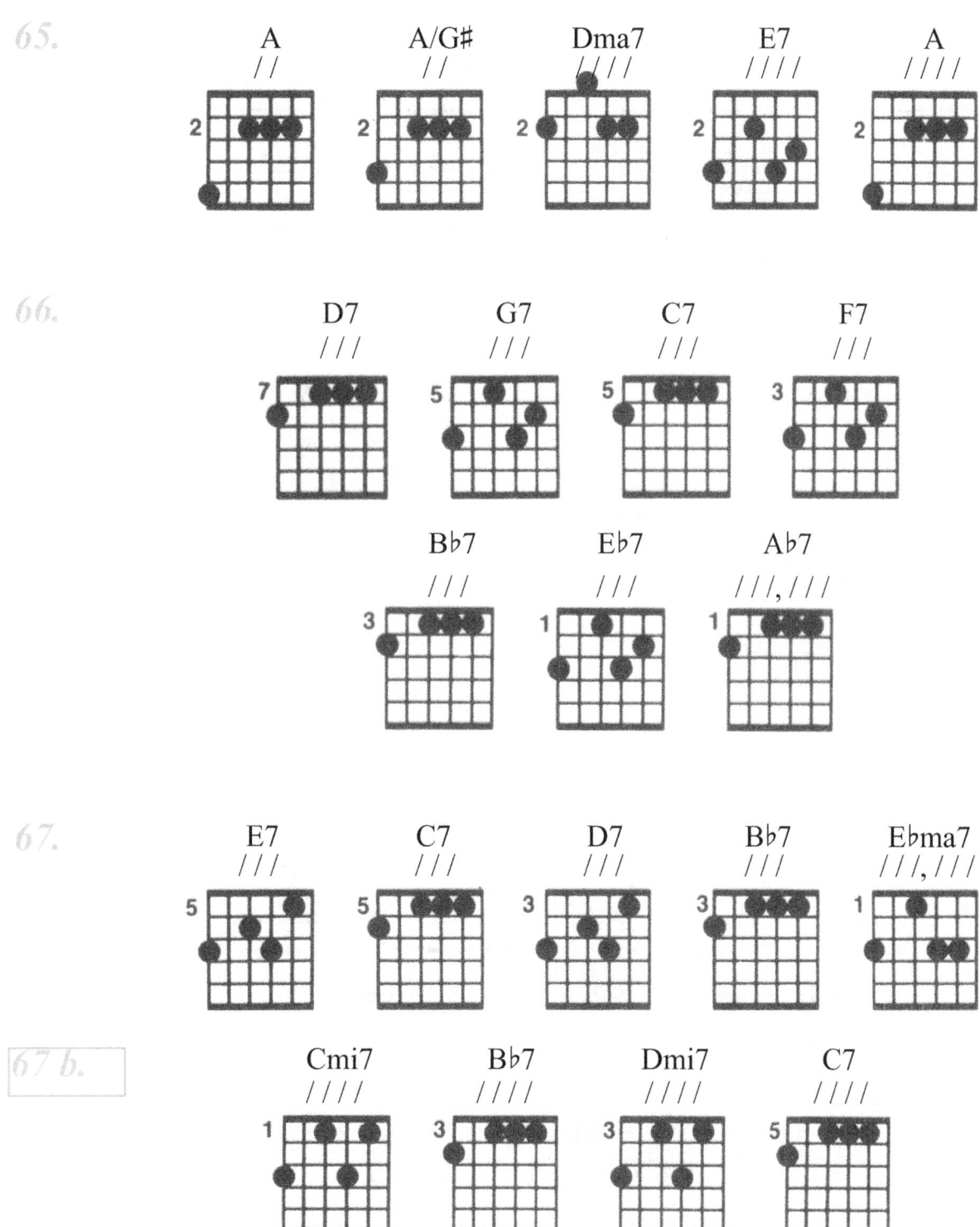

65. A / /   A/G# / /   Dma7 / / / /   E7 / / / /   A / / / /

66. D7 / / /   G7 / / /   C7 / / /   F7 / / /

Bb7 / / /   Eb7 / / /   Ab7 / / / , / / /

67. E7 / / /   C7 / / /   D7 / / /   Bb7 / / /   Ebma7 / / / , / / /

67 b. Cmi7 / / / /   Bb7 / / / /   Dmi7 / / / /   C7 / / / /

Chord Systems 40th Anniversary Edition - by Leon White

The examples below can be strummed, played fingerstyle, or by using pick and fingers.

The progressions use chords from various stringsets, but you've probably played songs like this already. Check each chord fingering before playing to make sure you sound the correct *strings* for each chord (Bmi7 in line 1, A in line 2 and Gma7 in line 4).

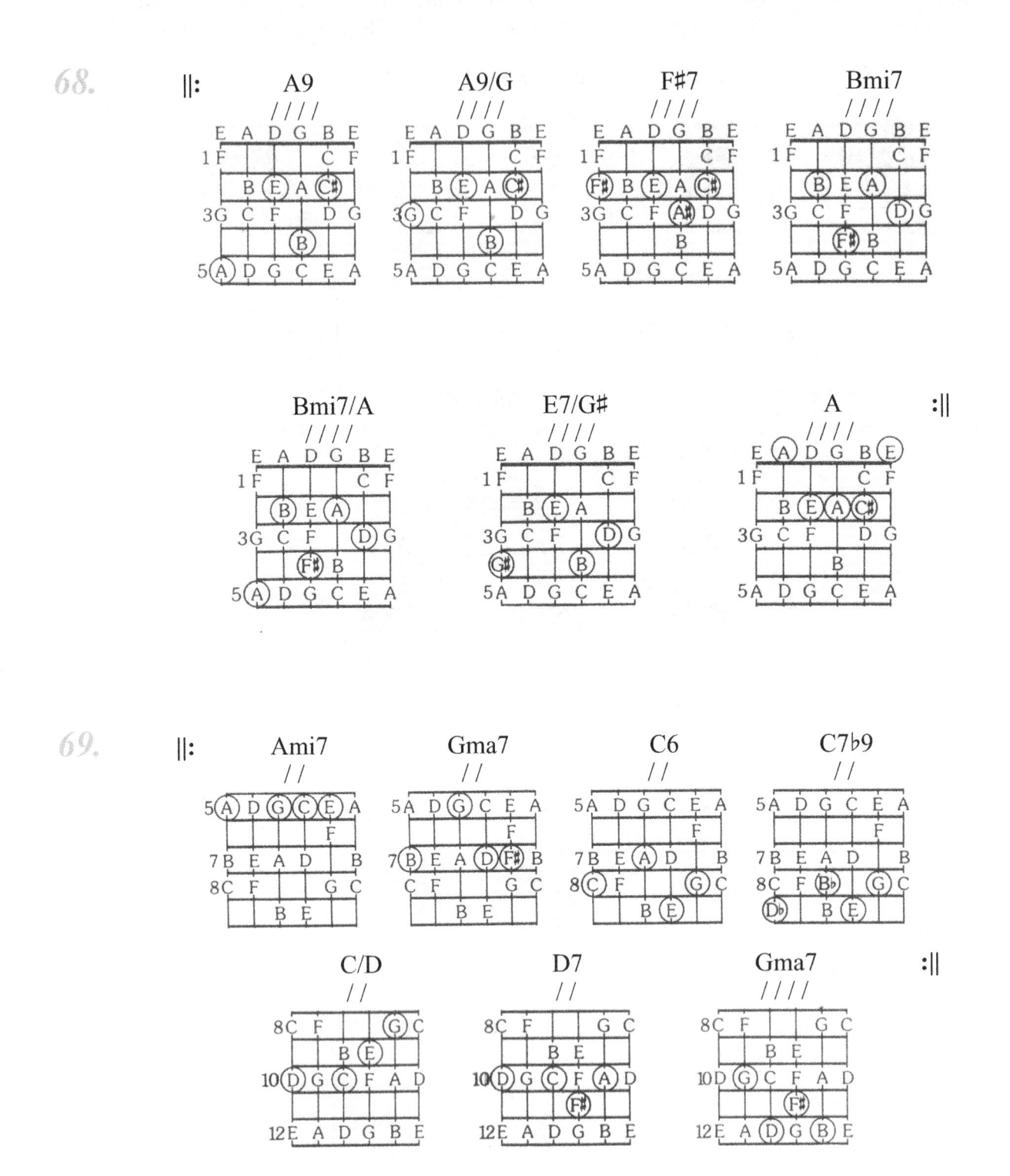

68. ‖: A9 | A9/G | F#7 | Bmi7 |

Bmi7/A | E7/G# | A :‖

69. ‖: Ami7 | Gma7 | C6 | C7♭9 |

C/D | D7 | Gma7 :‖

Chord Systems 40th Anniversary Edition - by Leon White

70.

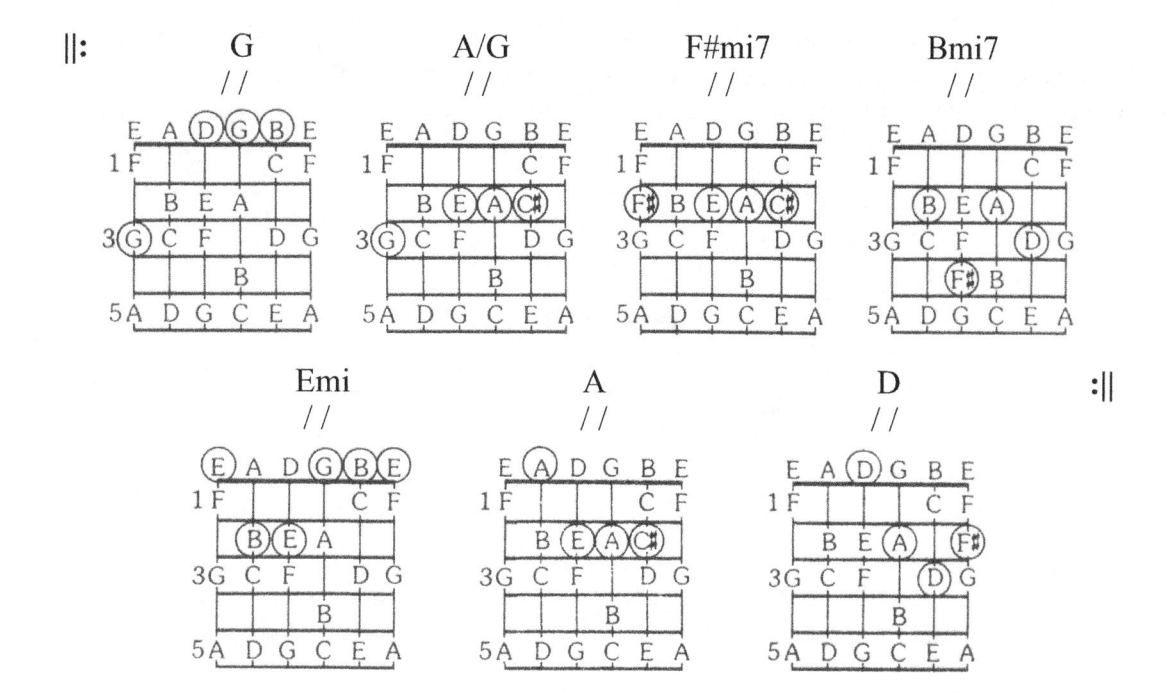

||: G   A/G   F#mi7   Bmi7

Emi   A   D   :||

The example above started as a 6432 stringset example, but then morphed. Which strings would you play on the bottom three chords? Don't answer with logic, listen and see which sounds you prefer.

71.

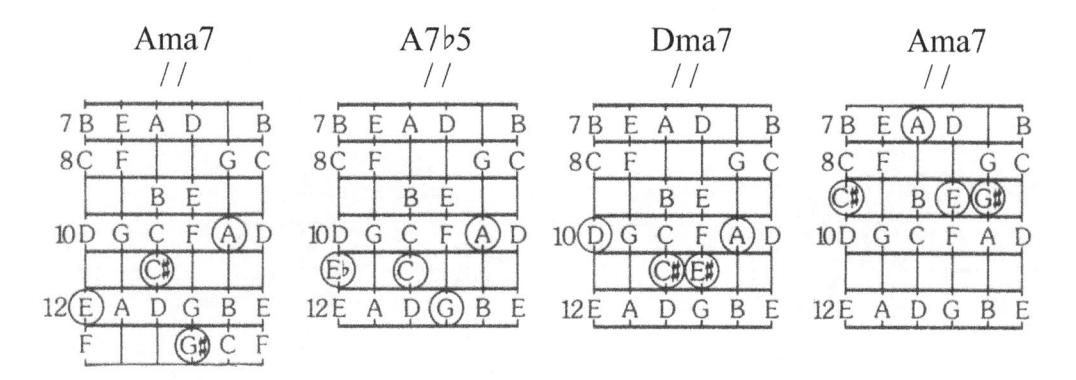

Ama7   A7♭5   Dma7   Ama7

At least one of the chords in the example above is new to you. But, because all the chords are on the 6432 stringset, you don't have to reposition your right hand. Keep that in mind as you move forward. You can begin to ignore your right hand position when you have chords that are consistent in location. Even when you do have to move, it will be easier because the stringset practice is establishing locations for you.

Comparing the 4321 and 6432 Stringsets

This page is a review and comparison of the two stringsets. As you can see, three of the notes are the same in each fingering. Only the outside note moves from the 1st string to the 6th. Once again the logic of stringsets and 4 note chords connects the chords to reinforce your memory and visualization.

72.

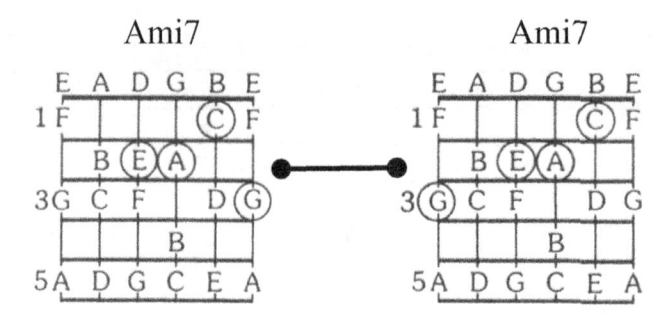

Ami7   Ami7

Shown below are three sets of columns with chord fingerings. Each column has a 4321 chord fingering next to the 6432 version of the chord. All three chord families are illustrated. Once again, notice how the chords and their fingerings all relate and interlock.

73.

Ami7   A7   Ama7

Chord Systems 40th Anniversary Edition - by Leon White

Essential Chord Fingerings on 6432

The Major Chord Family

As before, we're going to explore systematic inversions for other chords found in each chord family. Try to identify the name of the note that is moving as well as the degree (5th, 7th, or 3rd). (A7 is included to show the passing tone, although technically it is a dominant family chord.)

As before there is a ii - V progression you can use to play the A fingerings - Bmi7 to E7. Play each chord for four beats and then play four chords in a row with *one beat for each fingering* (ii - V - I). Try to choose fingerings on the same stringset for Bmi7 and E7.

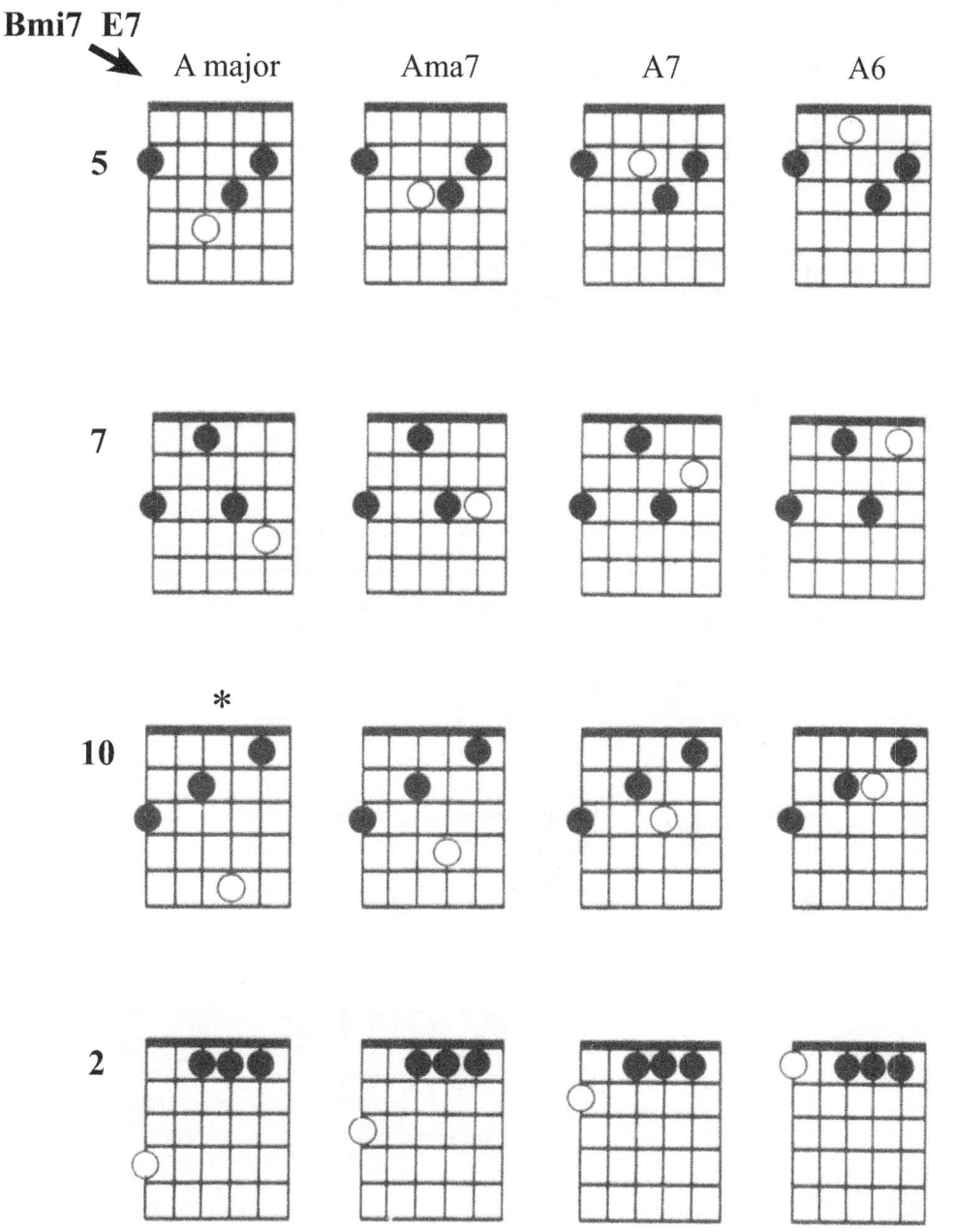

74. **Bmi7 E7**

        A major   Ama7   A7   A6

* Chords marked with this symbol may be very difficult to finger in that location. Try them higher up the neck before putting them aside.

In this table the changes to the "anchor chord" (Ama7) are cumulative - the root moves to the 9th, and then keeping the ninth, the major seventh drops to the sixth. As you've seen earlier though, all the fingerings share common notes and locations for each inversion. Review and experiment as before.

We've provided a ii - V progression for you to use to play the A fingerings - Bmi7 to E7. Play each chord for four beats and then play four beats over the three A chords in one of the rows. Try to choose fingerings on the same stringset for Bmi7 and E7. Be sure to try each row!

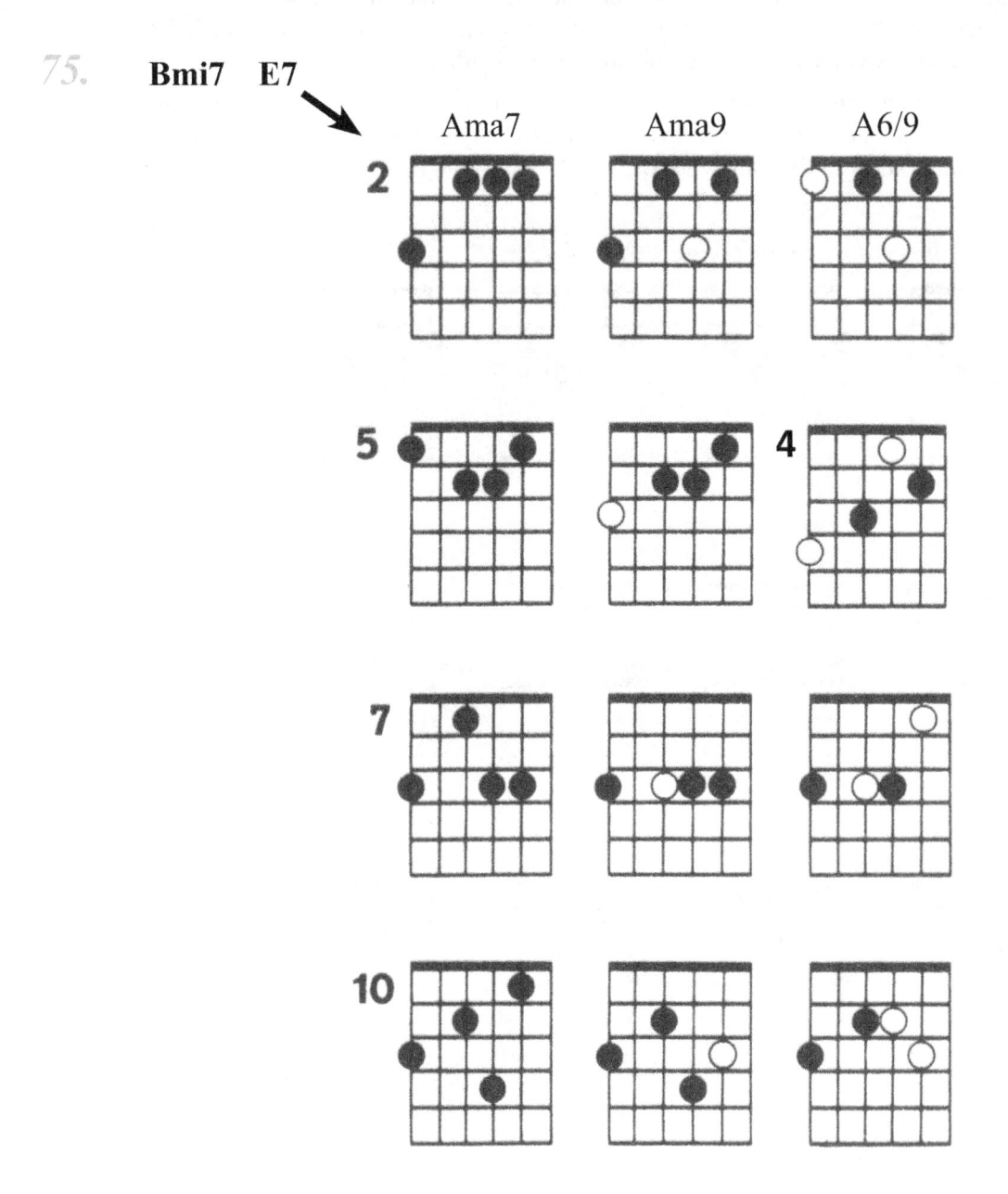

75. **Bmi7   E7**

The Minor Chord Family

Here we're seeing the root move down through the sevenths to the 6th. As before this is a reference section, but you'll find some simple chord licks with these moving voices.

For a progression sample consider these minor chords to be ii chords. At the bottom of the page there are V and I chords. Use one beat for each minor chord, and four beats each for the V and the I chord. Try to start out by using only 6432 fingerings in the progression samples.

76.

	Ami	Ami/ma7	Ami7	Ami6
5				
	*	*		
7				
	*			
12				

D7 Gma7

Once again we begin with our "anchor chord" - the minor seventh, but we're comparing related minor chord fingerings in each of the four inversions.

Compare the minor seventh column to the minor 6th, where you see the seventh move to a sixth. Then compare the same chord to minor seven flat five, where the regular 5th moves down to a flatted fifth. Lastly, compare the minor seventh fingering to the minor ninth, where the *root* has moved *up* a whole step to the ninth.

Playing these comparisons should be helping you to hear the chords and recognize them, although you can use this as a reference page.

For a progression sample consider these minor chords to be a ii chord as before. At the bottom of the page is a V and I chord. Use one beat for each minor chord, and four beats each for the V and the I chord. Try to start out by using only 6432 fingerings in the progression samples.

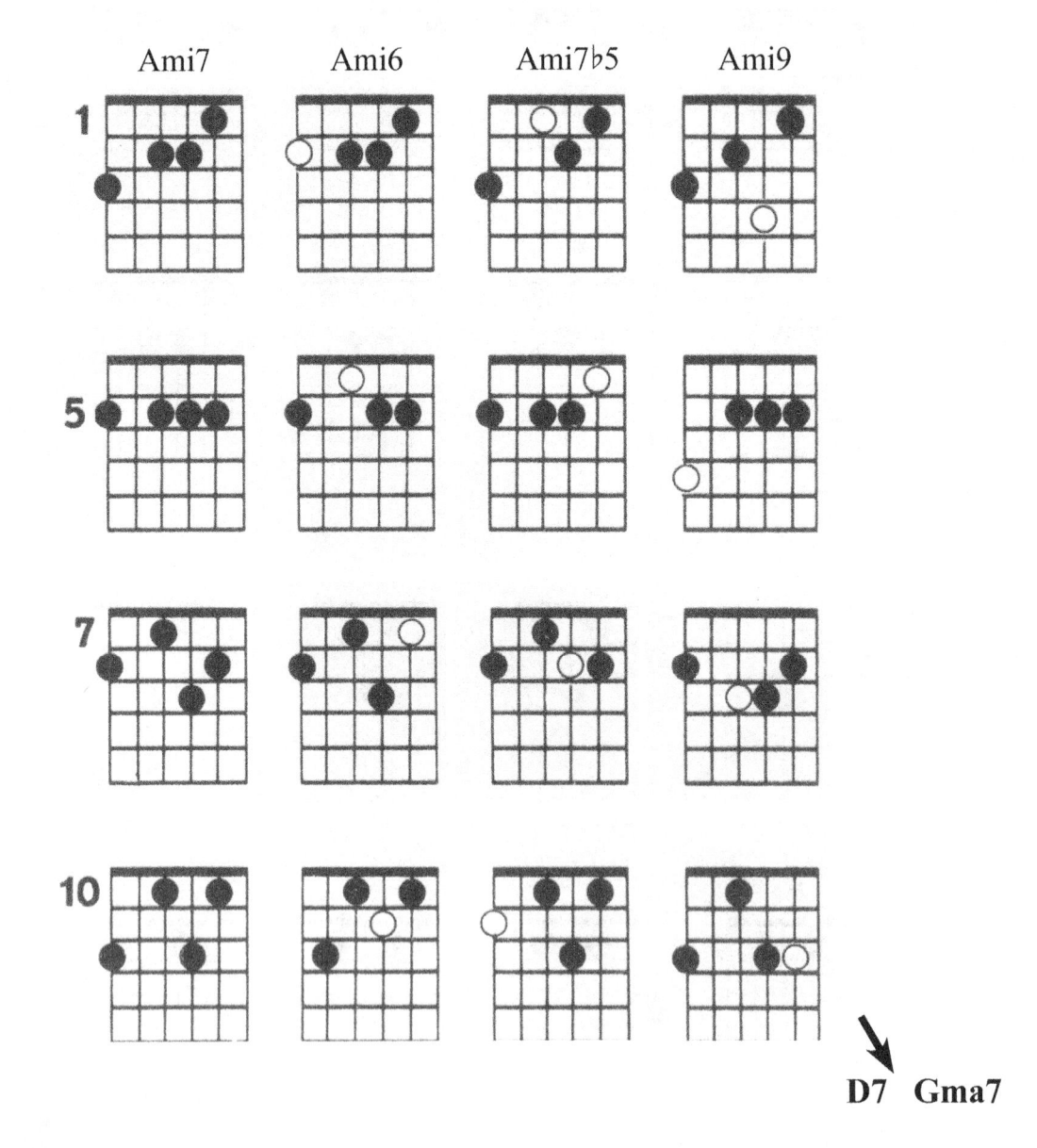

77.

Ami7   Ami6   Ami7♭5   Ami9

D7   Gma7

By now you should be able to change up the rhythmic feel of the progression samples you're creating. Sometimes a fingering needs extra time to play - that can be a place to change the timing.

On this page the Ami7 chord is shown moving the fifth to the flatted fifth and then the minor seven-eleven chord. (The eleventh is created by having a 4th, in this case a D note, included with the third and seventh.)

As before, this is a reference page, but it should lead your ear to the minor seventh sound with an eleventh or sus 4 note. The mi7/11 chord is colorful, but less well defined without some context from other chords.

As before, treat these minor chords as ii chords for a progression sample. At the bottom is the V - I part of the progression. Use four beats for the three minor chords, and four beats *each* for the V and the I chords.

78.

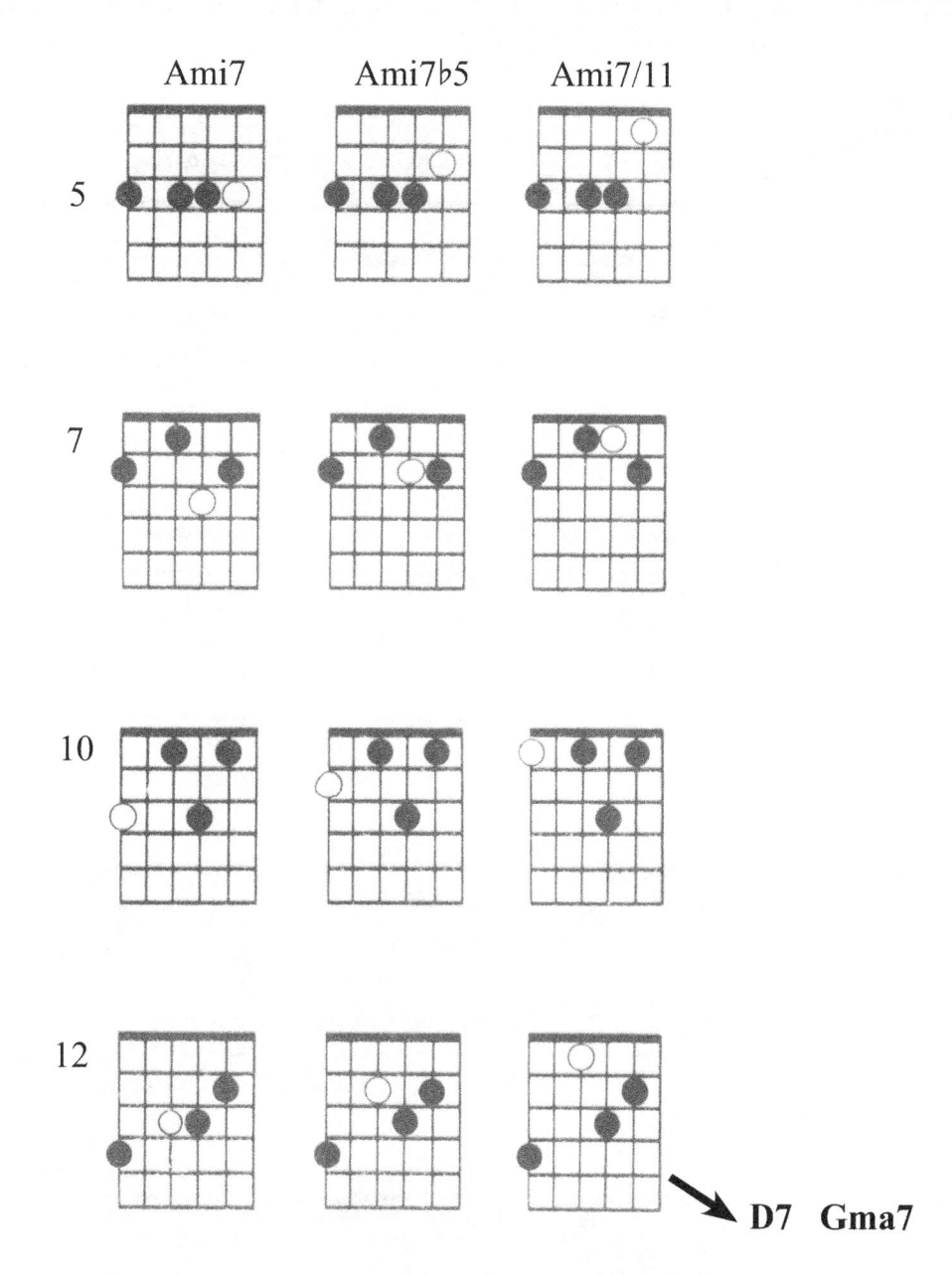

Ami7   Ami7♭5   Ami7/11

D7   Gma7

When comfortable, select some more colorful chords to play for the D7 and Gma7 (D9? Gma9?)

The Dominant Chord Family

As mentioned earlier, the three basic chord families can be considered to reflect a basic chord progression: ii - V - I. Minor chords can represent the ii chord, dominant chords the V chord, and major chords the I chord.

For progression samples consider these dominant chords to be a V chord. At the top is a ii chord. At the bottom is a I chord. Give the Emi7 four beats. Use four beats for the set of dominant chords, and four beats for the I chord to produce a ii - V - I example

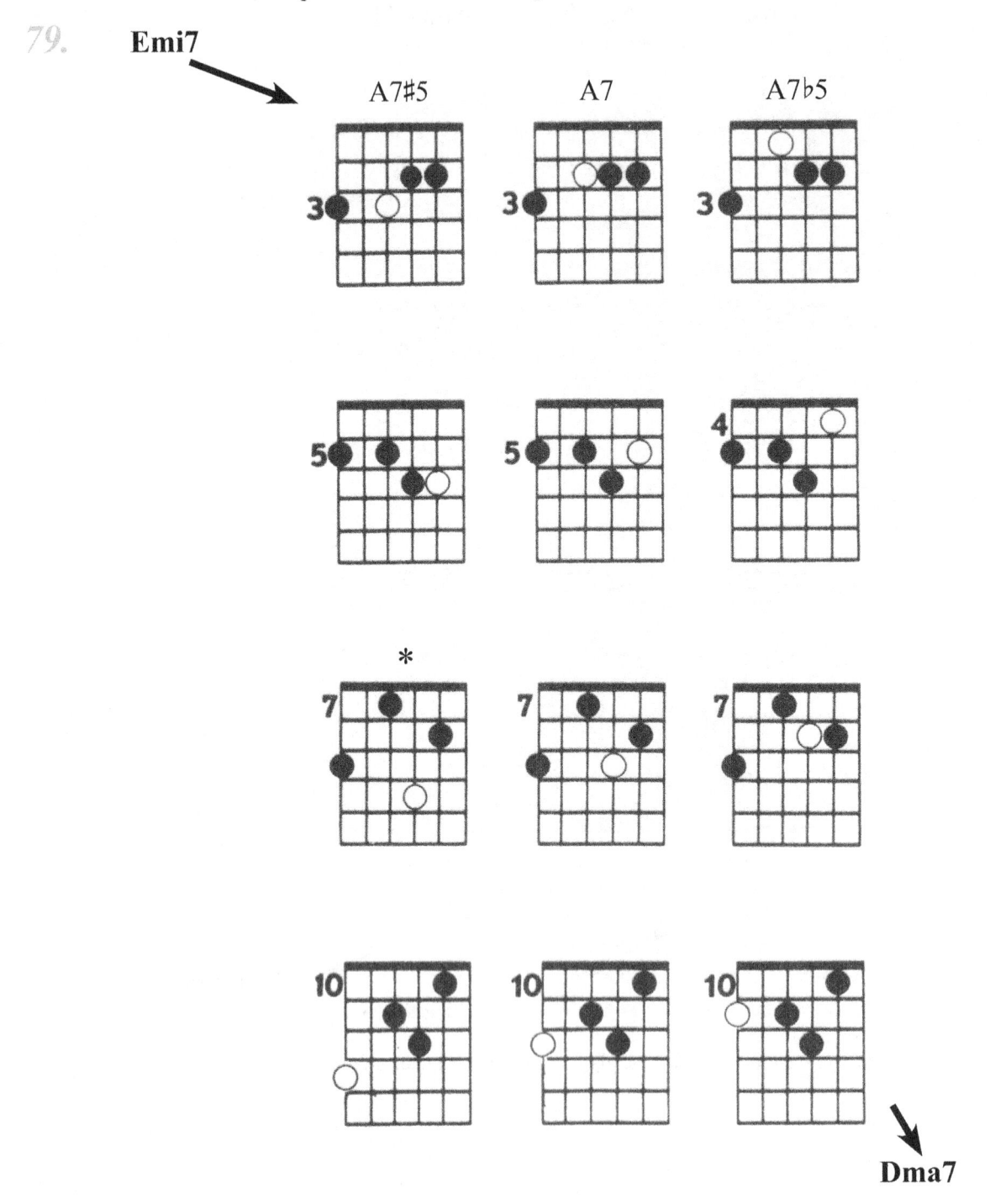

79. **Emi7** →   A7#5   A7   A7♭5

*

→ **Dma7**

There are two groups of chords shown. The left hand columns show movement of the 9th. The right hand columns show 9th chords with the 5th moving.

The notes that are moving are often referred to as "passing tones," and are all candidates for short chord licks. For progression samples, consider these dominant chords to be a V chord. Above the table there is a ii chord. At the bottom is a I chord. Give the Emi7 four beats. Use four beats for a left hand row or a right hand row of dominant chords, and four beats for the I chord to produce a ii - V - I progression.

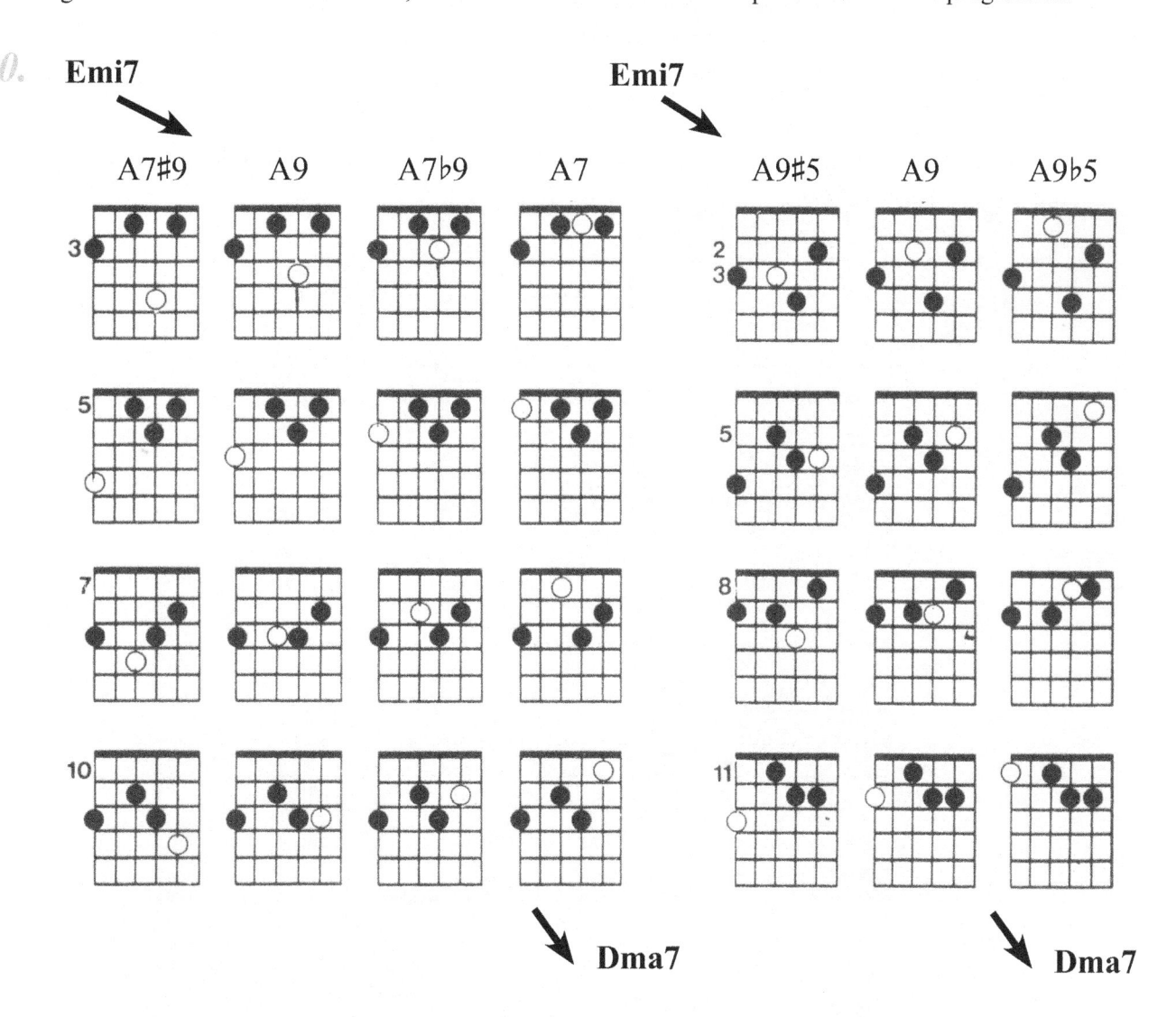

80.

Emi7 ↓

A7#9   A9   A7b9   A7

Emi7 ↓

A9#5   A9   A9b5

↓ Dma7

↓ Dma7

How Can a Person Remember All These Chords?!?

It is really pretty simple. You can't just memorize them. When you *use* them you'll remember them. It's no different than open or barre chords. What I'm trying to do is expose your musical brain to the *sound* of the chords (and their passing tone licks), and give you practice in fingering them.

Some chord fingerings will "stick" the first time through, while others won't until later. The 6432 stringset gets used a great deal in jazz and American standards styles of music. If you play that a lot, you'll learn a "go-to" group of fingerings for most songs, and add other chords when called upon. If you can finger the new chords, you'll be able to play them on demand, even if you have to look them up to find them. It all works out.

Chord Systems 40th Anniversary Edition - by Leon White • 65

The 5432 Stringset

Introductory Examples

We'll start with the systematic inversions of the seventh chords, but below are some short progressions using these chords. You can strum these fingerings or play them fingerstyle. As before, the following examples are a sort of a "meet 'n greet" with some 5432 fingerings. Just play them and enjoy them.

The 5432 stringset is like the 4321 in that there are four adjacent strings.

The first example below shows a common progression with a descending bass line. It starts with 54321 and then continues with other stringsets. Play and listen to see the mix of voicings.

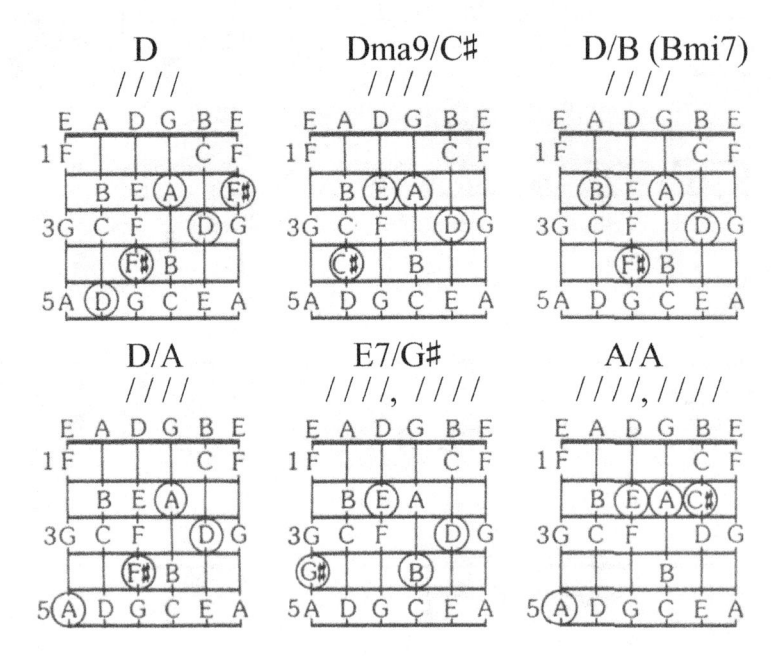

81.

D / / / /
Dma9/C# / / / /
D/B (Bmi7) / / / /

D/A / / / /
E7/G# / / / /, / / / /
A/A / / / /, / / / /

Back in the day* . . . my 1952-53 Telecaster. The sweetest lap-steel tele sound I'd heard.

Systematic Inversions

Proceed as before. There are some stretches and some more unappealing chords, but the examples that follow show where those chords fit in progressions and sound useful.

As before
1. Play one family at a time.
2. Note the fingerings you already know.
3. Continue to work on these while playing through the examples.

Ama7

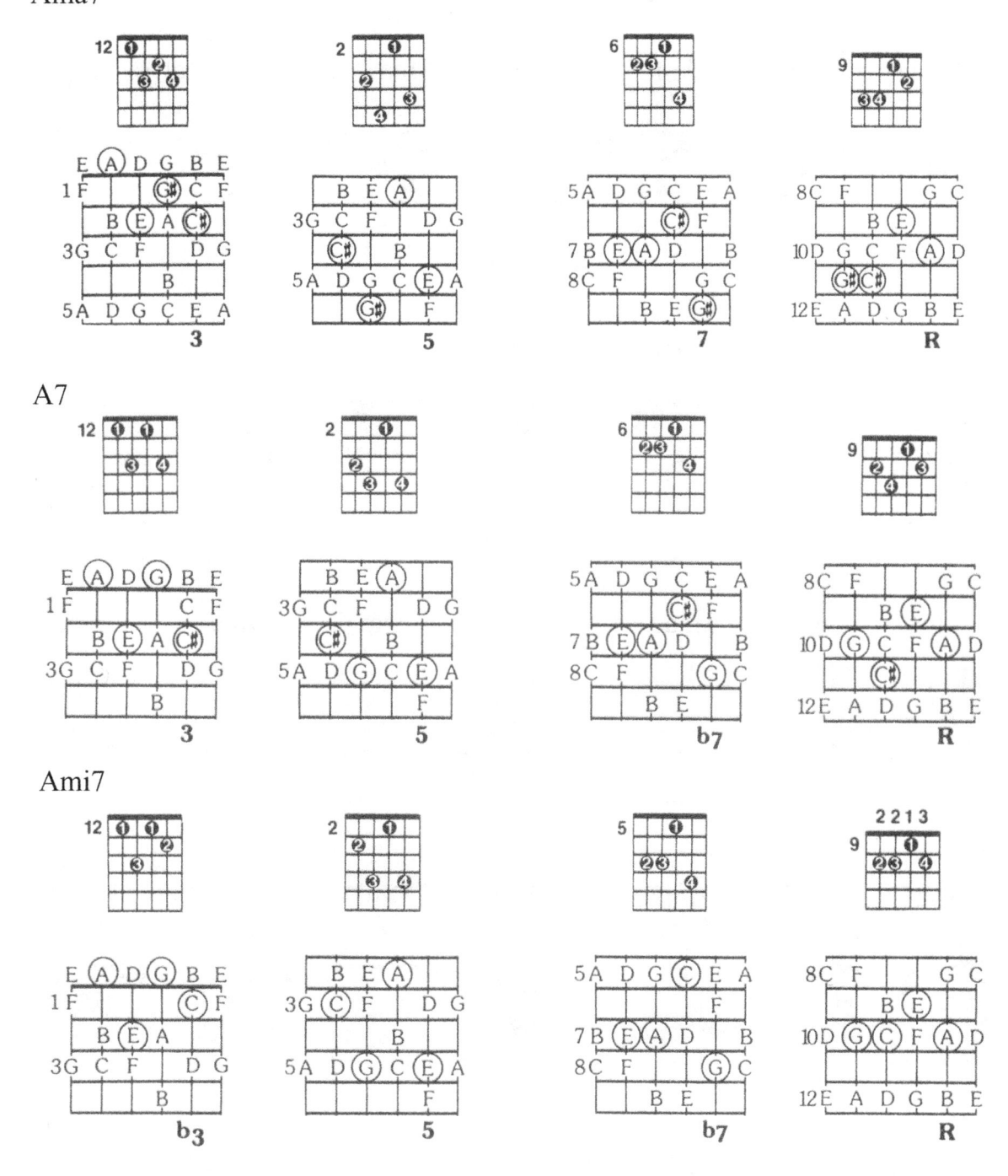

A7

Ami7

Progression Examples

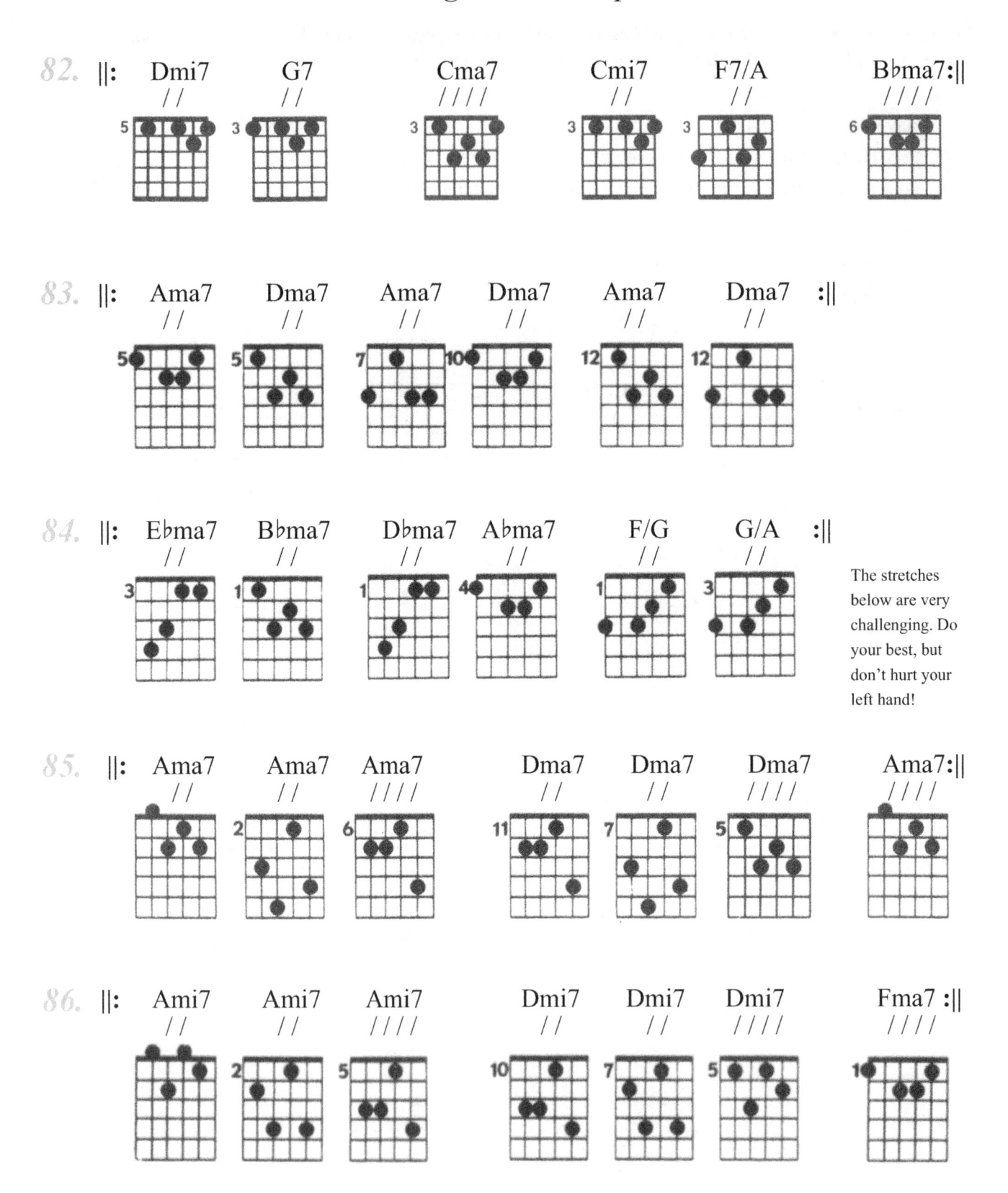

82. ||: Dmi7 G7 Cma7 Cmi7 F7/A B♭ma7 :||

83. ||: Ama7 Dma7 Ama7 Dma7 Ama7 Dma7 :||

84. ||: E♭ma7 B♭ma7 D♭ma7 A♭ma7 F/G G/A :||

The stretches below are very challenging. Do your best, but don't hurt your left hand!

85. ||: Ama7 Ama7 Ama7 Dma7 Dma7 Dma7 Ama7 :||

86. ||: Ami7 Ami7 Ami7 Dmi7 Dmi7 Dmi7 Fma7 :||

Play each fingering for two beats. The first example is a turnaround starting on the I chord and then starting from the vi chord.

87. Cma7   C#dim7   Dmi9   G7

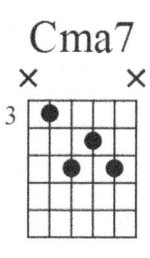

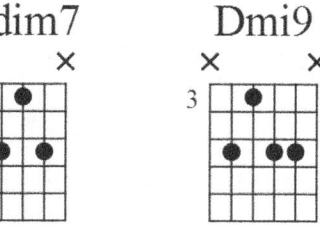

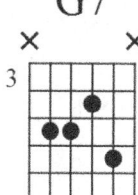

88. Em7   A7   Dmi7   G7

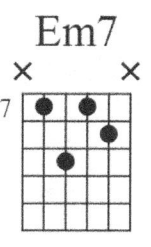

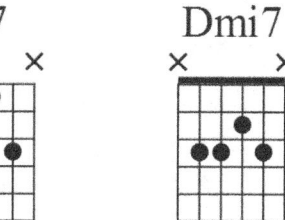

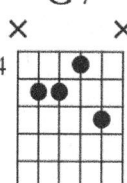

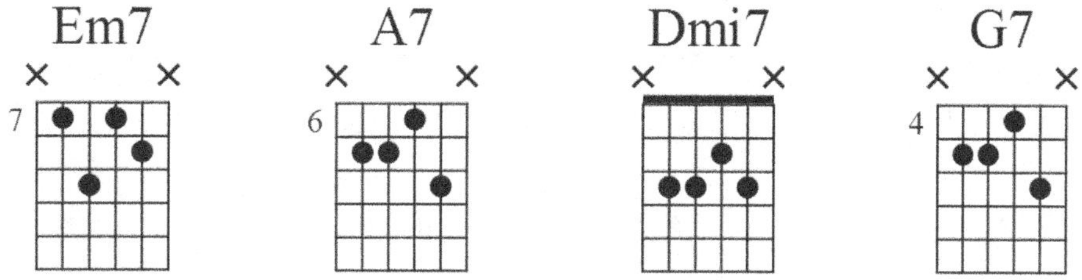

The next example is a little more colorful. You may wish to check the notes being used in each chord.

89. Ama7   Ama7   Dma7   Dma7

Gma7   Gma7   Cma9 $C^6/_9$

Fma9   Fma7#11   G7sus   Cma7

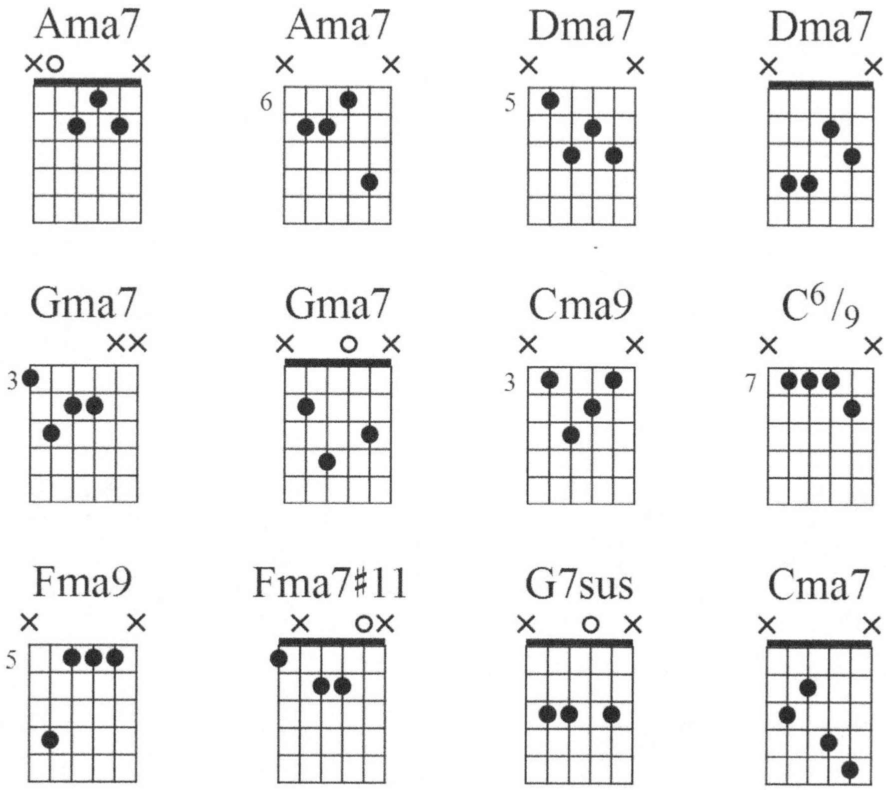

This example might be found in a jazz bossa nova type of arrangement. What is the tonal center? Could the progression end on some E or F root chords? Could the B7#9 chord be treated as a Bmi of some kind?

90.

Emi9   Eb7#9   Dmi9   Db7#9

Cmi9   B7#9   Gma7   G6/9

Comparing the 5432 Stringset and Barre Chords

Everything is connected when it comes to chord fingerings.

Compare the chords below and see how these fingerings are really parts of barre chords you already know. The first fingering in each pair is the 5432 chord. The barre chord is the second fingering.

91.

Comparing the 5432 and 4321 Fingerings

In these examples we're comparing the fingerings of two stringsets - 5432 and 4321. Both stringsets are composed of four adjacent strings, and so the fingerings resemble each other. However, the root of the chord moves up a fourth, like the tuning of the A and D strings.

As usual the four inversions of each chord are shown in each column. Compare the chords in columns 1 and 2 by playing each chord - A and then D. The second pair of columns (3 and 4) show the dominant seventh fingerings.

Ama7   Dma7   A7   D7

Remember that fingerings that are awkward on lower frets are easier to finger and sound different on the higher frets. On the next page the minor seventh fingerings are compared.

Chord Systems 40th Anniversary Edition - by Leon White

Review the minor seventh fingerings on the two stringsets. As before, the B string's tuning a 3rd above the G means one finger has to be adjusted.

One way to play the examples is to imagine the top 4 chords form a box. Play the first Ami7, and then the one below it. Then play the Dmi7 adjacent to the second Ami7 and then back to the top Dmi7. You can move the box down the inversions as well.

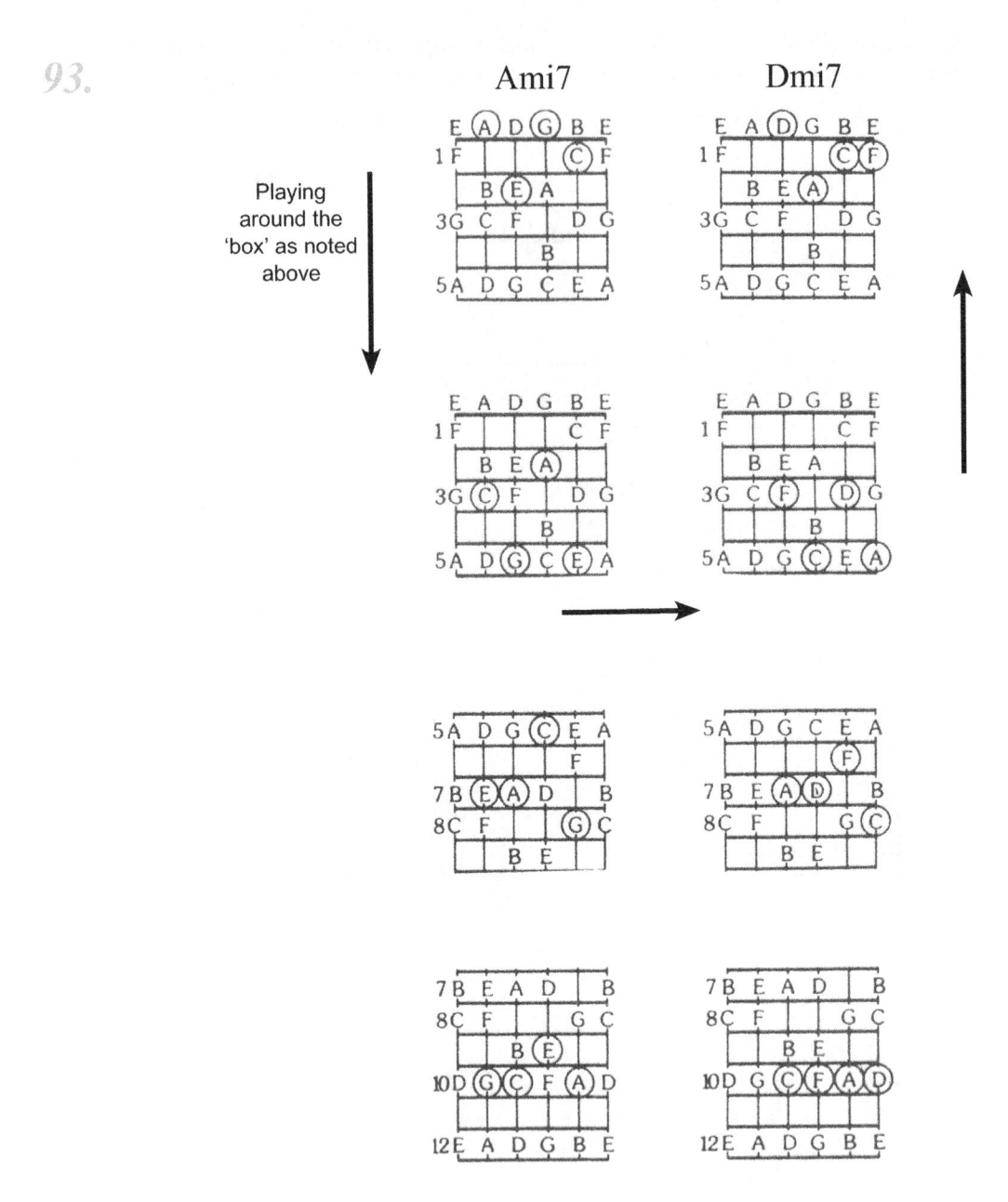

93.

Ami7 **Dmi7**

Playing around the 'box' as noted above

"Practice in all keys and positions." I just had to write that once in the book. No one ever does it, but do try it on higher frets so you can hear these chords in the upper registers.

Essential Fingerings on 5432

The Major Chord Family

Review the four chord types by playing across the rows. As noted earlier, I've included the A7 chord (a dominant family chord) to show the moving voices by half steps. We've provided a ii - V - I sample progression. Play each chord for four beats and then play four chords in a row with one beat each.

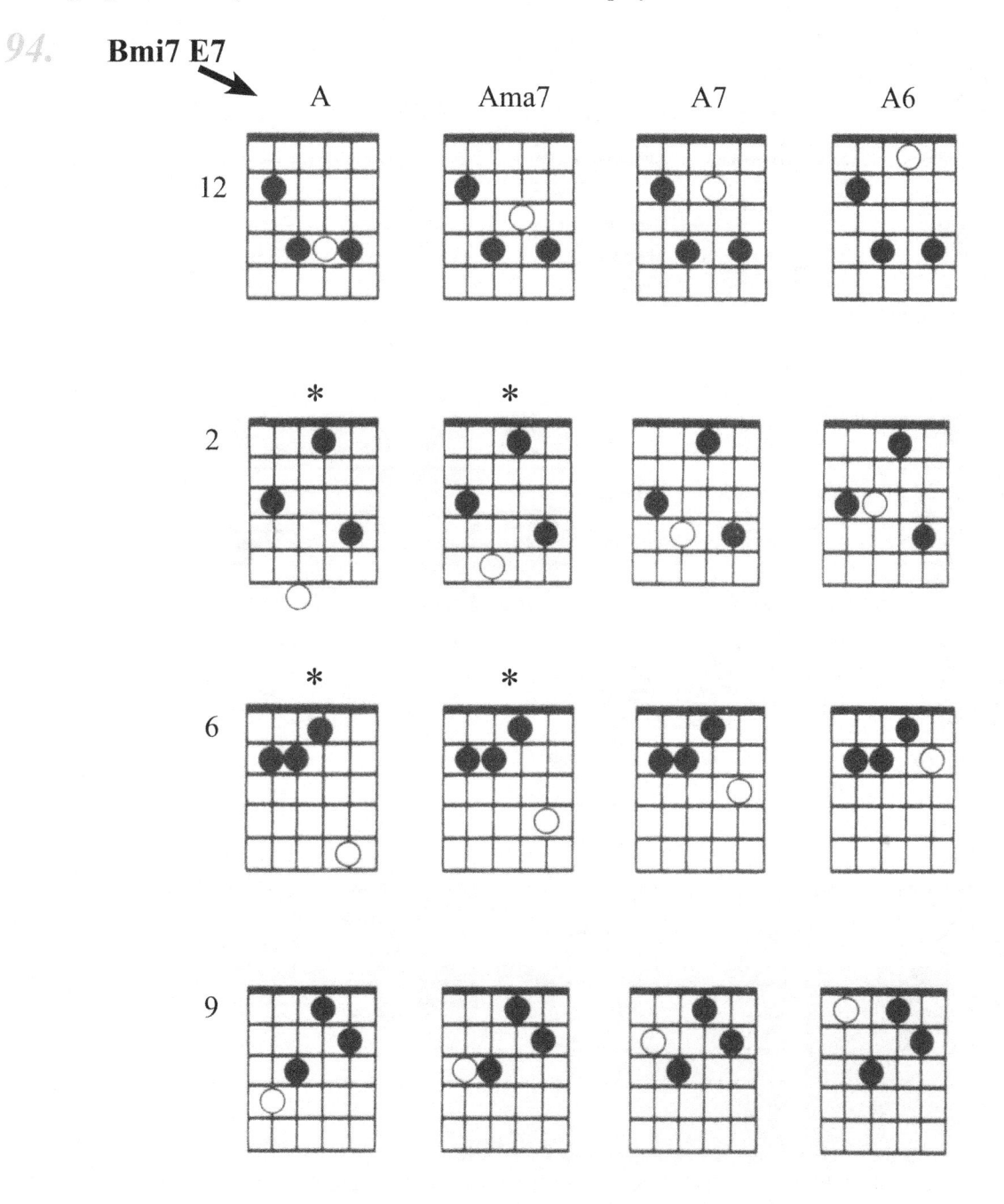

94. **Bmi7 E7**

	A	Ama7	A7	A6

(Chord diagrams at frets 12, 2, 6, and 9)

As you can see, the 5432 stringset has a number of chords with big stretches. Learn the chords you can finger first, and then work on the longer fingerings. Try them on higher frets for shorter stretches.

The major family of chords are continued on this page. As before, you can play down the columns to see the inversions, or across the rows to hear the different chords in each position.

A6 and A6/9 fingerings should look like some other chords from a different root . . . (F#).

Things just keep overlapping and re-enforcing each other.

As before we've provided a ii - V - I progression (Bmi7 to E7 to Ama). Play the first two chords for four beats each and then play four chords in a row with one beat for each fingering. Try to use chords on the 5432 stringset.

95. Bmi7 E7

Ama7   A6   Ama9   A6/9   Aadd9

One reason I titled the book "Chord Systems" is because there are several different structures I use to show the chords (like stringsets, inversions, and passing tones). Another reason is that once you can see how the chord fingerings are located, it should become clear that the whole *subject* is one big system.

The Minor Chord Family

Once again the three columns of chords illustrate the movement of one voice, hear the fifth. Play down the columns to hear the inversions or across the rows to hear the voice moving. And again, some chord fingerings look like other chords. (Ami7/11 = D7sus; Ami7♭5 = ?).

Learn the easy chords first and then experiment with the longer stretches. For the progression sample, use these minor chords as a ii chord. At the bottom are the V and I chords. Use four beats for one minor chord *row*, and four beats *each* for the V and the I chords.

96.

        Ami7   Ami7♭5   Ami7/11

→ **D7   Gma7**

You might consider playing across the rows as a way to find moving voice chord licks automatically.

Remember you can mark the book up, so highlight easy fingerings, or moving voice chords that are good licks or whatever. If you're trying to memorize the whole book, let me know when you do.

The moving line appearing in these chords is an extremely popular phrase for composers such as the Beatles, and Henry Mancini. And don't forget Leon Russel's composition "Masquerade."

Proceed as before - easy fingerings first, then others. Play across the row to hear the composer's usage.

For the progression sample use these minor chords as a ii chord. At the bottom is a V and I progression (D7 to Gma7). Use one beat for each minor chord, and four beats each for the V and the I chords.

97.

| Ami | Ami/ma7 | Ami7 | Ami6 |

D7   Gma7

Later in the book we're going to discuss something called "Chromatic Common Tone Chord Substitution." All these passing tone examples ARE chromatic common tone substitution when you use them to "fill" in one chord - such as A minor here.

The Dominant Chord Family

These example show moving the fifth down in half steps. This can help you remember the sounds of #5 or ♭5 chords.

For progression samples consider these dominant chords to be a V chord. At the top is a ii chord (Emi7). At the bottom is a I chord (Dma7). Give the Emi7 four beats. Use four beats for one row of A dominant chords, and four beats for the I chord to produce a ii - V - I progression.

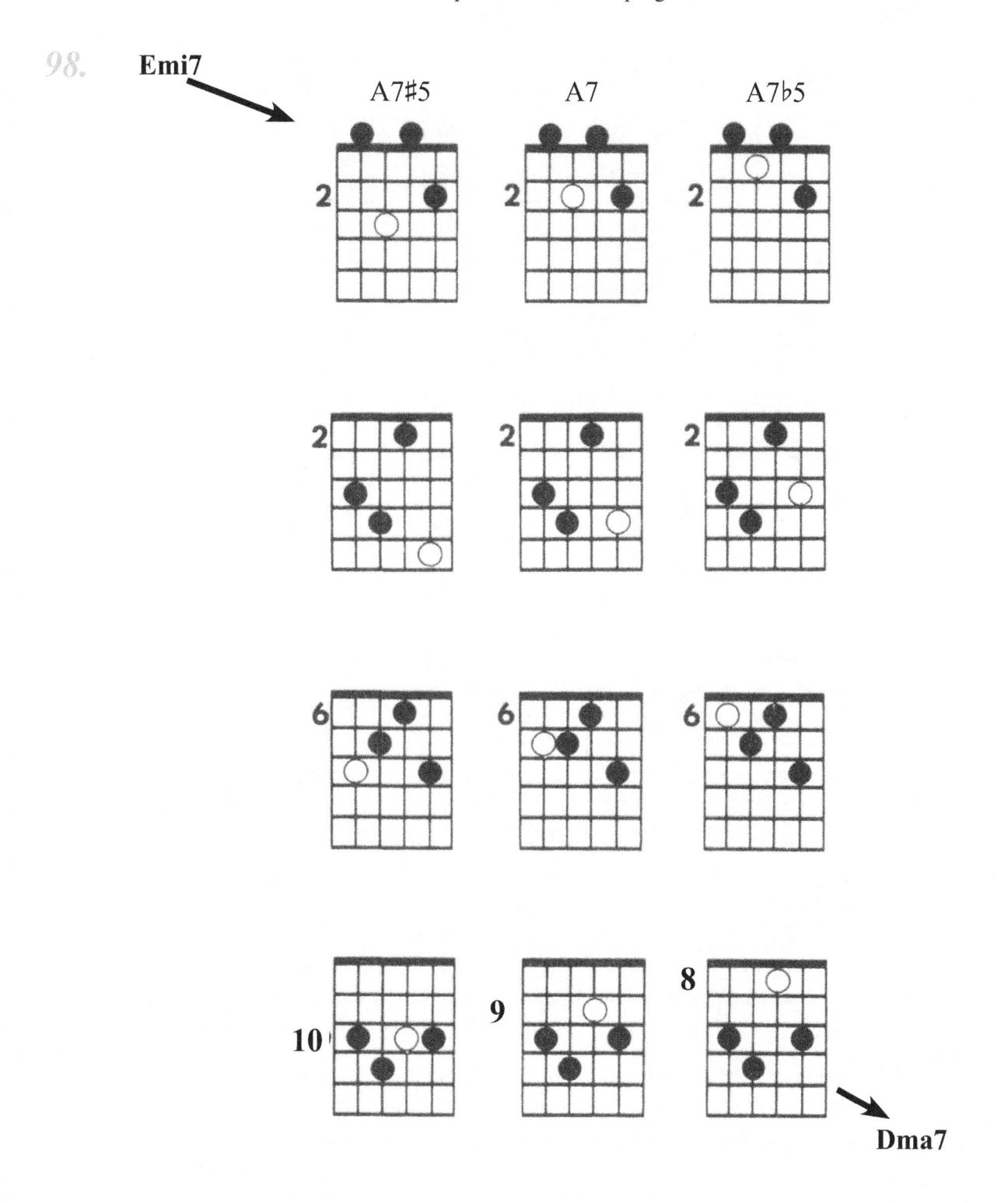

98. **Emi7** →   A7♯5   A7   A7♭5

(chord diagrams leading to) **Dma7**

Chord Systems 40th Anniversary Edition - by Leon White • 77

Here the 9th is the note moving through the A7 chord. While it is a different voice from the 5th (prior page) the same approach applies. Like earlier examples, you'll find fingerings that have appeared as other chords. (A9 for C#mi7b5).

For progression samples consider these dominant chords to be a V chord. At the top is a ii chord (Emi7). At the bottom is a I chord (Dma7). Give the Emi7 four beats. Use one beat for each dominant chord, and four beats for the I chord to produce a ii - V - I progression.

99.

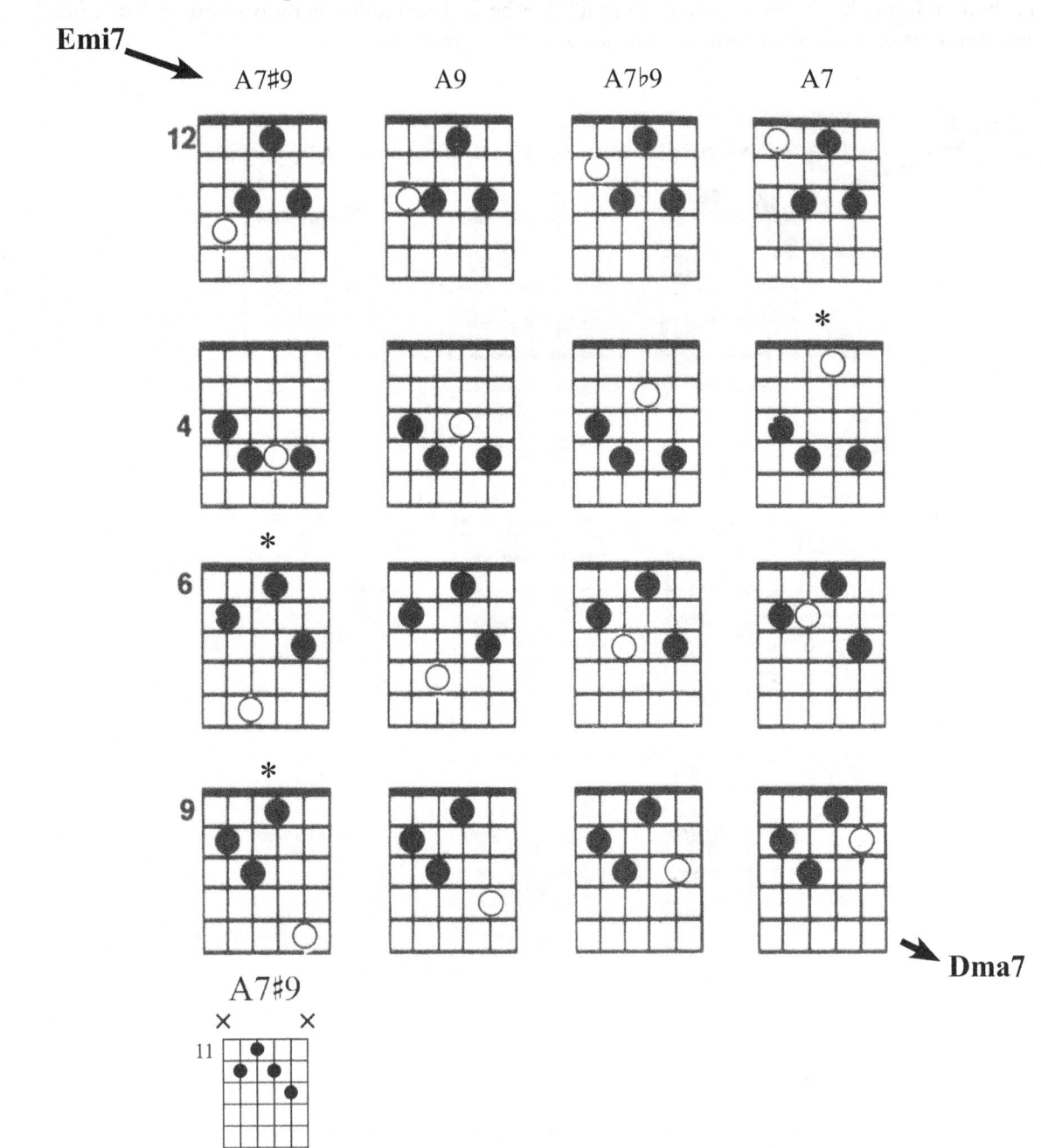

Emi7 →

A7#9 A9 A7b9 A7

[chord diagrams arranged in a 4x4 grid at frets 12, 4, 6, and 9, with asterisks marking certain chords; bottom right arrow points to **Dma7**]

A7#9
[additional chord diagram at fret 11 with x markings on two strings]

If you have trouble recognizing a four note voicing by sound, try moving it so that you have an open string as the root. A chords could be moved up to the root E so you can add a low open E string to the chord and hear it less ambiguously.

Playing these ii - V - I samples may be repetitive, but it's good for your ear, good to hear the moving voices, and good for finding fingerings on this stringset to complete the progression.

We could also use four different Emi7 fingerings on this page - one for each row.

Here the 9th is not moving, but the fifth steps along. A9#5 has some interesting fingerings on this stringset.

As before, play down the column to hear the inversions, play across to hear the voice moving. Mark the easy ones (or familiar ones) and try the five fret fingerings on the higher part of the neck. Are you recognizing some fingerings you've already played with a different chord name?

For progression samples consider these dominant chords to be a V chord. At the top is a ii chord (Emi7). At the bottom is a I chord (Dma7). Give the Emi7 four beats. Use four beats for one row of dominant chords, and four beats for the I chord to produce a ii - V - I progression

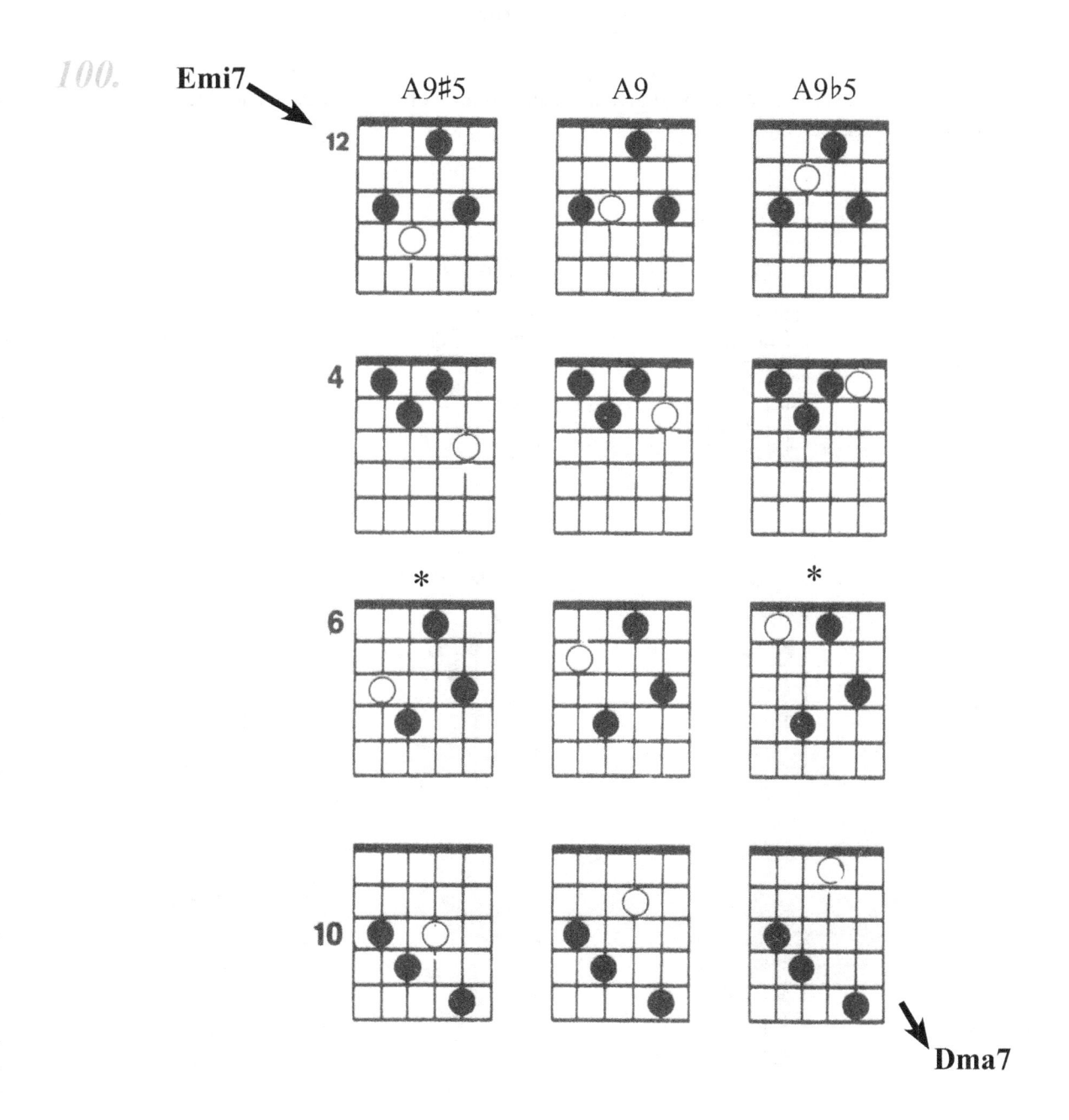

100.   **Emi7**   A9#5   A9   A9♭5

Dma7

The 5321 Stringset

This stringset is like the 6432 stringset in that there is one muted string in the fingerings. The fingerings include the B string, and therefore some of the fingers have longer stretches for the left hand. Learn the ones you can, and then revisit any fingerings that might be troublesome.

Introductory Examples

Play the examples below to see similarities between fingerings and stringsets, and hear the 5321 voicings in context. Each row is one example. You should give the same number of beats for each chord (two or four beats, your choice, your feel, and your tempo).

101. Dmi7   G7   Cma7   A7/E

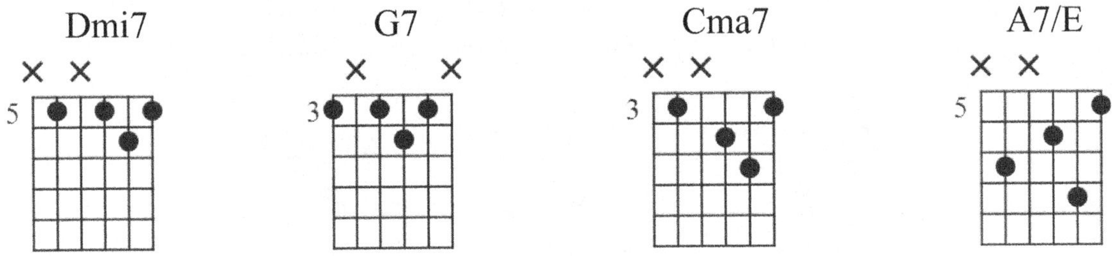

102. Ami7   D7   G/F#   G

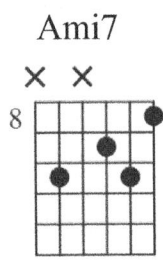

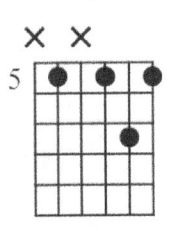

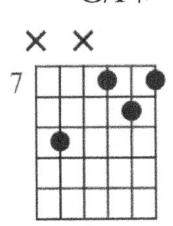

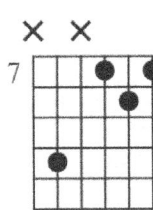

103. Emi7   A7   Dma7   B7#5

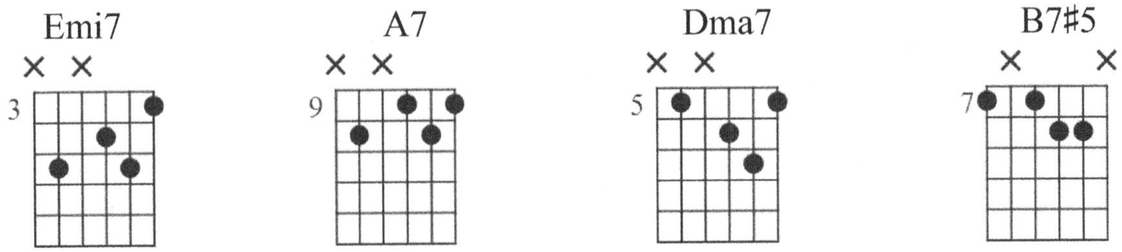

Systematic Inversions

The 5321 stringset has the same arrangement of strings and notes as the 6432 stringset, but moved over one string. Because of the B string being a different interval, the fingerings all adjust. And the stringset can be a bit more difficult to strum as you must avoid the 6th string as well as the fourth. As a result, the fingerings with the 3rd in the bass (the first column) tend to be used less frequently. As you review these, allow a little more time to get comfortable with those fingerings - that's typical for most players.

Ama7

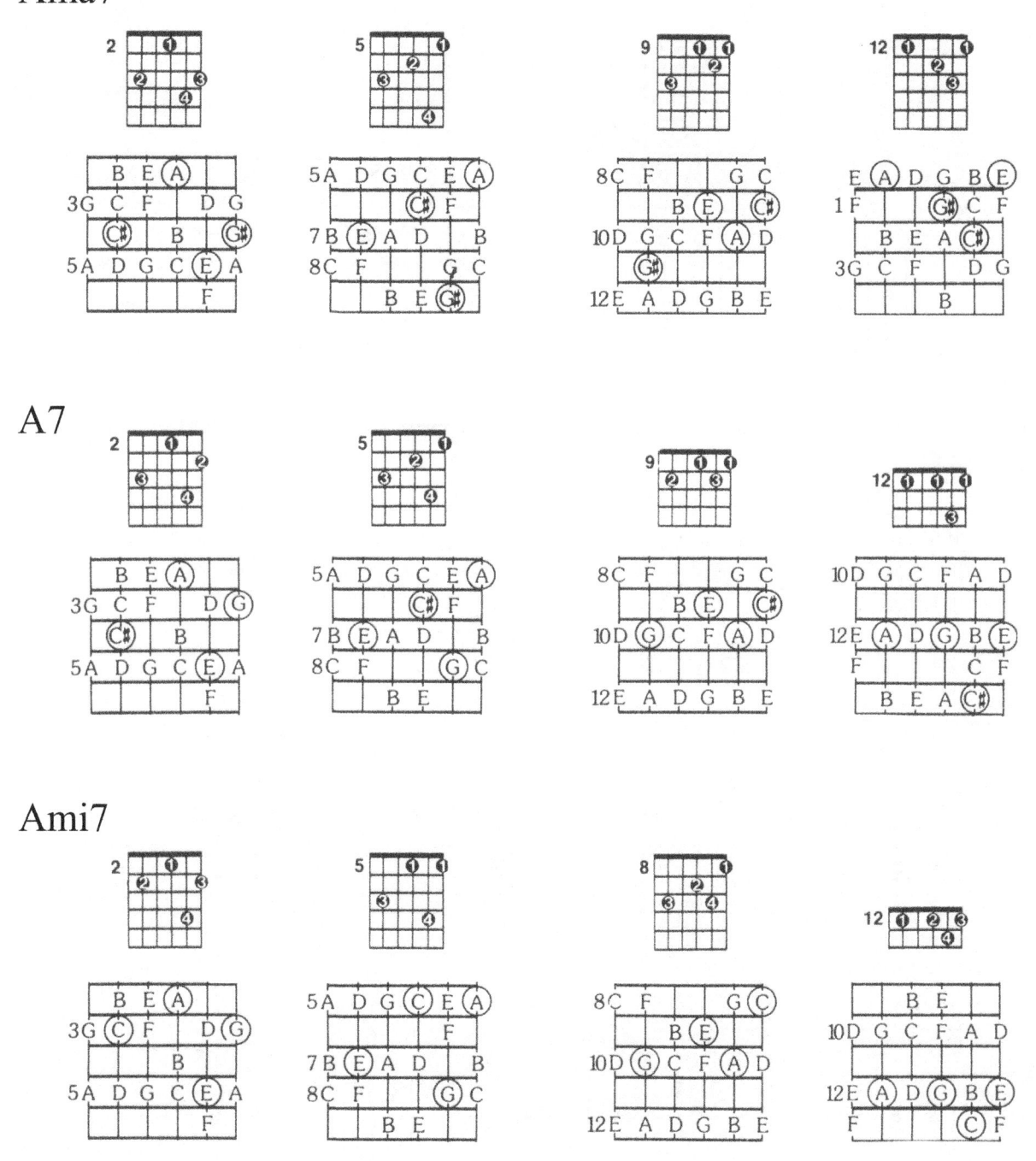

A7

Ami7

Progression Examples

Shown below are the chords found on each note of the C major scale, and using the 5321 stringset. This set of voicings has the root in the bass of each chord. Play each chord for two beats.

104. Cma7 — Dmi7 — Emi7 — Fma7 — G7 — Ami7 — Bmi7♭5 — C6/9

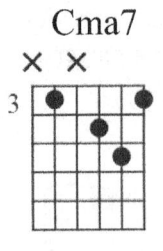

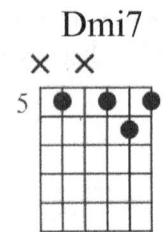

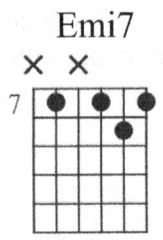

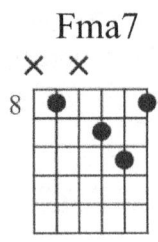

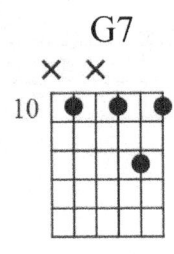

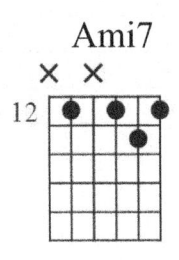

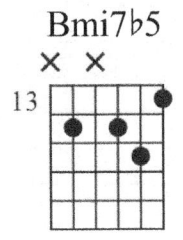

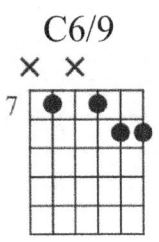

More colorful sounds are found in the example below. Two beats for each chord and four for the last one.

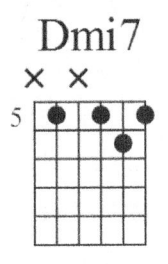

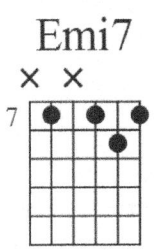

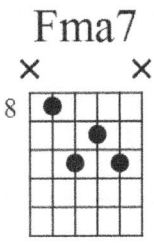

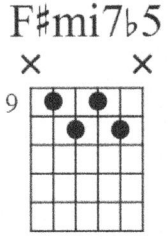

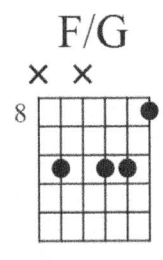

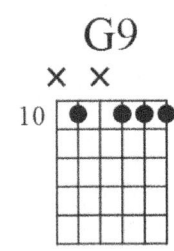

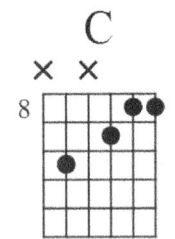

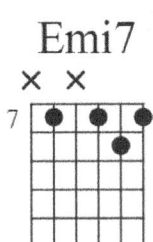

105. Dmi7 — Emi7 — Fma7 — F♯mi7♭5 — F/G — G9 — C — Emi7 — Dmi7 — G13♭9 — C — G/C — D/C

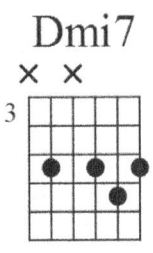

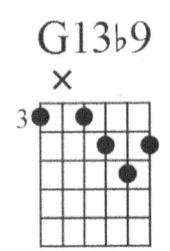

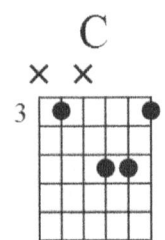

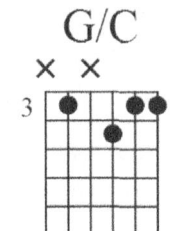

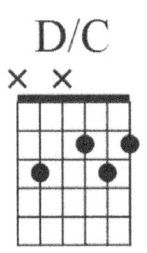

These examples are meant to be played at a medium slow tempo with each chord receiving two beats. There are chords with names that include bass notes, and chords that don't. If it seems random, it's because that is the way they occur in songs.

106. D   Dma7   D7/C   Bm7

G7   G7/F   A7   A7

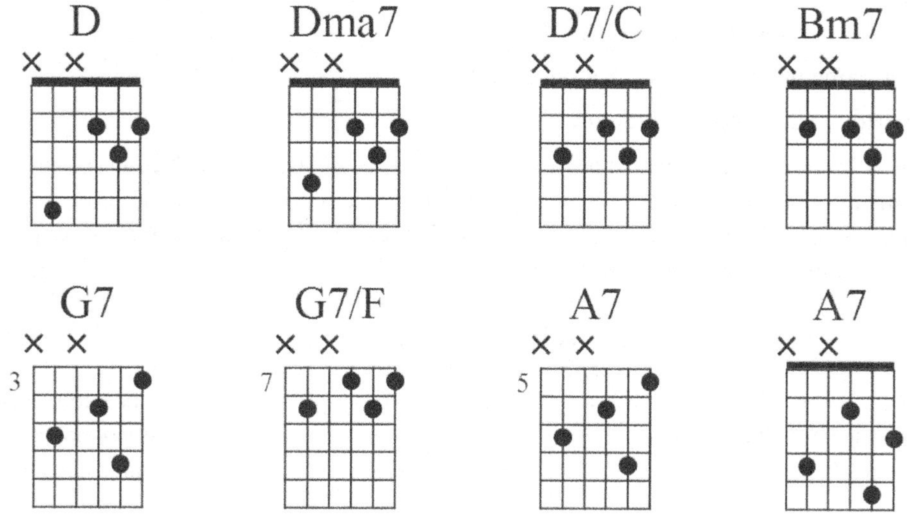

107. Cma7   C#dim7   Dmi7   G7/F

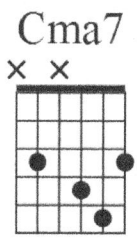

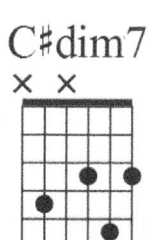

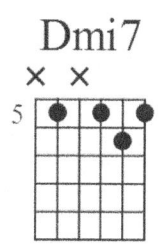

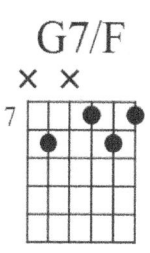

108. G/F   C9   F7/Eb   Bb9

D11   A9b5   Gadd9

Chord Systems 40th Anniversary Edition - by Leon White • 83

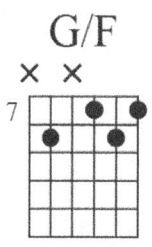

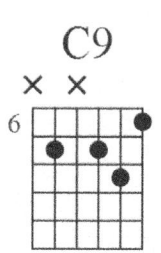

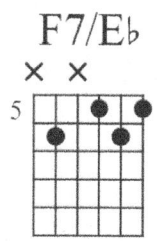

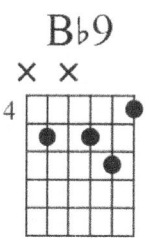

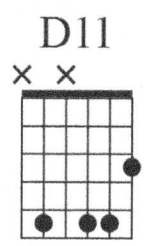

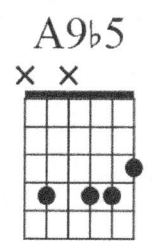

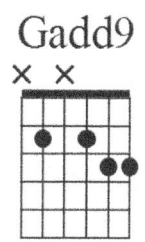

Comparing 5321 and 6432 Fingerings

In the examples below you'll see the fingering shapes in pairs, side by side. Study the shapes and see the similarities and the differences. The important things to understand are that

- the fingerings correspond to each other,
- they are the same inversions, and that once again,
- chords interlock into a logical structure.

From a practical point of view the tone of a fingering on one set of strings is different when moved to a different set of strings. The guitar, the string gauges, and the location on the neck all contribute to this difference. String bends and vibrato are also influenced. Depending upon the sound you're playing, this tone difference may influence which chord you select.

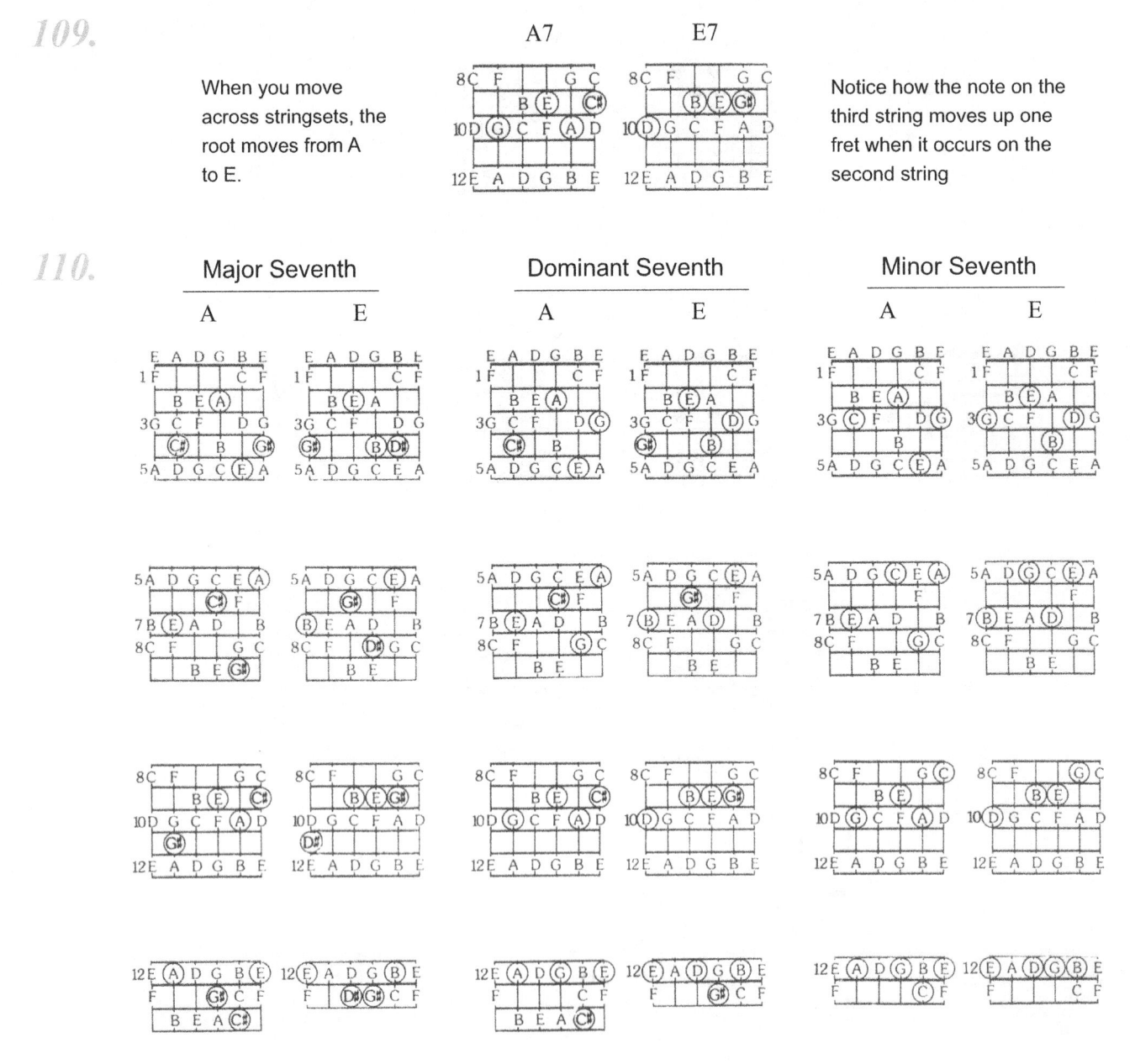

109. When you move across stringsets, the root moves from A to E.

Notice how the note on the third string moves up one fret when it occurs on the second string.

110. Major Seventh — Dominant Seventh — Minor Seventh (A and E fingerings shown for each)

Remember, you can play down each column to hear the inversions for one chord.

Essential Chord Fingerings on 5321

The Major Chord Family

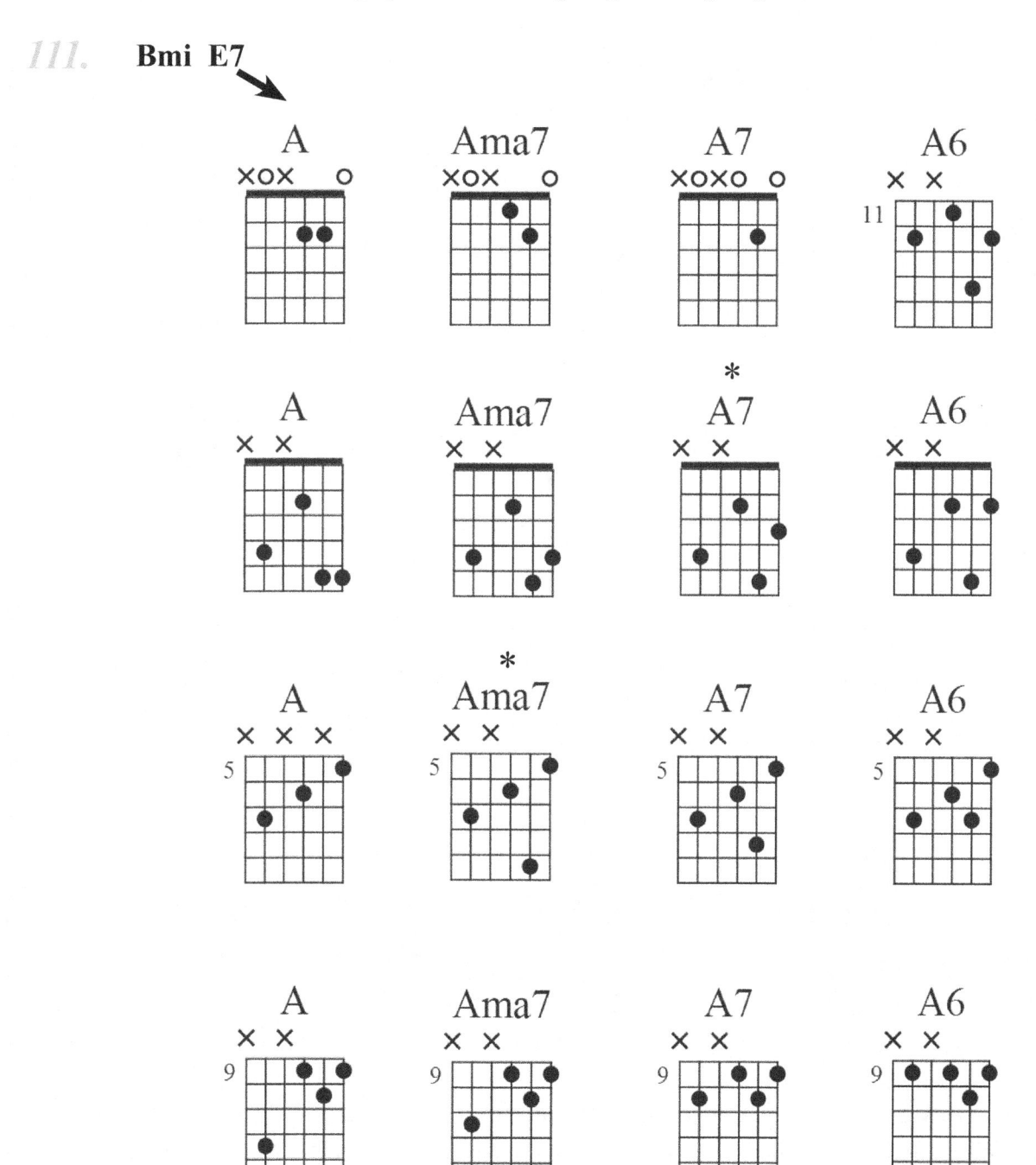

Proceed as before: review the four chord types by playing across the rows. Then play down the columns. The A major chords here act as I chords in a ii - V - I progression in A major. Play the Bmi7 and E7 for four beats each, and then play across the row giving each fingering one beat.

111.   **Bmi E7**

Chord Systems 40th Anniversary Edition - by Leon White • 85

Proceed as before: review the chord types by playing across the rows. Then play down the columns. Once again, the A major chords act as I chords in a ii - V - I progression in A major.

There are two sets of columns: columns 1 - 2, and columns 3 - 5. Treat them as two different sets of chords.

As before the progression consists of a ii chord (Bmi7), a V chord (E7) and a one chord (A ___). Use columns 1 and 2 for one ii - V - I example. You can repeat the process (Bmi7, E7, and A___) using the chords from the second grouping (A6, Ama7, and Ama9).

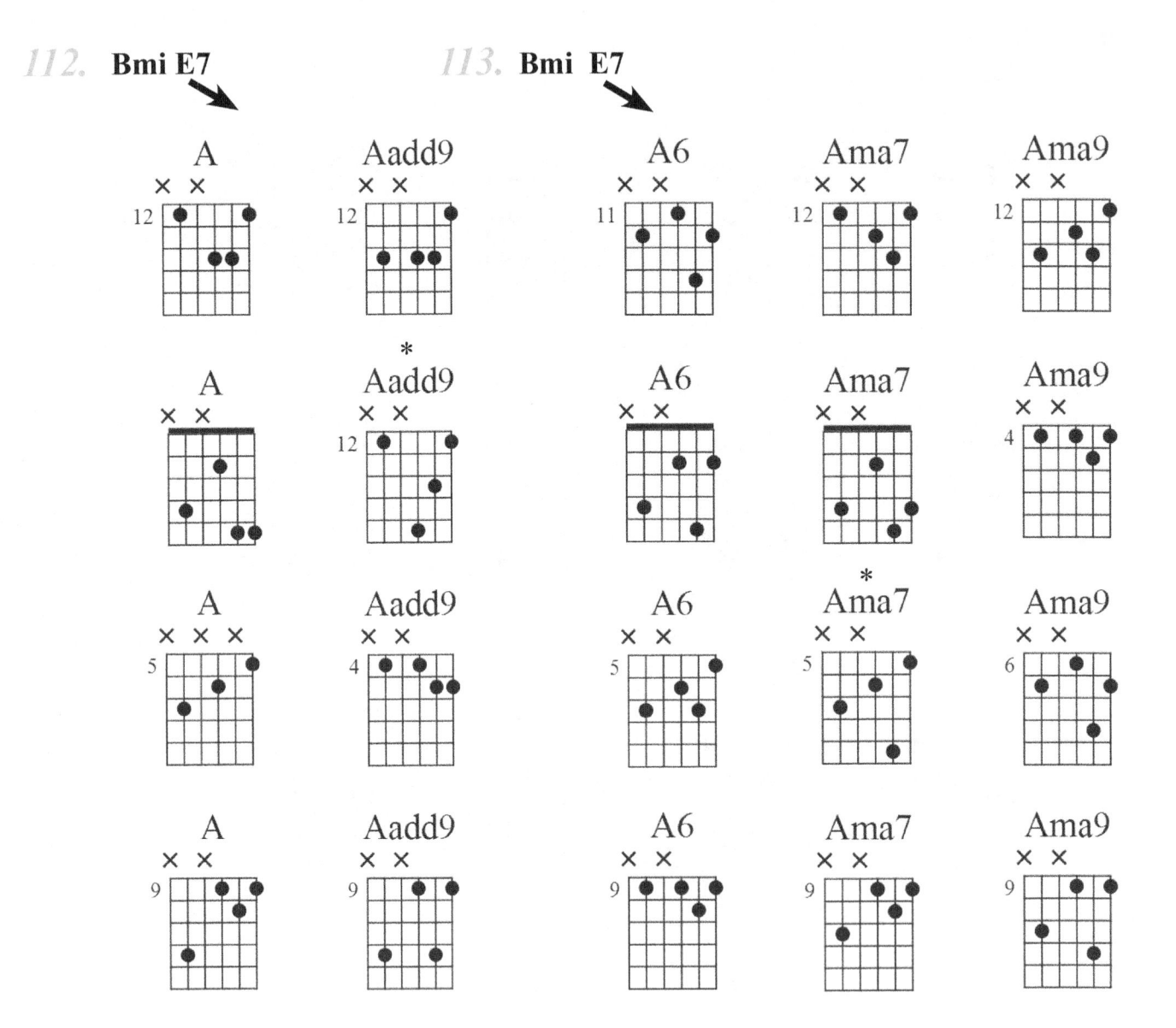

112. **Bmi E7** ↘   *113.* **Bmi E7** ↘

A	Aadd9	A6	Ama7	Ama9

"Why does the author keep repeating the instructions for playing the ii - V - I examples!?!"

Good question. Players will open the book over the years and just jump in to a page. So, I like each page to be complete in and of itself.

You should be using Bmi7 and E7 chords from the 5321 stringset if you're trying to familiarize yourself with that group of sounds. Don't be afraid to substitute Bmi9 or E7♭5 and other family chords too.

The Minor Chord Family

Proceed as before: review the three chord types by playing across the rows. Then play down the columns. The Ami chords here are a ii chord in a ii - V - I progression in G major. There are two sets of three columns: columns 1 - 3, and columns 4 - 6. Treat them as two different sets of chords. Play across the row (columns 1-3) for four beats and then four beats for each chord in the D7 and Gma7 part of the progression. Repeat the process for columns 4 - 6.

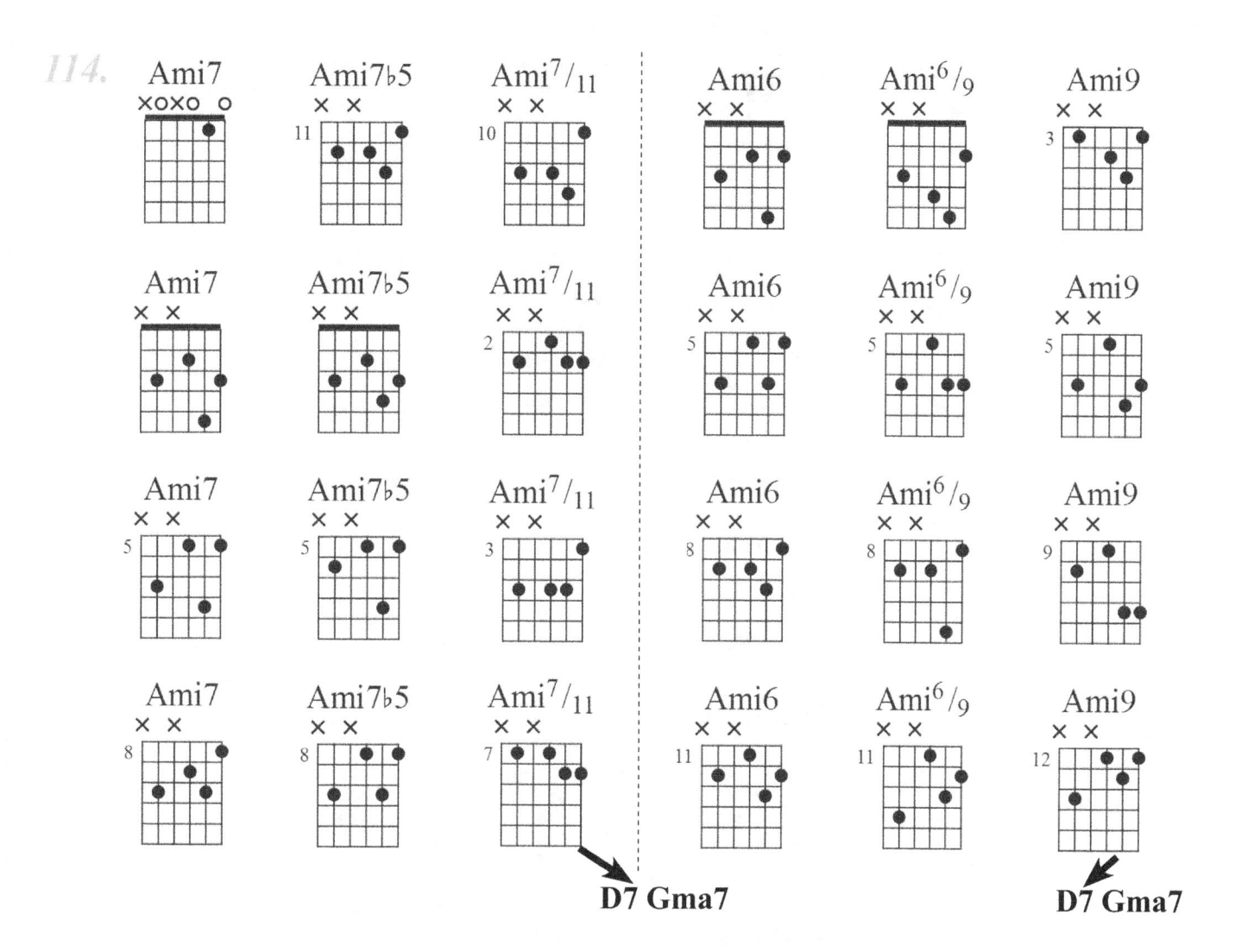

114.

Ami7	Ami7b5	Ami7/11	Ami6	Ami6/9	Ami9

(chord diagrams in four rows across six columns)

D7 Gma7   D7 Gma7

This stringset has a number of chord fingerings that are more difficult than other stringsets. I would recommend you highlight the chords you think you'll be able to play more easily, and postpone the very stretchy fingerings (especially on lower frets) until you've finished the first group.

Proceed as before: review the chord types by playing across the rows. Then play down the columns. These A minor chords can be seen as a ii chord in a ii - V - I progression in G major. Play across the row for four beats and then play four beats for each chord in the D7 and Gma7 part of the progression.

Feel free to substitute some other D dominant chord for D7, and another major chord for Gma7, and try to stick to the 5321 stringset at first. Doing so will keep your right hand in position as you concentrate on the left hand fingerings.

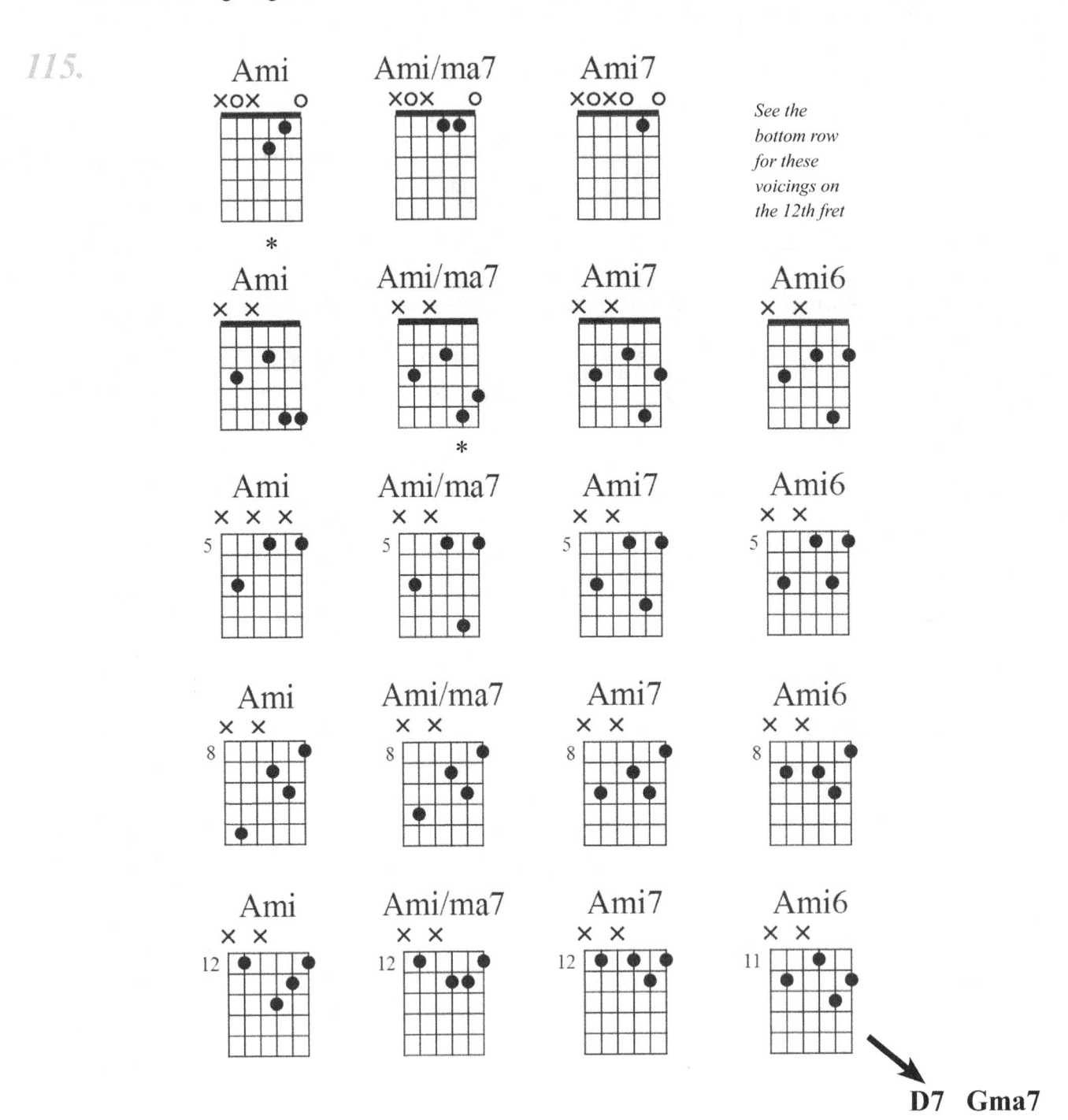

115.

Ami	Ami/ma7	Ami7	
Ami	Ami/ma7	Ami7	Ami6
Ami	Ami/ma7	Ami7	Ami6
Ami	Ami/ma7	Ami7	Ami6
Ami	Ami/ma7	Ami7	Ami6

See the bottom row for these voicings on the 12th fret

D7   Gma7

In row four, you might try playing the notes from high to low, with the bass note last.

The Dominant Chord Family

This page presents two groups of chords: columns 1 - 3, and columns 4 - 6. The first group illustrates the movement of a #5 to a ♮5 and then a ♭5. The second group repeats that melodic movement, but for A9 chords instead of A7. You should be able to hear the difference between the two groups.

As before, we have a ii - V - I progression with the A chords being used as the V chord. Play four beats of Emi7, four beats with the three A chords, and then four beats for the Dma7 chord.

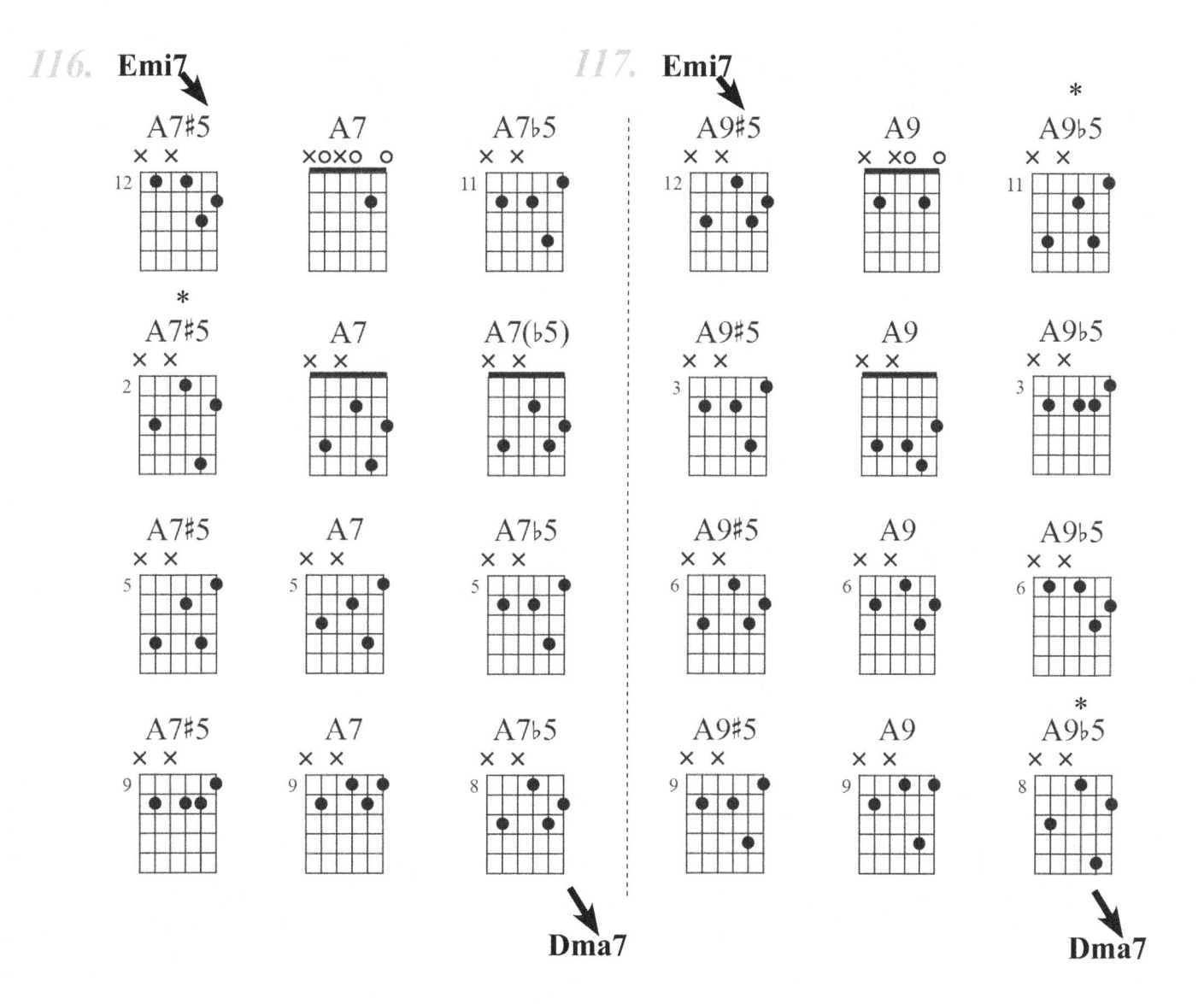

116. **Emi7** → A7#5, A7, A7♭5 (four positions each)

117. **Emi7** → A9#5, A9, A9♭5 (four positions each)

→ **Dma7**

We're going to be discussing chord substitution in a separate section of the book, but do you see any correspondence between the A7#5 fingerings and the A9♭5 fingerings? Between A7♭5 and A9#5?

Once again we have a ii - V - I progression with the A chords being used as the V chord. Play across a row to hear the moving voice, or down a column to hear the inversions of a chord. The moving voice is the A note, which moves up a half step in each chord. (B♭ is the ♭9, B♮ is the 9, and C is the ♯9 - B♯.)

Play four beats of Emi7, one beat for each A fingering, and then four beats for the Dma7 chord.

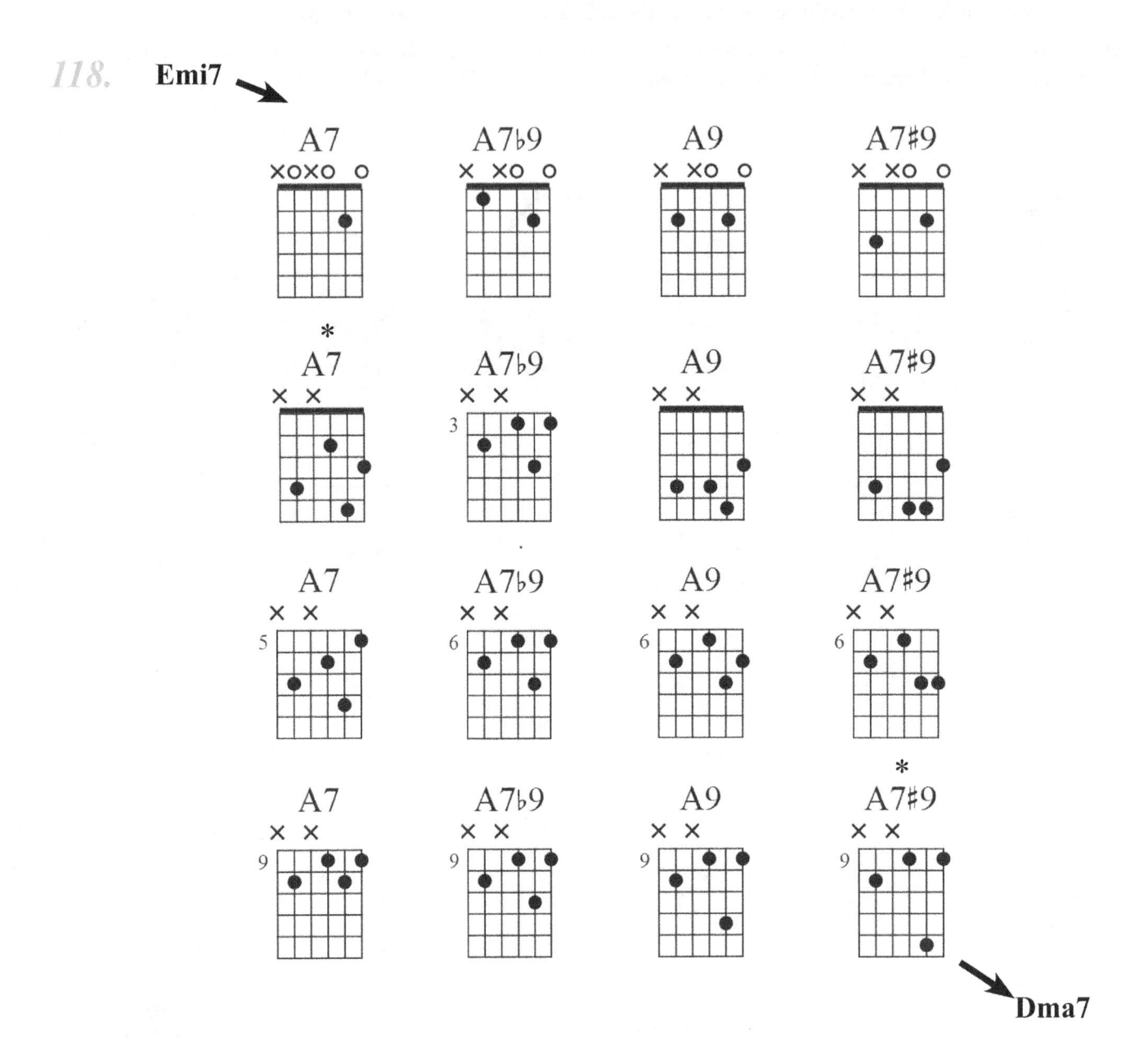

118. **Emi7** →

[Grid of chord diagrams: 4 columns (A7, A7♭9, A9, A7♯9) × 4 rows of fingerings at different positions, with asterisks marking certain chords and an arrow pointing to **Dma7** at the end.]

Those 7♭9 chords have a curios set of fingerings - the same fingering in each inversion. This is related to sharing these notes with a B♭ diminished 7 chord (a chord composed of equal intervals - a minor third - in which every note could be the root of a diminished 7 chord). Diminished seventh chords share notes with the 7♭9 chord, and hence fingerings. This is discussed elsewhere in the book in more detail.

For right now, listen to how the 7♭9 chords sound ***dominant.***

Strummable Altered Chord Fingerings

The Major Chord Family

This is a reference section of strummable "jazz chords" as they used to be called. The chords are either chromatic or rich in 9, 11, and 13 notes, and are often five or six string voicings. They're shown from the roots C and G so they should be easily transposable.

The chord types are generally placed in columns.

Explore the fingerings and mark any that you'd like to learn now.

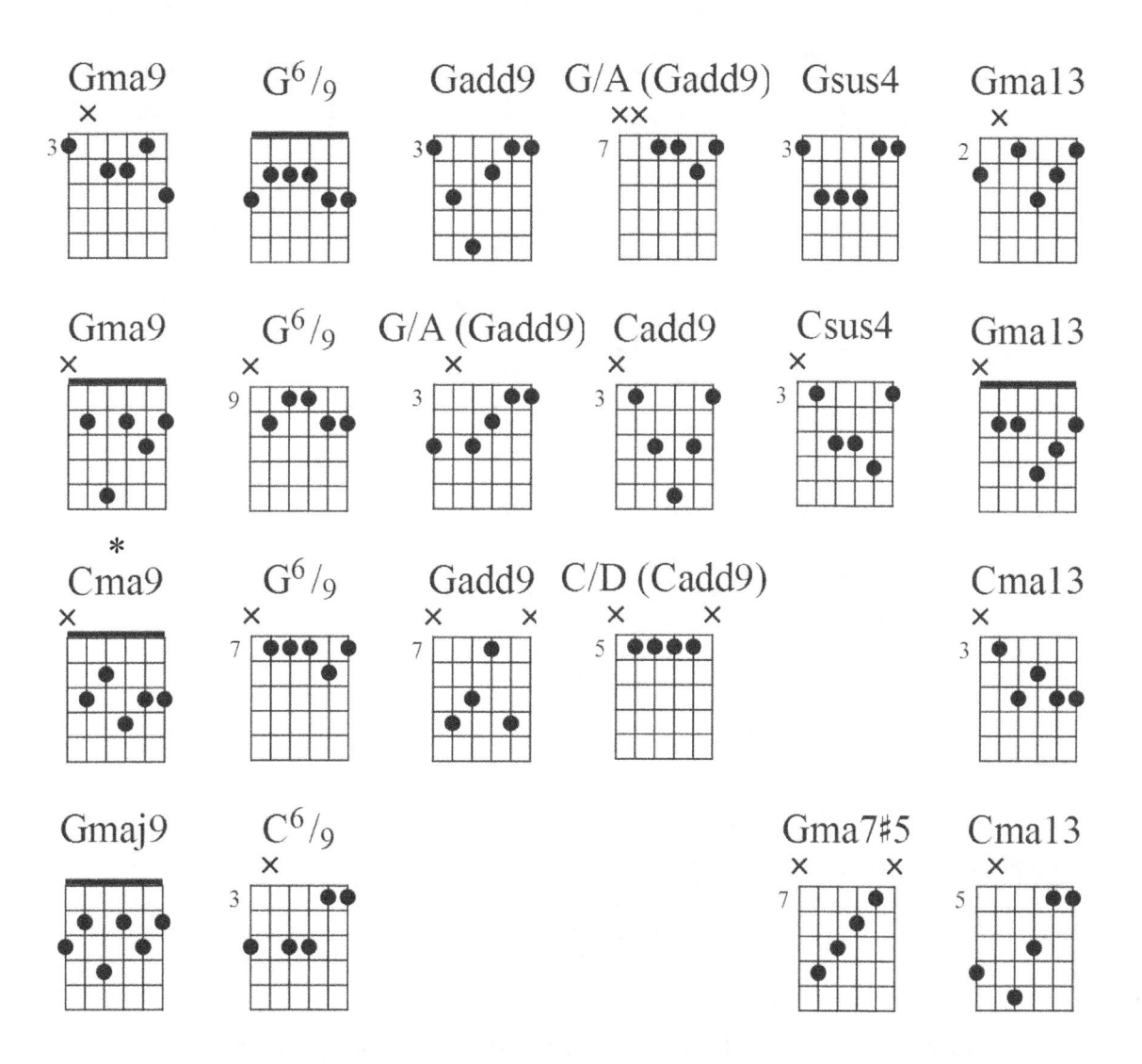

Gma9	G6/9	Gadd9	G/A (Gadd9)	Gsus4	Gma13
Gma9	G6/9	G/A (Gadd9)	Cadd9	Csus4	Gma13
*Cma9	G6/9	Gadd9	C/D (Cadd9)		Cma13
Gmaj9	C6/9			Gma7#5	Cma13

As we've already seen, four note fingerings can sound somewhat "ambiguous" - that is, they may not have as well defined tonal center. That's neither good nor bad. Just be aware this sound.

You may also recognize a fingering as being known by another name, as we've seen before (Ami7 and C6). Exploration is the key here - just try them on and listen. Shared names are interesting, but not critical to your learning.

The Minor Chord Family

Remember that these fingerings are mostly big "grab-able" chords that have a pretty definite sound with five or six strings. That can be good or bad. If you're in a large ensemble you may choose to go with a smaller sound to prevent clashes with other instruments. In a small ensemble, especially without a keyboard player, the larger fingerings should help deliver the harmony, and clashes are less likely.

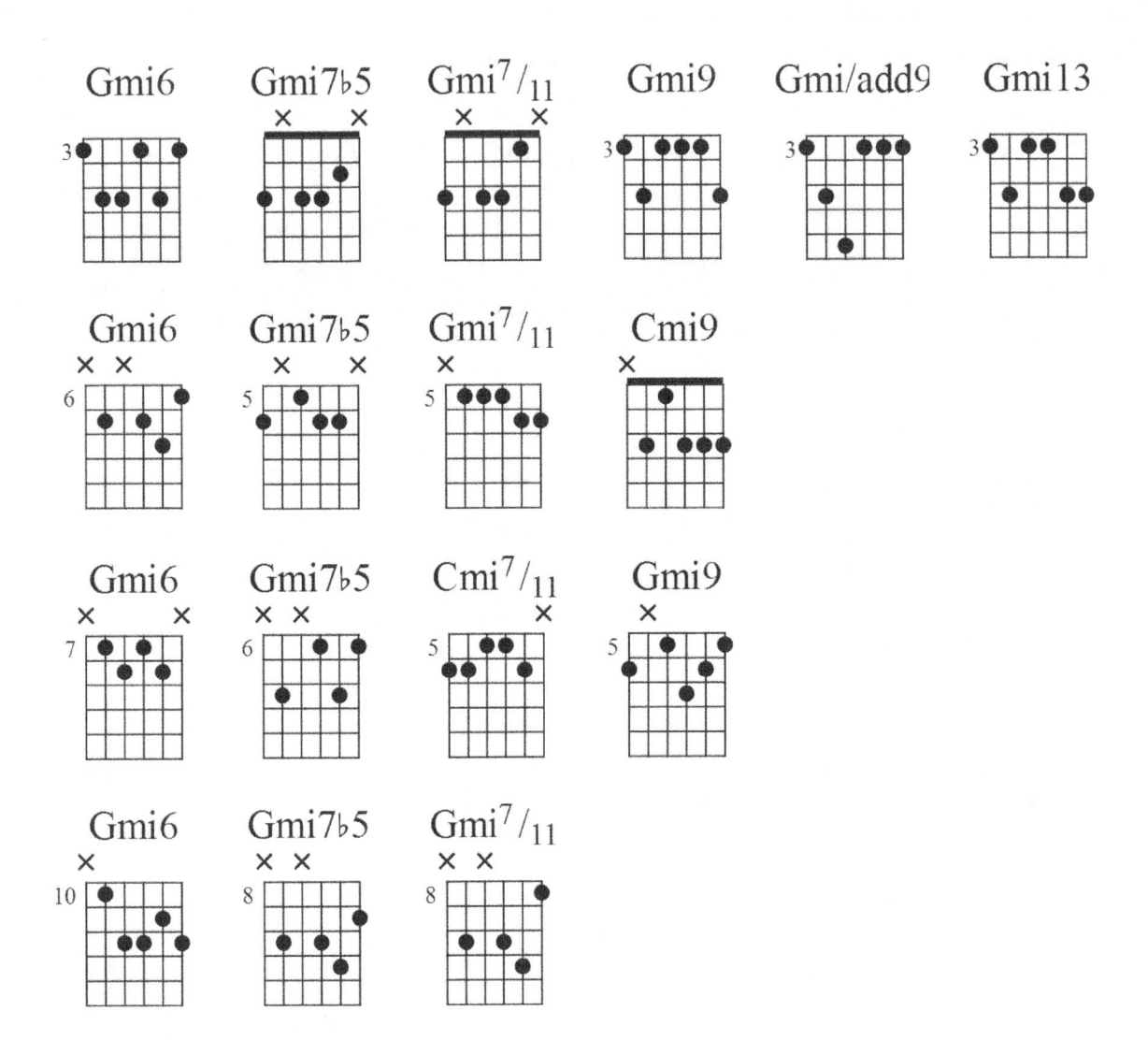

Gmi6	Gmi7b5	Gmi7/11	Gmi9	Gmi/add9	Gmi13
Gmi6	Gmi7b5	Gmi7/11	Cmi9		
Gmi6	Gmi7b5	Cmi7/11	Gmi9		
Gmi6	Gmi7b5	Gmi7/11			

Note: In large ensemble settings (lots of horns, strings, or even guitars) tuning may be an issue. If it is, the more instruments playing the same note, the less in tune you may all sound.

You should always let your ear be your guide, but one technique you might try is to shorten the sound of the chord. Your role may be to add a percussive *start* to the chord, where other instruments sustain it. In that case, shortening your sound (via muting) might be helpful if done subtly.

The Dominant Chord Family

The dominant family fingerings are divided up onto three pages:
- Seventh and ninth chords
- Very chromatic seventh and ninth chords
- Eleventh and thirteenth chords

As before, explore and listen, and then mark the fingerings you wish to start to learn now.

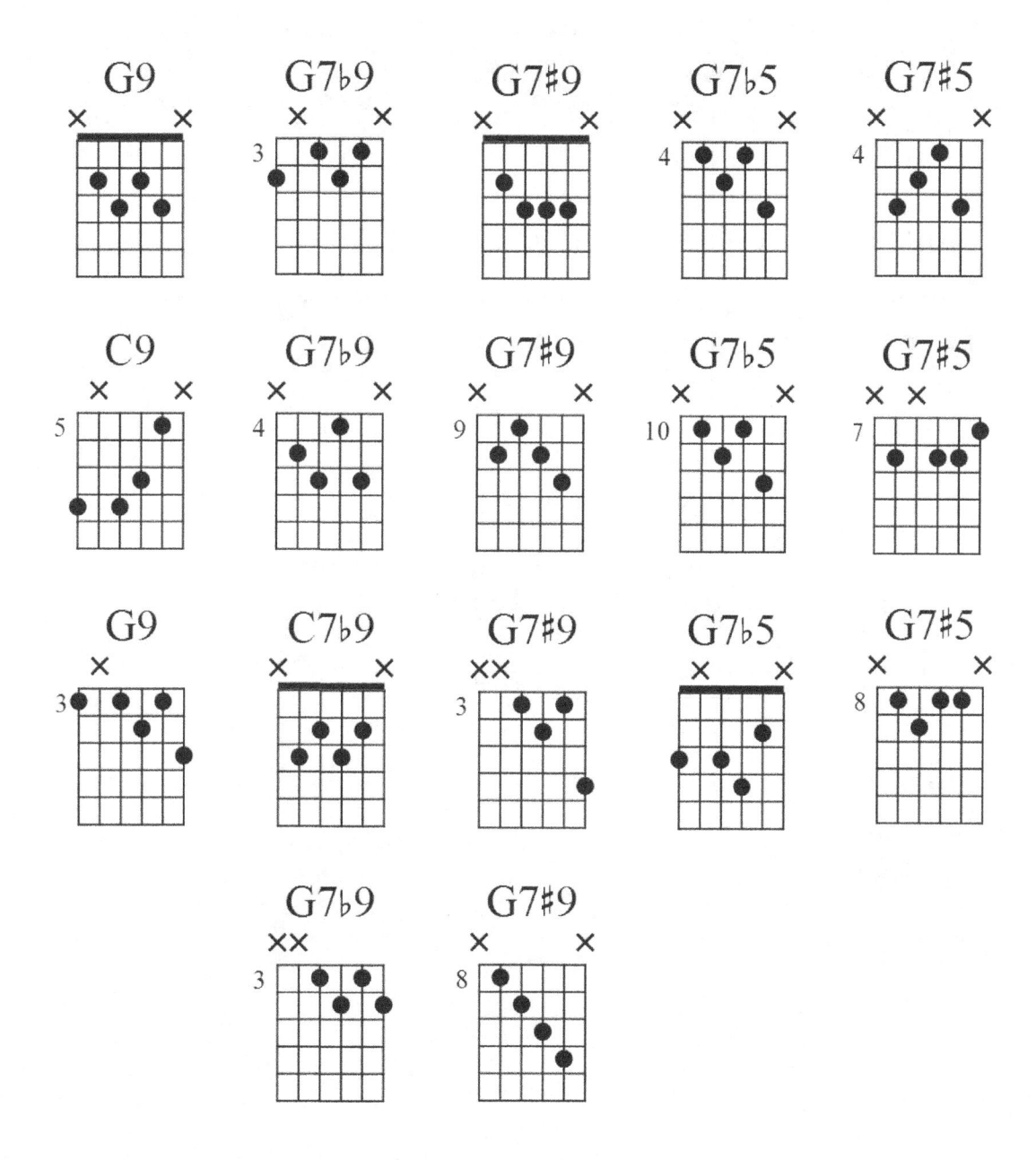

Chord Systems 40th Anniversary Edition - by Leon White • 93

The Dominant Chord Family Continued

In the fingerings below you may wish to compare the sound of 9♭5 fingerings and 9♯11 fingerings. You'll also find an F9♭5 fingerings next to a G9♯5. Check those two fingerings out too.

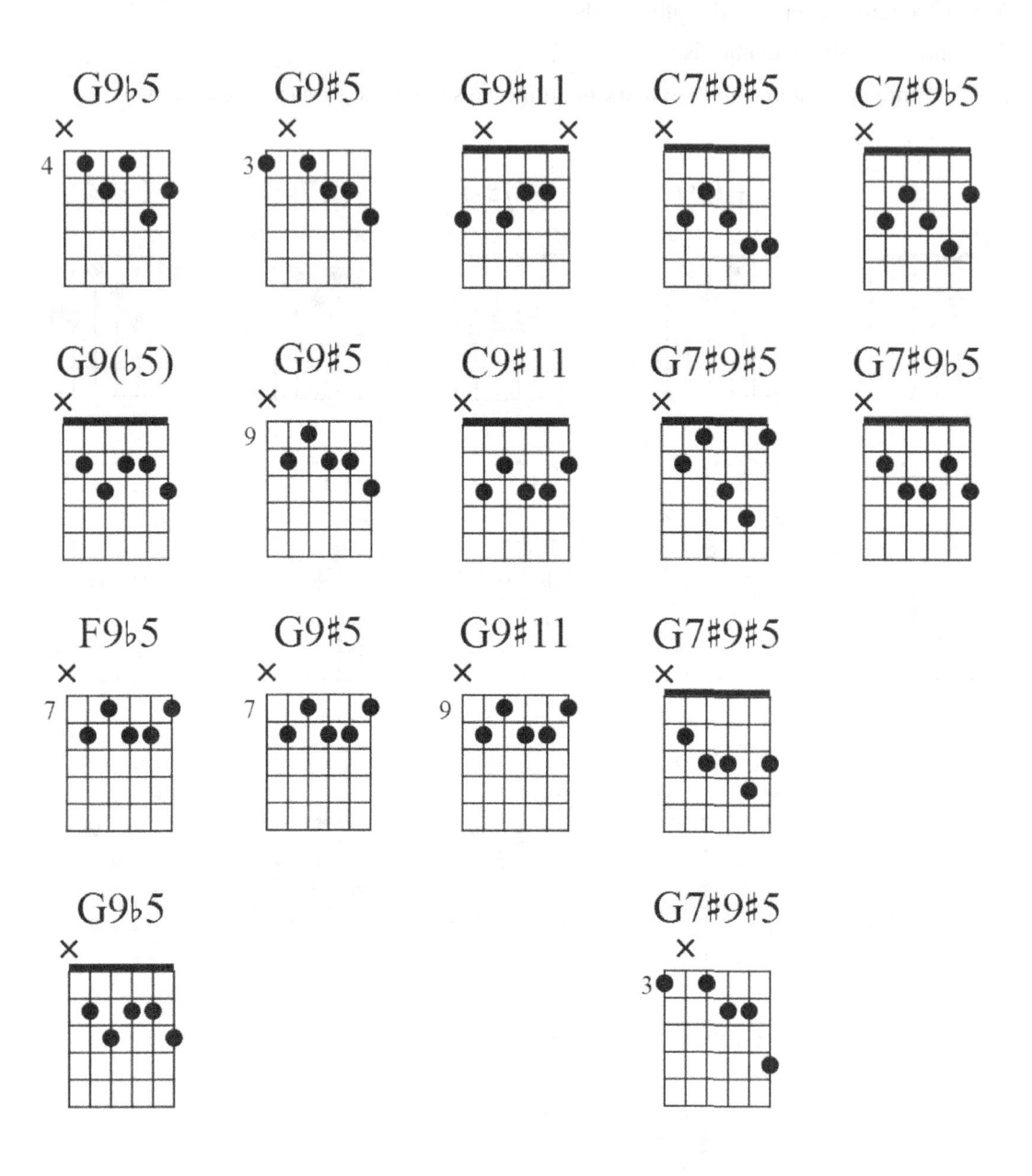

The Dominant Chord Family Continued

Keep exploring and listening in this reference section. Mark the fingerings you want to start learning now, but remember you can always come back here to grab a different fingering if you need it.

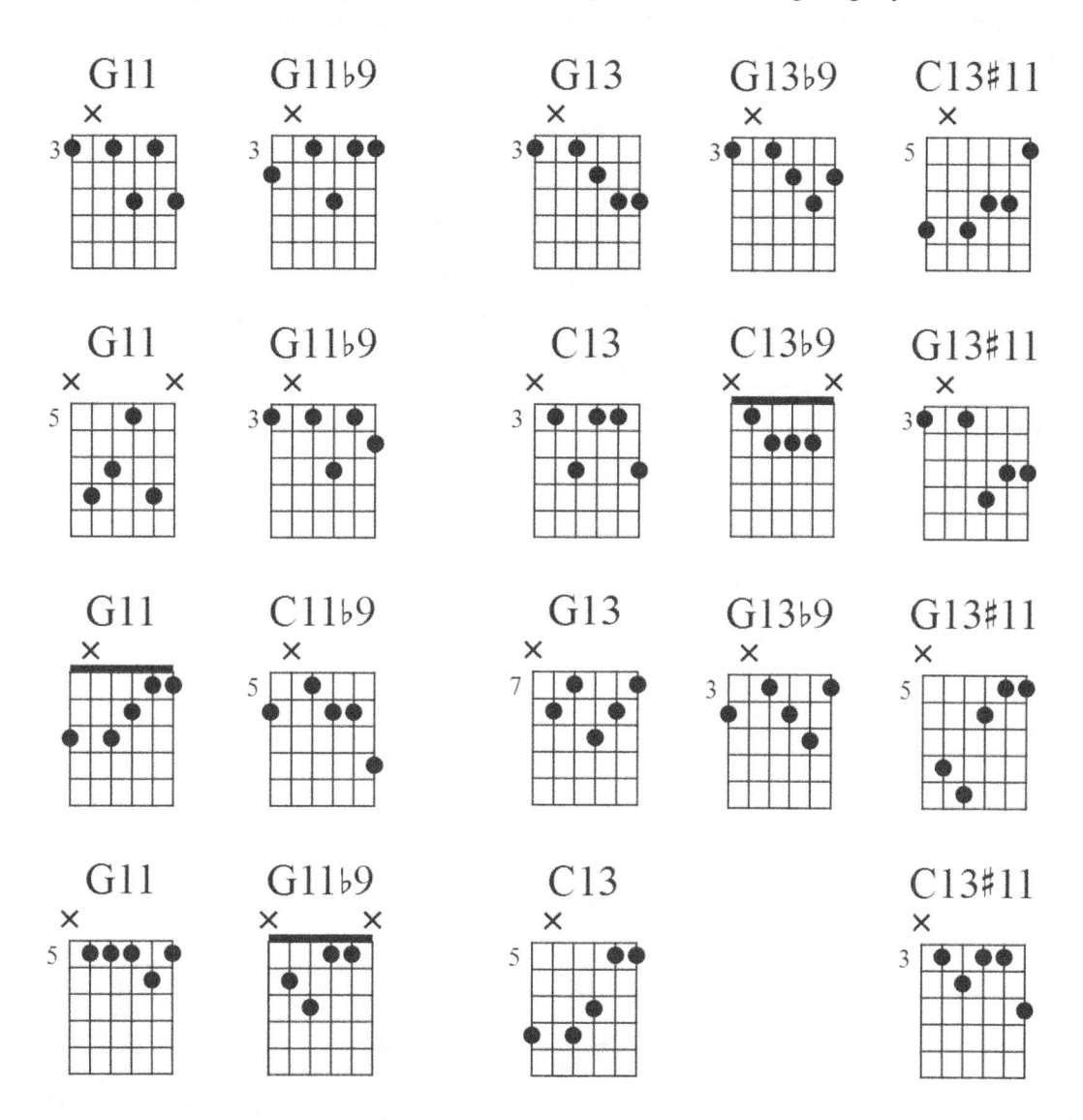

G11	G11♭9	G13	G13♭9	C13♯11
G11	G11♭9	C13	C13♭9	G13♯11
G11	C11♭9	G13	G13♭9	G13♯11
G11	G11♭9	C13		C13♯11

A Whole Lotta Chords

The earlier edition of Chord Systems (from the 1980s) had a chord dictionary as a separate volume (Volume Four). It had chords from only seven roots: A B C D E F G. The reason was size. Even with only seven roots, the dictionary was 288 pages long. That was barely printable and weighed a lot.

So - this reference section is meant to be for convenience and not completeness. At that size, to sit open, volume four had a comb binding, which is not always available from "on-demand" printers around the world. If you're interested, let us know. I'll try to figure out how to deliver it as a separate product. (It had all the chords arranged by all the stringsets.)

Playing ii - V - I Progressions

This page is a master progression that permits you to compare the strummable chord sounds in context. Start by playing a ii chord, and then any V chord fingering shown, and then any I chord. Try all the combinations!

The first example focuses on frets three through eight. The second example centers on fingerings above the eighth fret. Can you see how the different voicings have a role in the location of the fingerings?

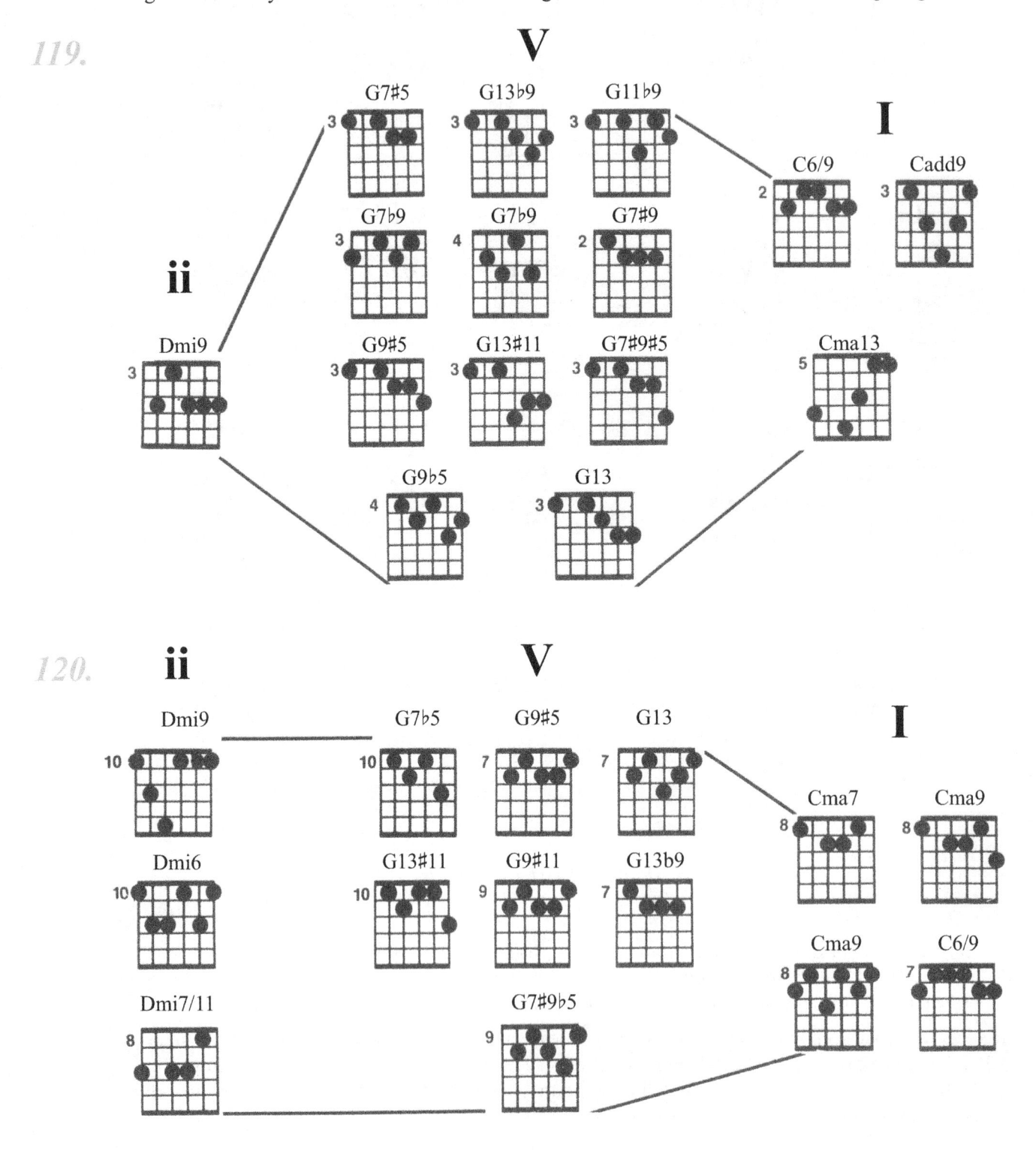

119.

ii — Dmi9

V — G7#5, G13b9, G11b9, G7b9, G7b9, G7#9, G9#5, G13#11, G7#9#5, G9b5, G13

I — C6/9, Cadd9, Cma13

120.

ii — Dmi9, Dmi6, Dmi7/11

V — G7b5, G9#5, G13, G13#11, G9#11, G13b9, G7#9b5

I — Cma7, Cma9, Cma9, C6/9

Ambiguous Chords

"Ambiguous" refers to chords that have multiple names (and are actually multiple chords), and chord sounds that are colorful but *not* defining (as plain major and minor chords).

Following are various chords that meet these criteria. You may have seen and heard them already, but I'm bringing them together so you may compare the sounds and the feelings they create in *you*. These are not all the chord sounds that may be labeled, but once you've heard these you'll recognize new chords when they appear.

Fourths, Ninths, and Elevenths

I categorize these chords as "ambiguous" because their sound and structure, while unique, do not suggest a tonal center. "Ambiguous" is not a standard term. The basic major, minor and dominant chords all seem to clearly suggest not only their individual sounds, but often also the *tonal center* - although sometimes they're less obvious than others. But they seem more readily acceptable to the listener. For instance:

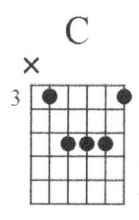

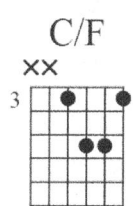

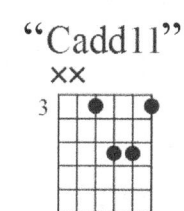

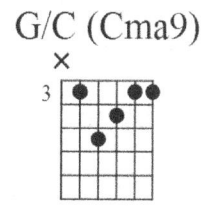

121.   C   C/F   "Cadd11"   G/C (Cma9)

Add 9 chords can also fall into the same type of sound:

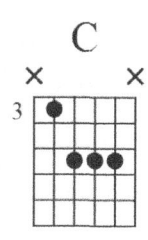

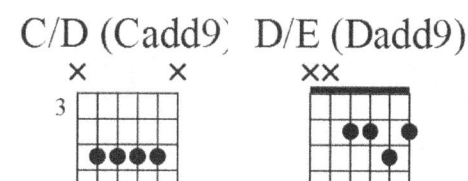

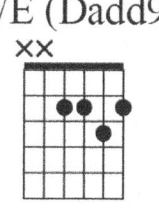

122.   C   C/D (Cadd9)   D/E (Dadd9)

Regardless of the words I've used to describe these chords, I think we can all agree they sound different from our basic three chord families. Words can't always describe sound, so perhaps the way to discuss the subject is to say "Well, it sounds like an Add 9, or a fourth in the bass - you know that sound? Like this: " and then you play it. Other chords that can get dragged into this area of sound include the so called "sus2" and sus4.

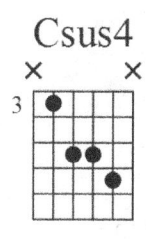

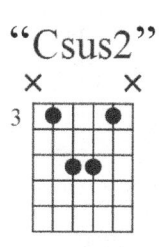

123.   Csus4   "Csus2"

I'm highlighting these sounds because they can be confusing when you see them in music, especially when they are mis-named. The key is to find out what notes the other musician is trying to communicate to you and work with that. If *you're* naming things, name them so they're obvious!

Some of these chords are also known as "chords built in fourths."

Minor Seventh ♯5 Chords

The 7♯5 chord certainly doesn't look like one of the major scale chords. However ... it really is! Watch:

    E   G   B   D   spells Emi7   A   C   E   G   spells Ami7

    E   G   ***C***   D   spells Emi7♯5   A   C   ***F***   G   spells Ami7 ♯5

You can see that both the vi chord and the iii chord can have a raised fifth degree and remain diatonic. Play the progressions below and then tuck this bit of information away for now.

This chord is heard prominently in the song "Peg" by Steely Dan, where the chord helps create a pedal tone. It can also be used as a substitution for a plain minor seventh chord. Part of its appeal is the ambiguity - the Emi7♯5 could also be a Cadd9 - C E G D. The Ami7♯5 could be considered an Fadd9 - F A C G. Play each chord for two beats. The last two rows are a single progression example.

124. Fma7   Gmi7   Ami7♯5   B♭ma7

125. B♭ma7   Ami7♯5   Gmi7   Ami7♯5

126. Ami7♯5   D7♯9   Gmi7   C7sus

127. G7   G7/6   Ami7♯5   Ami7

128. B♭mi13   G/B   Cma7   Cma7/6

129. Dmi7♯5   Dmi7   E♭mi6   C/E

Diminished Seventh Chord

The basic diminished seventh chord fingerings are shown on our four main stringsets:

130.   Gdim7   Gdim7   Gdim7   Gdim7

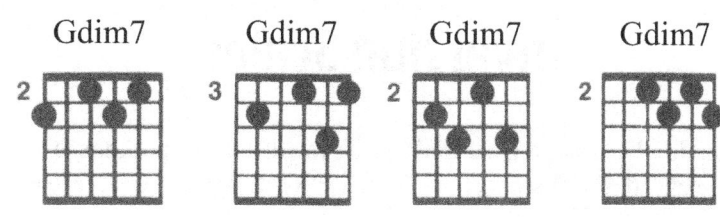

The diminished seventh chord is a pretty well defined sound in popular music. Its ambiguity comes from what the chord is actually *doing*. The diminished seventh chord is also a 7b9 chord. Examine the following fingerings.

131.   F#7b9   C7b9   B7b9   G7b9

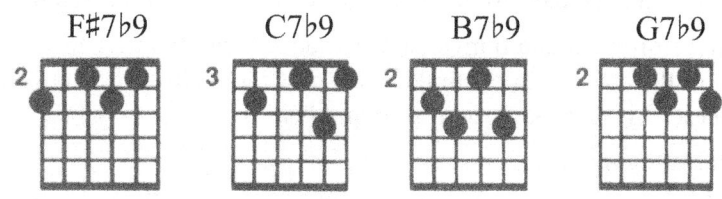

The diminished seventh chord can have any note in the chord as its root:

Cdim7	C	Eb	Gb	Bbb		B7b9	B	D#	F#	A	C
Ebdim7	Eb	Gb	Bbb	C		D7b9	D	F#	A	C	D#
Gbdim7	Gb	Bbb	C	Eb		F7b9	F	A	C	Eb	Gb
Adim7	A(Bbb)	C	Eb	Gb		Ab7b9	Ab	C	Eb	Gb	A

To the right there are four 7b9 chords that contain the *same* diminished 7th chord: C Eb Gb Bbb !

If that isn't confusing I don't know what is. The value here is that most of the diminished seventh chords written in music are really acting as dominant seventh chords.

132.   Gma7   "G#dim7"   Ami7   D7

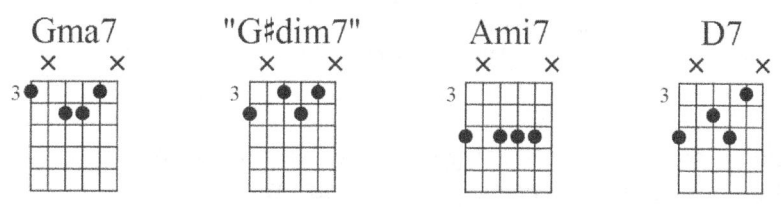

Above is a classic progression with a diminished 7th chord in it. The dim7 is often described as a "passing chord" but that dim7 chord could also be thought of as an E7b9 chord. Below, the G#dim7 suggests a vi chord of some kind (including VI7) in a I VI ii V progression. Once you hear the similarity it becomes clearer.

133.   Gma7   G7b9   Ami7   D7

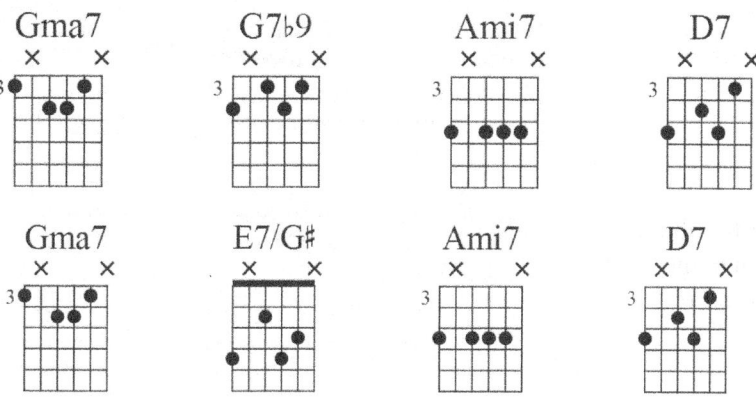

134.   Gma7   E7/G#   Ami7   D7

Section 3 - Four Note Chords in Action

Inversion Scales

As we said earlier, "inversion" is a word used to describe the different spellings (from top to bottom or bottom to top) of a single chord. For Instance: C E G, E G C, and G C E are all different inversions of the C major chord.

An inversion *scale* is a combination of a scale and a series of chord inversions which are played at the same time. To begin with we'll use only one kind of chord with one scale. The chord can be from anyone of our chord families. Our first examples use the major seventh chord and the major scale.

The scale is played with the different chord inversions as "accompaniment." The scale may be the top, middle, or bottom voice of the chord. Our examples will show the scale as the top voice and later as the lowest voice (because these outside voices are most easily heard).

There are two reasons for studying inversion scales.

1. The inversion scale is a powerful tool for accompaniment, especially when the guitar is the only chordal instrument being used. (I've always thought they sound good too.)
2. Inversion scales are an important fundamental tool for learning to play the solo chord melody guitar style (where the guitar plays both the melody AND the accompaniment).

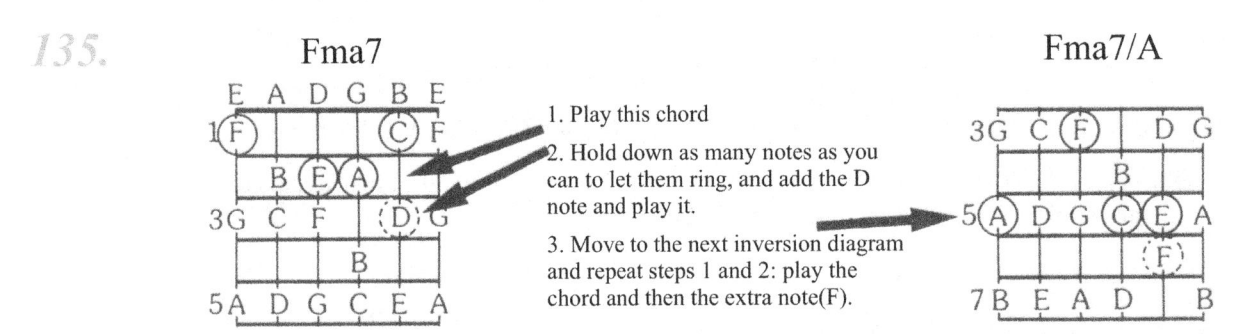

135. **Fma7**

1. Play this chord
2. Hold down as many notes as you can to let them ring, and add the D note and play it.
3. Move to the next inversion diagram and repeat steps 1 and 2: play the chord and then the extra note(F).

Fma7/A

When you are descending down the fingerboard, you will be doing things in reverse. The note that was added to the first grid will now be played *after the second grid*. Watch:

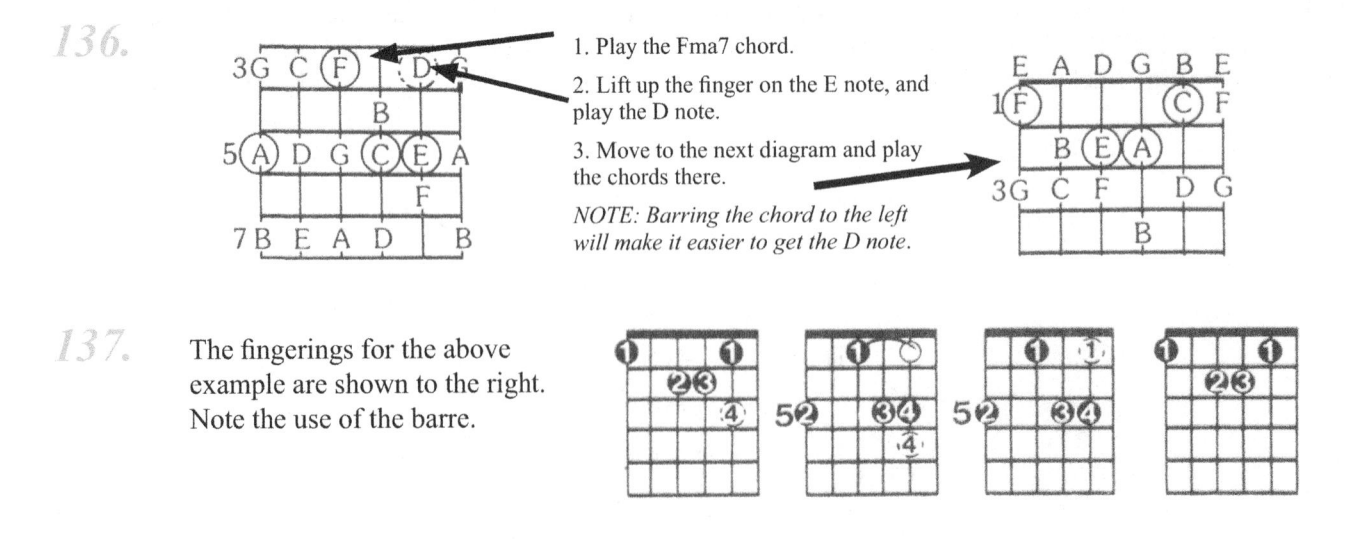

136.
1. Play the Fma7 chord.
2. Lift up the finger on the E note, and play the D note.
3. Move to the next diagram and play the chords there.

NOTE: Barring the chord to the left will make it easier to get the D note.

137. The fingerings for the above example are shown to the right. Note the use of the barre.

Major Seventh Chord Scale Examples

The inversion scales will be shown on different stringsets, and even across stringsets. Work slowly and carefully as you memorize each set of fingerings. SPECIAL NOTE: There are four fingerings for each chord in these inversion scales. We are playing one melody note in the chord itself, and adding one melody note afterwards. That means we're playing two melody notes with each chord fingering. However, there is one small issue.

Since there are *four* chords and *seven* melody notes in a major scale, one chord will have only one note. That's OK.

Play each of these examples as discussed. Sometimes to help the fingering of the chord scales we have begun on a 6th chord instead of the 7th. To help 'swing' the example, try playing the bass note *first,* and then the chord, and *then* the extra note. Even if you're a flat picker, you should be trying fingerpicking now.

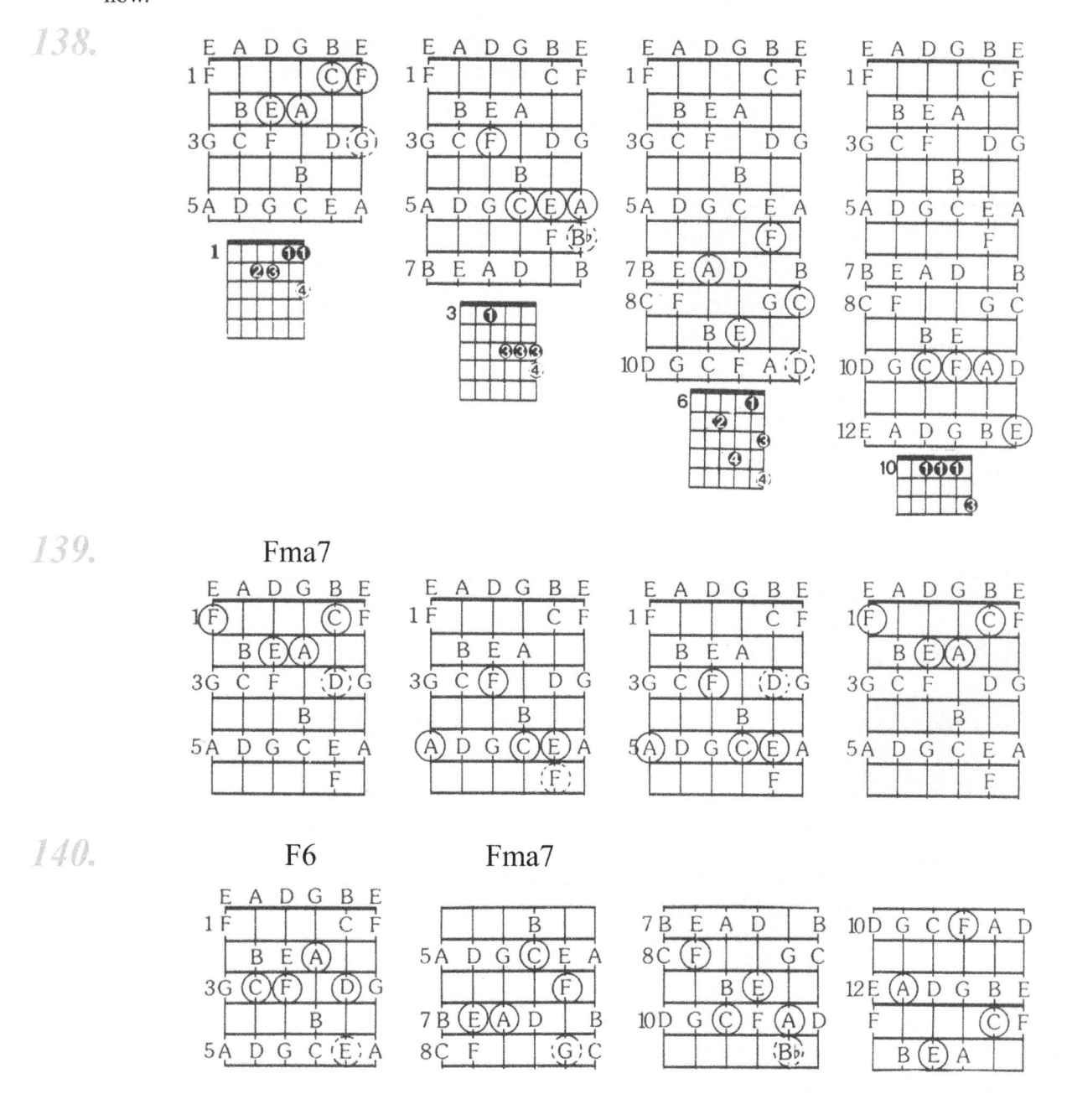

138.

139. Fma7

140. F6   Fma7

Chord Scales on Mixed Stringsets

You may play each row as an example, but connect the rows together and make the change in stringsets smooth. Use two or four beats per chord, try the 'swing' feel described earlier, and listen closely to the volume of each note in the chord. Balanced volume is the goal, although emphasizing bass or treble is also a good way to practice control . . . and have fun! You should be making music with these licks.

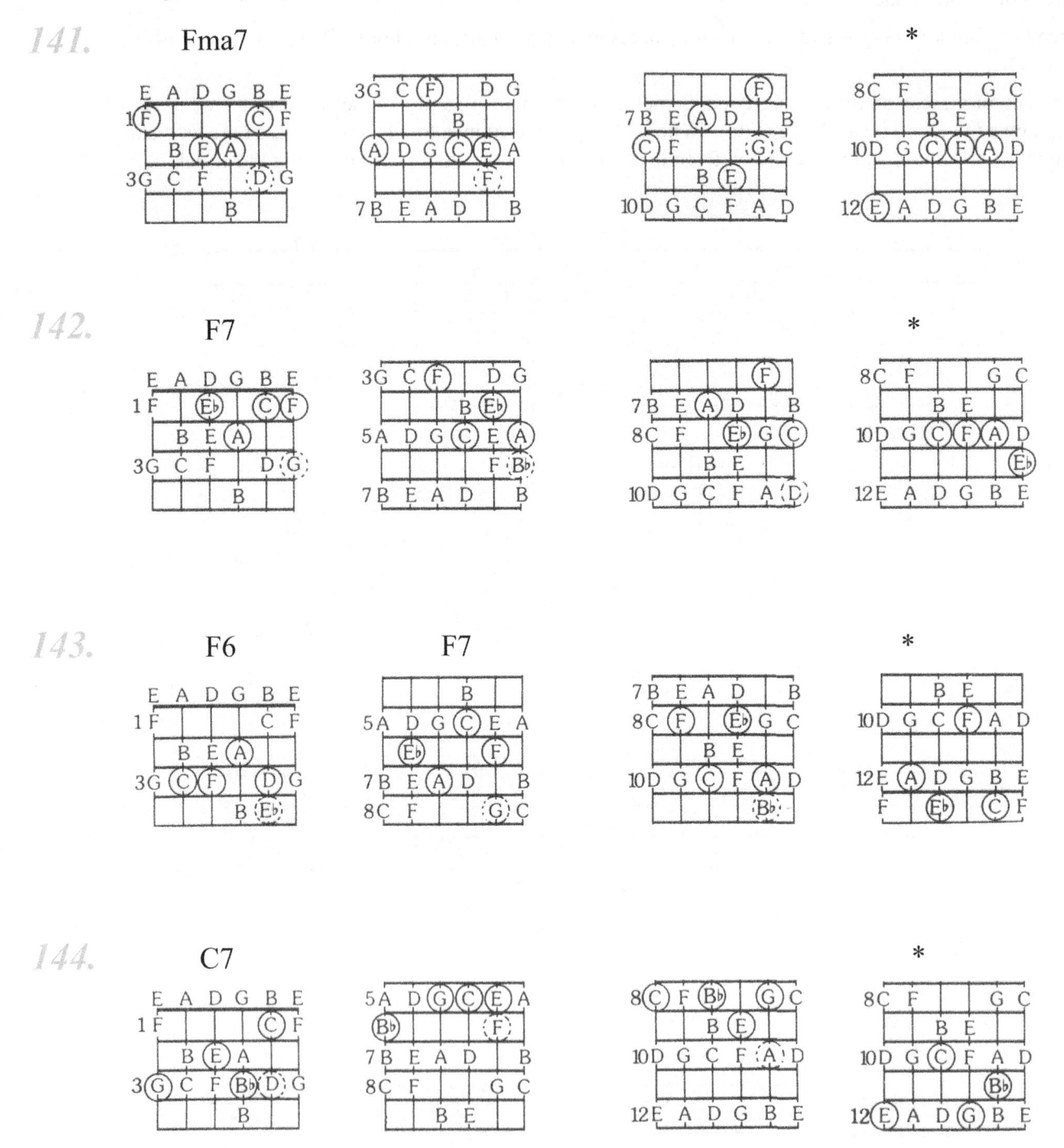

141. **Fma7**   *

142. **F7**   *

143. **F6**   **F7**   *

144. **C7**   *

* These fingerings have only one melody note.

Minor Seventh Chord Scale Examples

Repeat all the same processes as before for these examples. You should start to recognize these examples in chord melody style guitar playing. While I prefer to play these fingerstyle, you can still strum them.

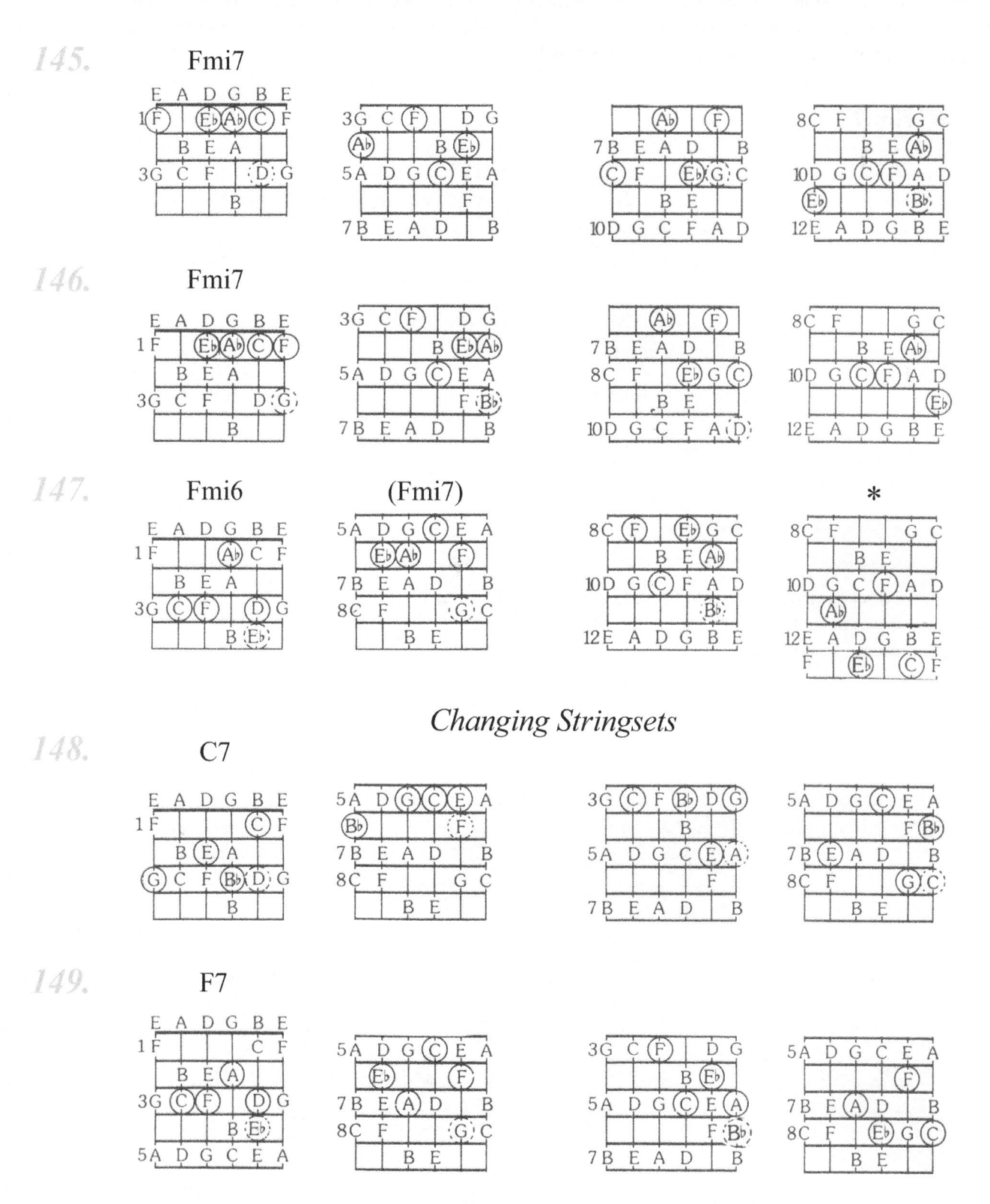

145. Fmi7

146. Fmi7

147. Fmi6   (Fmi7)   *

Changing Stringsets

148. C7

149. F7

Chord Scale Progressions by Stringset

Below are two examples of a ii-V-I progression in the key of F major. The top one uses the 4321 stringset while the bottom example uses the 6432 stringset. You can give each chord 2 beats, and use the techniques outlined earlier to make music from these. The 4321 voicings are common for chord melody jazz guitar as played by musicians like Herb Ellis and Joe Pass.

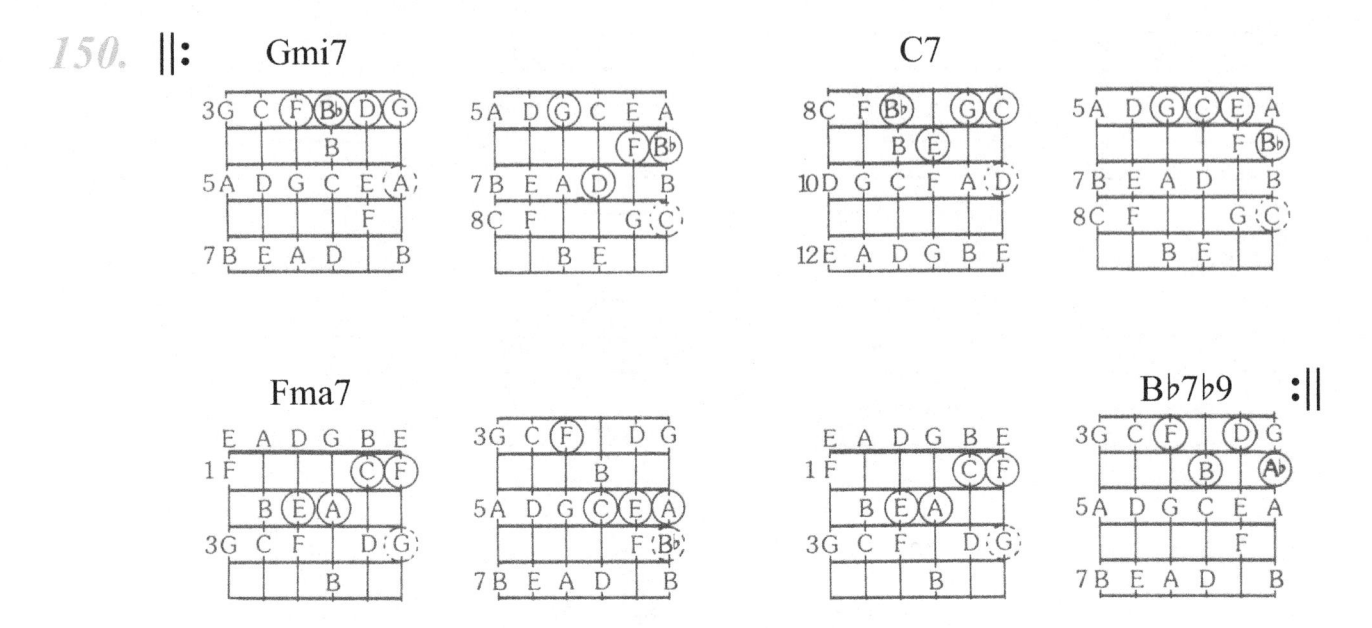

150. ||: Gmi7   C7

Fma7   Bb7b9 :||

In the phrase directly above, the melody is always going UP - even when the voicings are going down. You don't have to have the melody follow the voicings movement. Could you have the chord in the 3rd box (in the row right above) move the melody from F to D? Sure. This is music, not geometry.

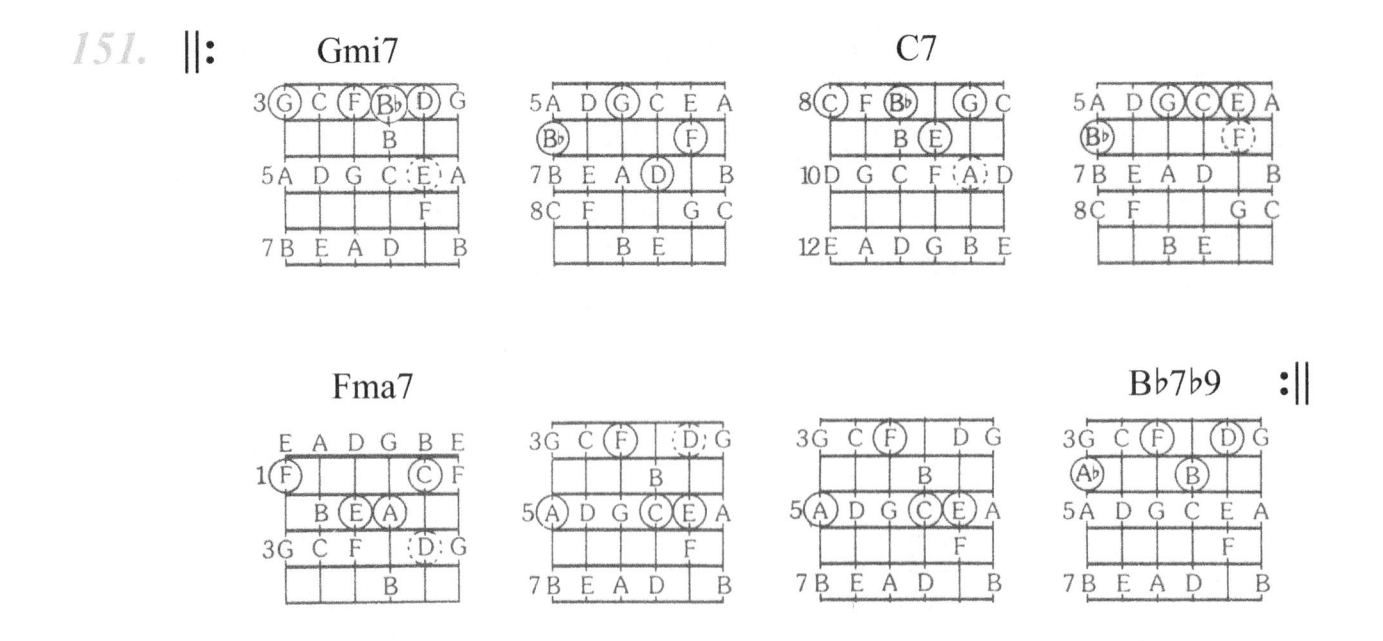

151. ||: Gmi7   C7

Fma7   Bb7b9 :||

Inversion Scales in the Bass

You have now seen how to add melodies to the top voice of a chord progression. You can repeat the process for the lowest voice - the bass voice. This introduces a popular accompaniment tool called "Walking Bass," often heard in swing style jazz.

Walking Bass Lines

Shown below are the scale tones placed in the bass voice of the chord fingering on the 6432 stringset. You do the same thing here as you did when the scale tone was the top note. For the walking bass effect do the following:

1. Finger the chord.
2. Play the bass note alone.
3. Then play the chord.
4. Then play the added bass note (shown in a broken circle).
5. Then move to the next position and repeat: bass note-chord-bass note.

(Ted Greene's album Solo Guitar has many examples of this style of playing.)

The notation is the same as before. In these bass examples, the second "bass note" in each diagram is shown by a broken circle. Practice the mechanics on these examples. Go slowly at first, and make sure you're getting all the notes sounded. The first row stays on one stringset. The second row crosses stringsets.

152. A7

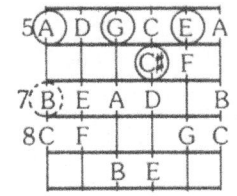

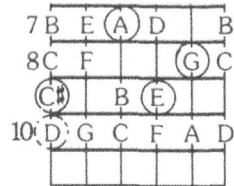

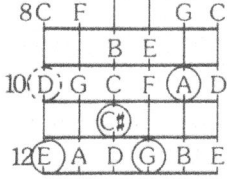

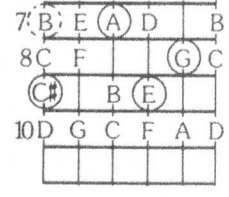

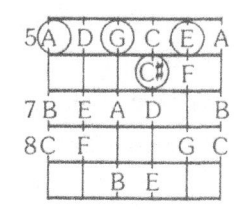

153. A7

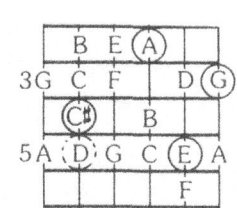

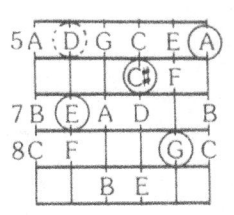

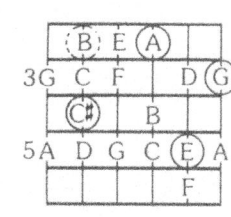

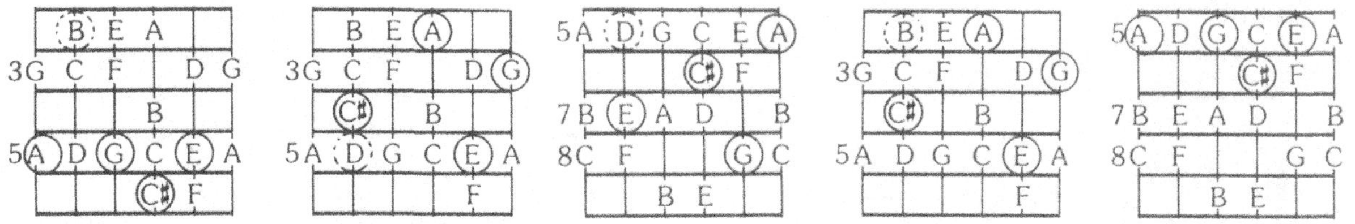

A note on fingering: When adding the second bass note shown in a diagram you can choose to add the note to the chord you've fingered, *or*, anticipate the *next* chord fingering by moving your left hand to play that second note (the B note) in the shape of the *next fingering*.

In the first example above the B note can be added to the A7 by using the 3rd finger (box #1). *Or*, you can play that A7, move your left hand so that the B note is played by your *first* finger, and position your hand for the A chord with the C♯ in the bass (box #2). In effect, you've placed a barre behind the A/C♯ fingering and played the B note there.

This is definitely a fingerstyle technique because you're barring notes that should NOT be sounded.

154. A7

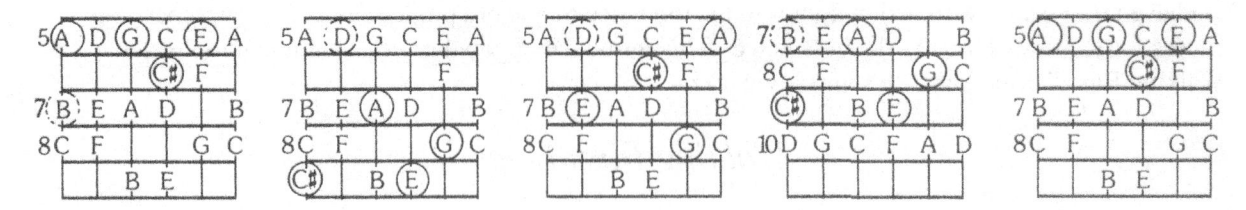

The key to getting a good sound with walking bass lines is to think and play like a bass player. This kind of playing is NOT some version of fingerpicking accompaniment! You want to convey two independent sets of sounds. The bass notes can be held and played legato, for instance, while the chord tones are short and muted. Or all the notes could be sounded legato.

Ted Greene really set the standard for these techniques.

1. He played his guitar tuned down a half-step, whole-step, or even a step-and-a-half.
2. He used the *side* of his right hand thumb to hit the bass string - not the tip - to get a more bass-like attack.
3. Ted would purposely slide into selected bass notes because upright basses don't have frets, and it was common to slide into a note.
4. He wasn't afraid to repeat a bass note to keep good time in the bass line if another pitch was not available. He understood the importance of the bass player keeping a good rhythmic feel.
5. He would introduce chromatic notes to approach a chord, or to create movement in the bass line.
6. He would create rhythmic variety by varying the number of bass notes played with each chord to help show two independent 'players' at work.
7. He would often create simple melodies between chords to deliver a smooth connected harmonic sound with the moving bass.
8. He developed lots of chord colors with fingerings that would support playing the bass line, so the harmony was interesting while the groove was steady.

Introduce some of Ted's ideas as you play the minor seventh chords with bass lines, below. Note the C# chromatic note in the second chord box. Think about the fingerings.

155. Dmi7

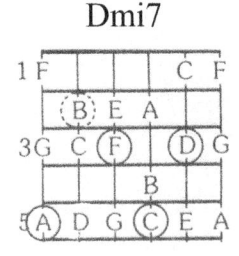

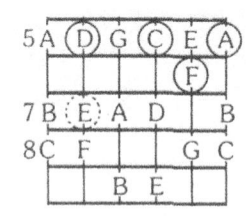

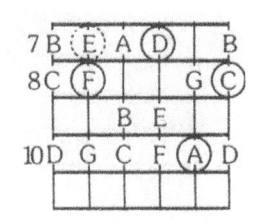

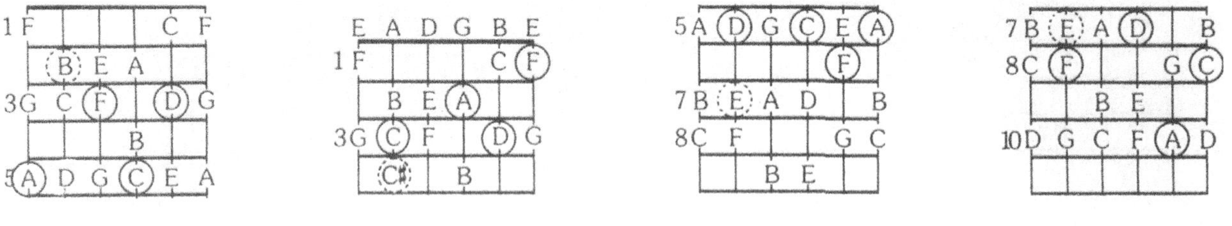

Dmi7

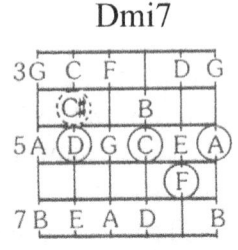

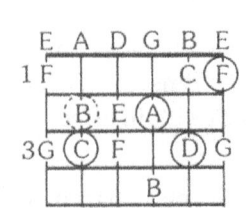

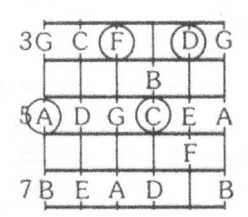

In the first examples below focus on diatonic scale tones in the walking bass line, and the chords are basic seventh chords. Play each example as before.

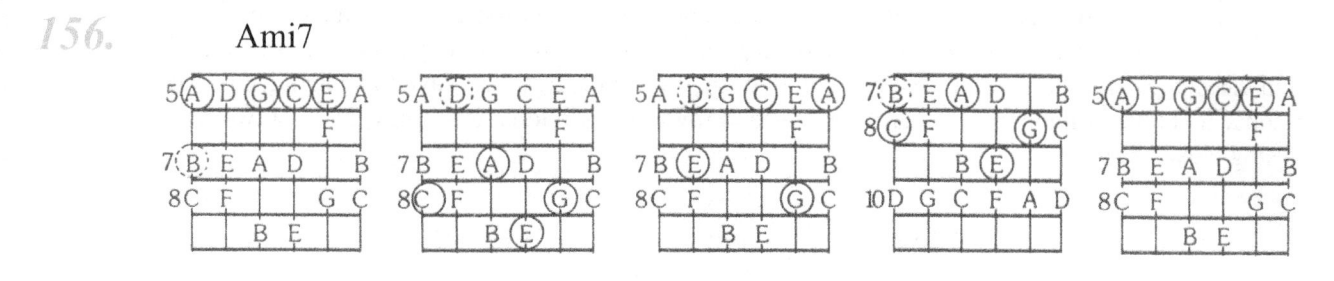

156. Ami7

Play each chord for two beats.

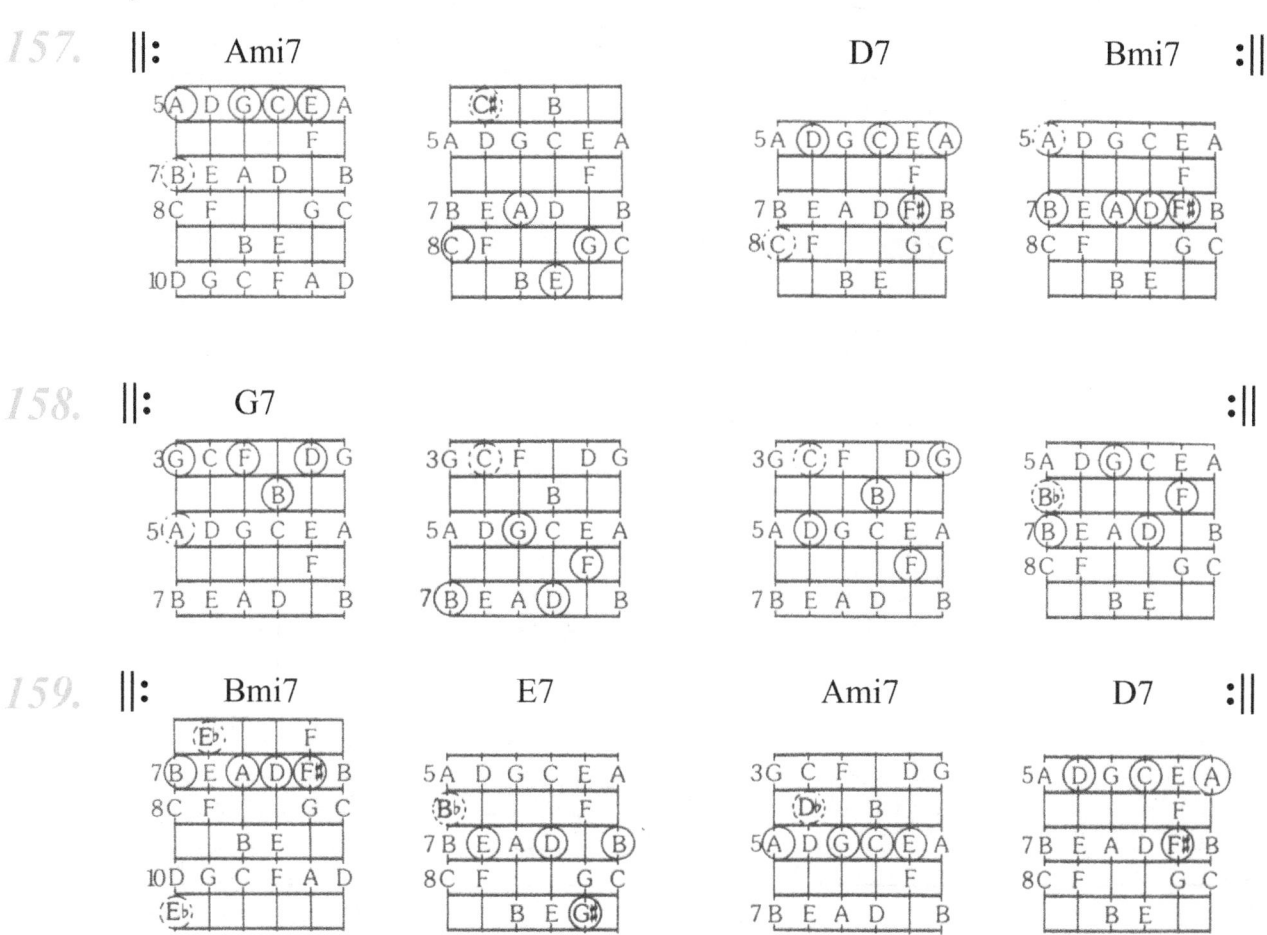

157. ||: Ami7   D7   Bmi7 :||

158. ||: G7   :||

159. ||: Bmi7   E7   Ami7   D7 :||

This last example introduces a different way to create the bass line. It is mostly a jazz sounding technique, and simply involves selecting a bass note that is one half-step above or below the next chord. Often you can grab the next chord fingering, but one fret low, and play the bass note and then slide up to the chord with the new bass note. Play the example slowly and think about which notes are used.

The half-step approach should have some thought on your part. Mixing half step below and half step above may not "sell" the sound to the listener as well as repeating the "below, below, below." The direction the voicings are moving may also influence your choice of bass note: put the note below chords as you ascend, and above as you move the voicings down again. Your choices should govern, but be the bass player!

Mixed Stringset and Bass Lines

The first example introduces more colorful chromatic chords and the half-step approach bass line style. In addition, we're moving between stringsets to keep the tone more uniform. Pay attention to your guitar tone in various parts of the neck. Unhappily for all of us, some voicings may have to be avoided because of inconsistent tone or intonation. The first and second rows are individual examples. The last two rows are a single example.

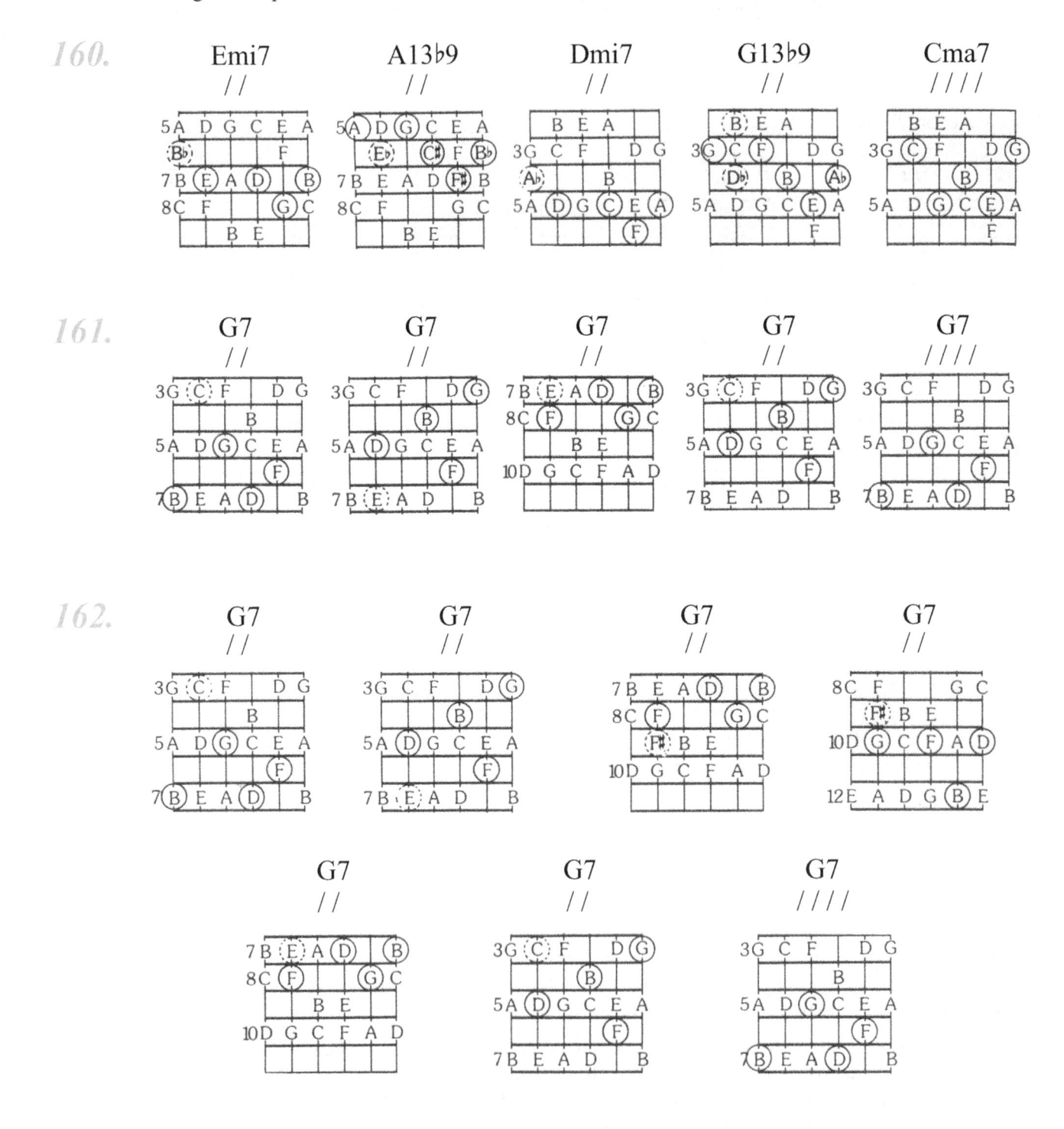

160. Emi7 / /   A13♭9 / /   Dmi7 / /   G13♭9 / /   Cma7 / / / /

161. G7 / /   G7 / /   G7 / /   G7 / /   G7 / / / /

162. G7 / /   G7 / /   G7 / /   G7 / /

G7 / /   G7 / /   G7 / / / /

12 Bar Blues in G - Chord Bass Style

The main focus in this example should be on the bass line. I've kept the voicings fairly diatonic so you can see the chord fingerings being played. The key here is the fingering. The next page shows my recommended fingerings. You'll see the use of half-step slides into chords as well as lots of simple substitutions, but I reduced the chromatic sounds. Give each chord two beats.

163.

[Chord diagrams for a 12-bar blues progression in G, chord bass style:]

Row 1: G7 — C7 — G7 — C7 — G7
Row 2: C7 — G7 — G7 — C7 — C7
Row 3: C7 — C7 — G7 — C7 — G7
Row 4: Emi7 — Ami7 — Ami7 — D7 — D6
Row 5: G7 — E7#9 — Ami7 — D11

Chord Systems 40th Anniversary Edition - by Leon White • 109

G Blues Fingering Example

The fingerings below are suggested. I've used partial barres, double stops, and selected stringsets to try to 1) achieve a consistent guitar tone, 2) save jumping around, and 3) stay moderately diatonic (seventh chords mostly). This works best for some version of fingerstyle where you can emphasize notes.

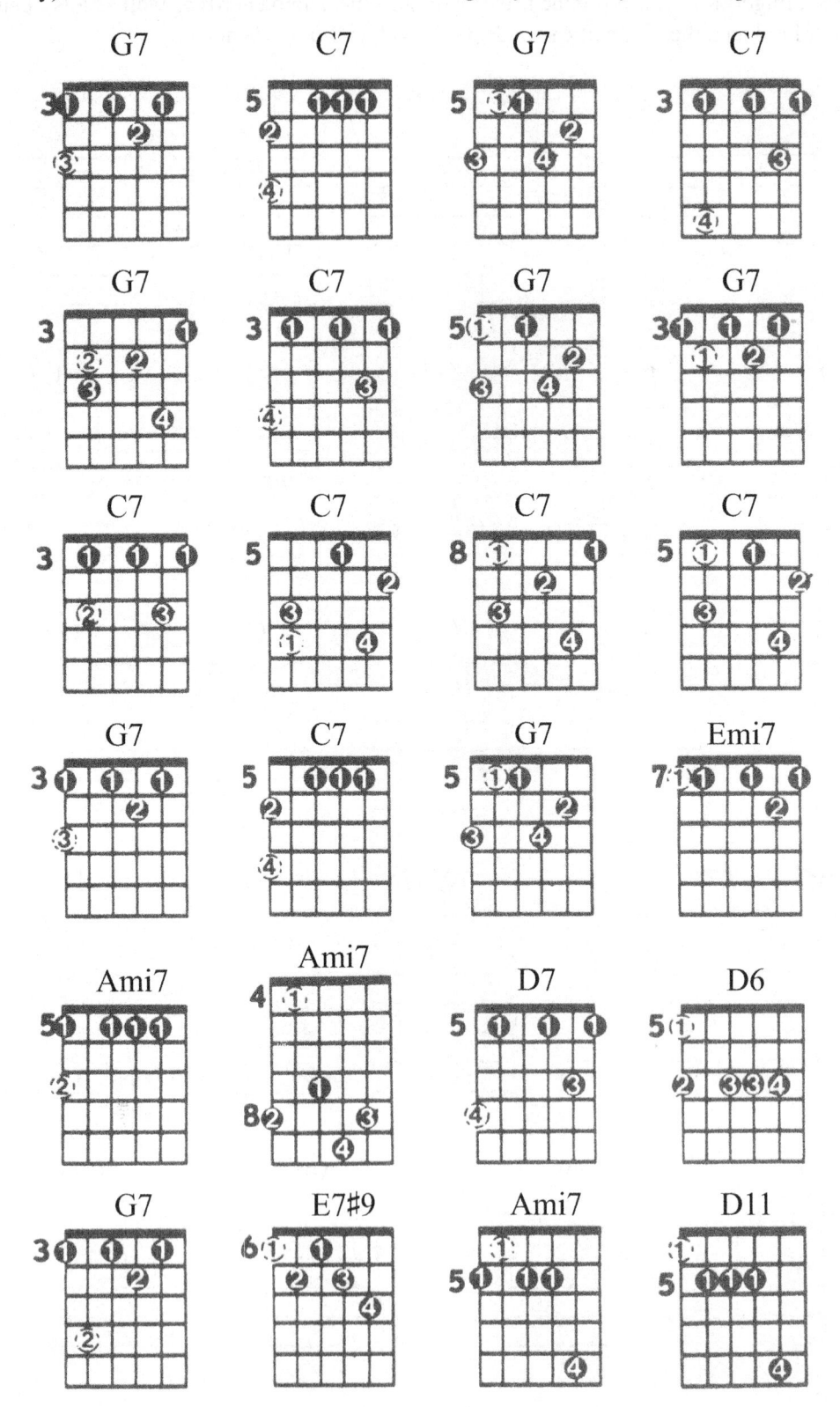

164.

Section 4 - Three Note Chords: Triads
Introductory Examples

A triad is a three note chord. They're small and powerful groups of notes.
- Master guitarist Ted Greene taught triads to thousands of students, and used the triad throughout chord melody arrangements and Bach passages that he composed and improvised "on the spot."
- Triads in rhythm 'n blues guitar are used in comping and soloing.
- Triads fill thousands of songs in country, western, bluegrass, folk and classical styles of music.
- In jazz, the triad appears in complex chord structures and arrangements, as well as throughout improvised solos.
- Improvisers such as guitarist Larry Carlton use triads throughout stunning solos in various styles. (Steely Dan recordings are a masterclass in triad use).

While the subject of triads could fill a multi-volume encyclopedia, I'll use musical examples, our stringset logic, and a few harmony ideas to layout a road map for your playing and investigations.

As before, here are some simple triad chord licks to remind you of where we've seen these types of sounds. This is the "meet 'n greet" segment. Just play these, listen very closely, and pay attention to the notes.

Here are some chordal accompaniment progressions for A7 that employ chords up a fourth - here D or D7. Play the rows over an A major or A7 chord.

165. A7

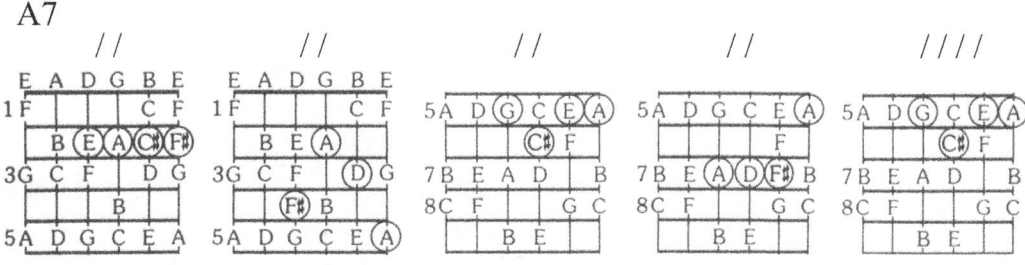

The example above uses four note triads. Look at the following examples, also for use over A or A7, and hear how the basic triads sound in the same kind of progression.

166.

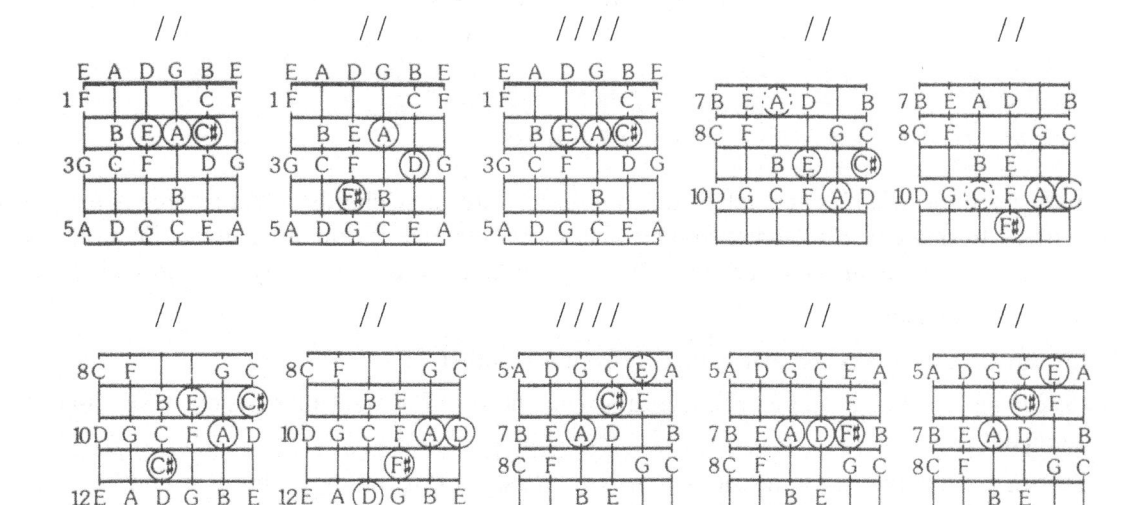

167.

The example below also uses triads, and you've probably heard this chord lick in blues progressions. The triads are quite colorful when played over A7, although technically they don't come from the root A.

168.

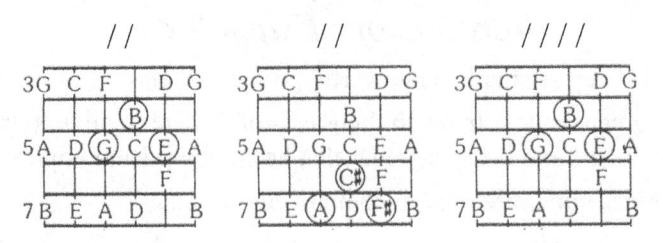

Any chance you can name the two triads used here?

The example below expands on the two chords above, but this is still to be played over an A or A7.

169.

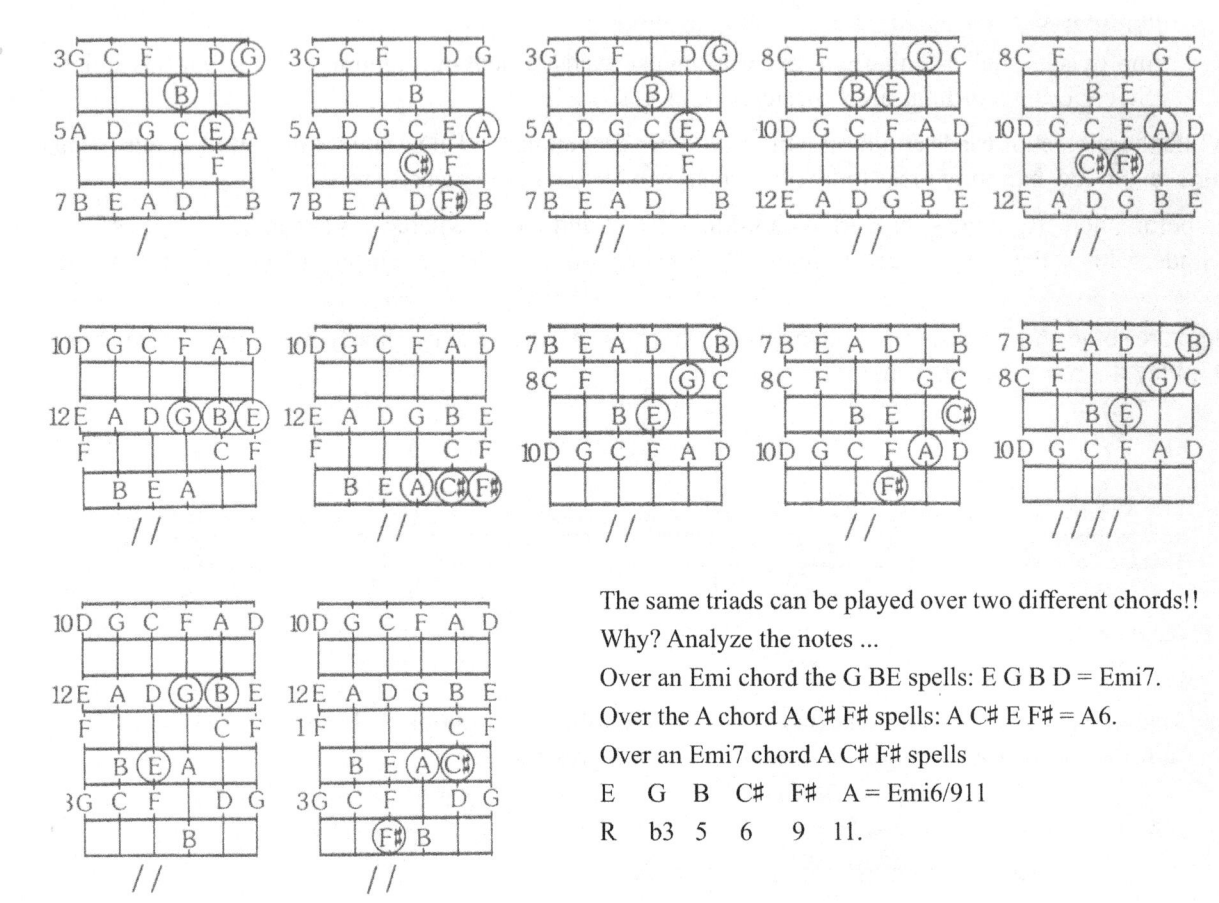

The same triads can be played over two different chords!!
Why? Analyze the notes ...
Over an Emi chord the G B E spells: E G B D = Emi7.
Over the A chord A C# F# spells: A C# E F# = A6.
Over an Emi7 chord A C# F# spells
E   G   B   C#   F#   A = Emi6/911
R   b3 5   6   9   11.

Triad Rules

In chord study, the term "triad" is generally used to refer to "three note chords" - that is three notes played at the same time. In single line (melodic) soloing "using triads" refers to thinking and hearing triads in your head and playing them *one note at a time*. We're going to focus on notes played at the same time.

1. Triads can contain any notes.
2. Triads can have the notes any distance apart from each other.
3. Triads can be used like any other chord form - with chord scales, walking bass, chord streams, chord melody, etc.
4. Triads can be ambiguous, having multiple names and suggesting multiple chords in context with other chords.

Let's look at triads on adjacent strings (the easiest to play and to hear).

Adjacent String Triad Fingerings on the 321 Stringset

Shown below are the five types of basic triads and their inversions on the 321 stringset. Play across the row to hear the inversions. Play down the columns to hear the different chords in each location. The first fingering occurs in the open position, so I have repeated it at the 12th fret so you can see the shape.

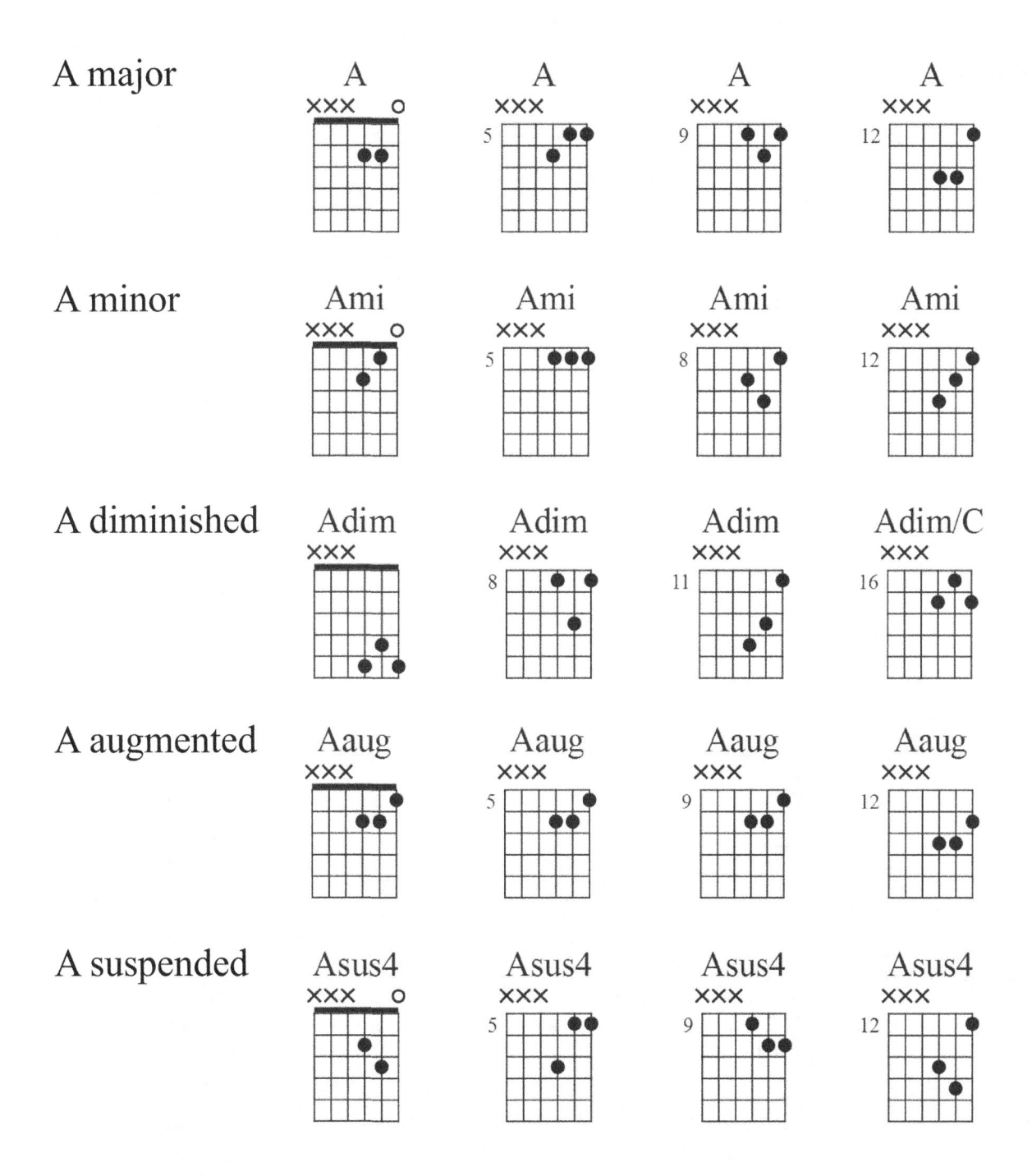

A major

A minor

A diminished

A augmented

A suspended

Triads are often played with double stops so that related triads are easier and faster to play. Review the fingerings here and note places where you can use one or more double stops.

Chord Systems 40th Anniversary Edition - by Leon White • 113

Triads on the 432 Stringset

Here are the five types of basic triads and their inversions on the 432 stringset. Play across the row to hear the inversions. Play down the columns to hear the different chords in each location.

A major

A minor

A diminished

A augmented

A suspended

Triads on the 543 Stringset

Here are the five types of basic triads and their inversions on the 543 stringset. Play across the row to hear the inversions. Play down the columns to hear the different chords in each location.

A major	A	A (5)	A (9)	A (12)
A minor	Ami	Ami (5)	Ami (9)	Ami (12)
A diminished	Adim	Adim (5)	Adim (8)	Adim (13)
A augmented	Aaug	Aaug (6)	Aaug (10)	Aaug (14)
A suspended	Asus4	Asus4 (5)	Asus4 (9)	Asus4 (14)

Chord Systems 40th Anniversary Edition - by Leon White

Triads on the 654 Stringset

Here are the five types of basic triads and their inversions on the 654 stringset. Play across the row to hear the inversions. Play down the columns to hear the different chords in each location.

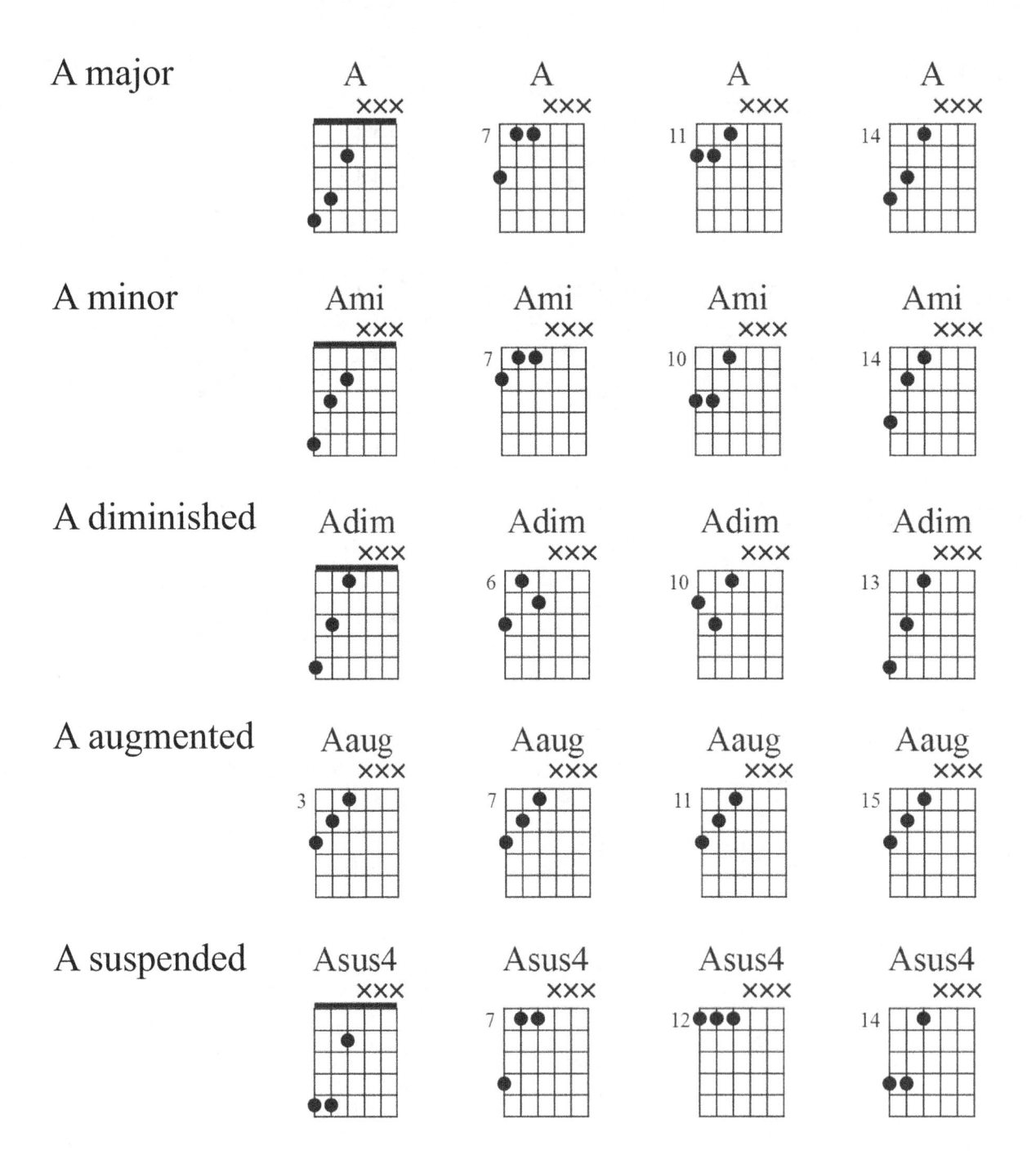

A major	A	A	A	A
A minor	Ami	Ami	Ami	Ami
A diminished	Adim	Adim	Adim	Adim
A augmented	Aaug	Aaug	Aaug	Aaug
A suspended	Asus4	Asus4	Asus4	Asus4

Ted Greene routinely had students learn all the triads on the guitar, and asked that they be played in all keys. Do the best you can. Many of the triads are parts of chords you've seen so that might help you remember them.

Chord Systems 40th Anniversary Edition - by Leon White

Triad Licks

The examples below show licks for an A chord that include the chord up a fourth from A(D). First we have examples from A to Asus4. The sus sound can suggest the D chord sound as shown.

I've also added a sus2 chord in there for variety. Each fingering can be played for two beats. This single progression is shown on all stringsets. Each row is one example.

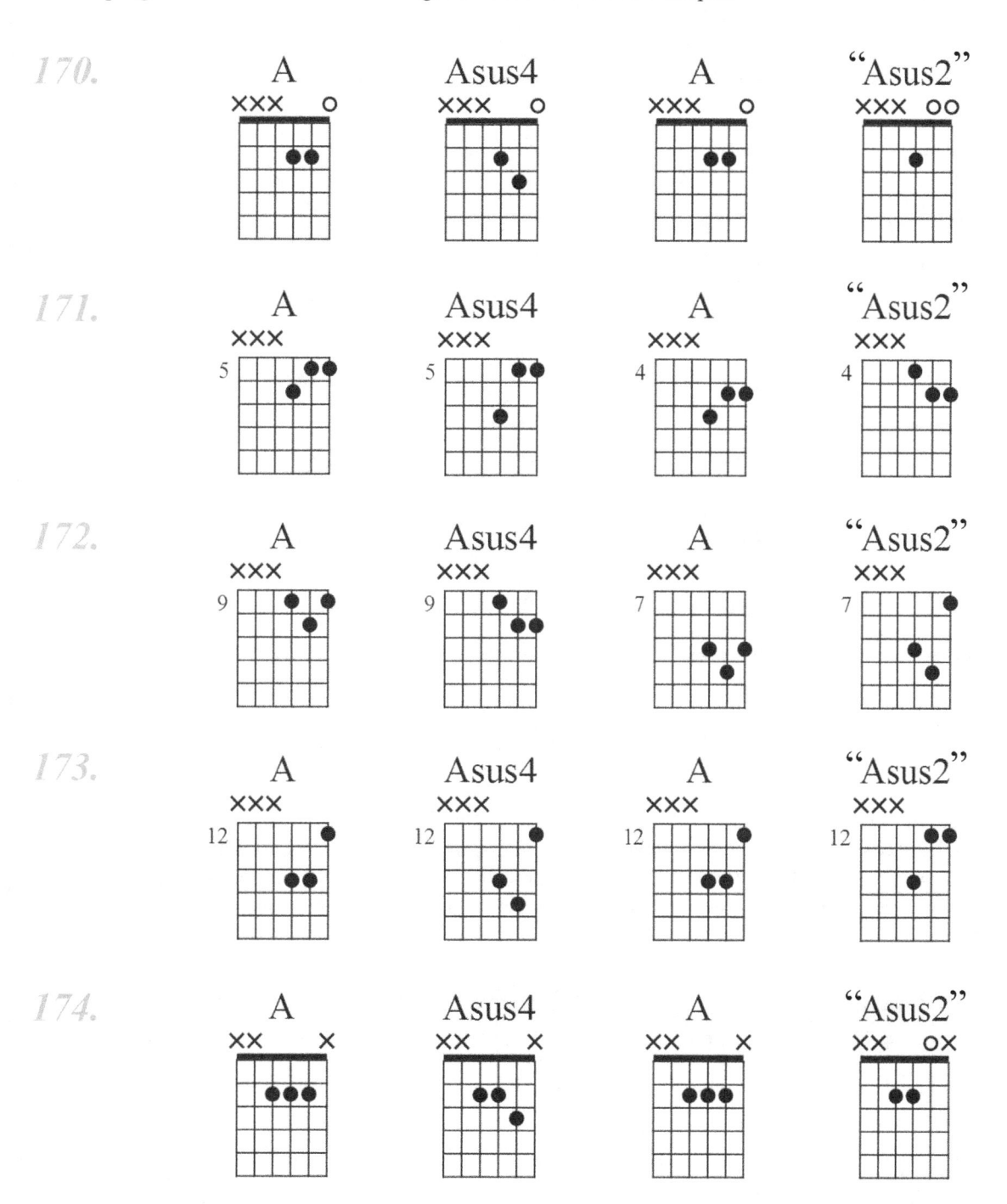

170. — A   Asus4   A   "Asus2"

171. — A   Asus4   A   "Asus2"

172. — A   Asus4   A   "Asus2"

173. — A   Asus4   A   "Asus2"

174. — A   Asus4   A   "Asus2"

Chord Systems 40th Anniversary Edition - by Leon White • 117

The examples below are a continuation of the prior progression showing the major to sus4 sounds. As before play each chord for two beats. Each row is one example.

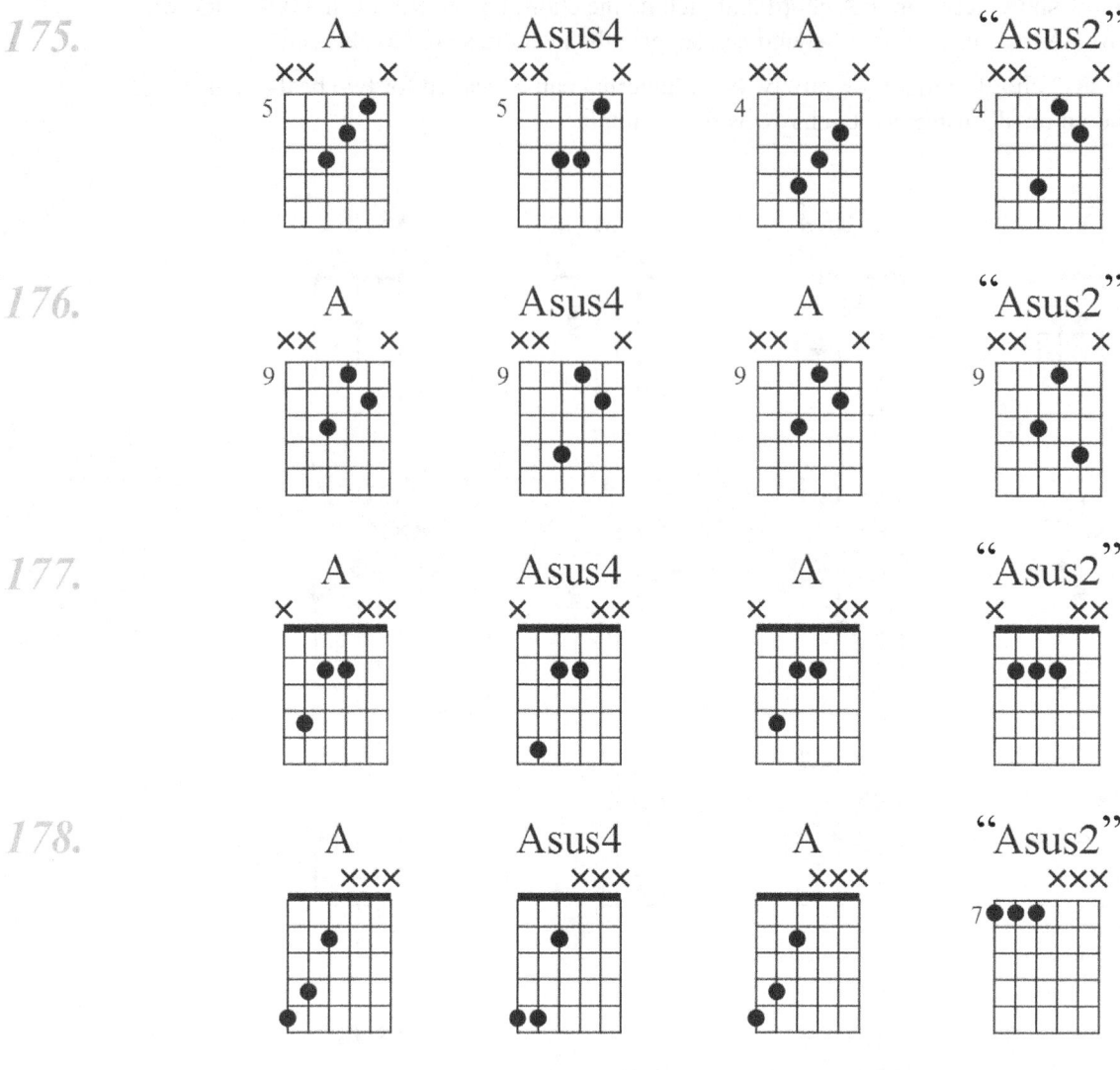

175. A — Asus4 — A — "Asus2"

176. A — Asus4 — A — "Asus2"

177. A — Asus4 — A — "Asus2"

178. A — Asus4 — A — "Asus2"

The next example enlarges the sus sound by providing the D chord (the IV) in the progressions instead of the Asus4 sound. You've probably heard and played these sounds, often inside barre chord fingerings. For the second row, use a barre for D, and double stops elsewhere so you can hold the notes as long as possible. There are hammer-on fingerings too. Each chord gets 2 or 4 beats. Each row is one example.

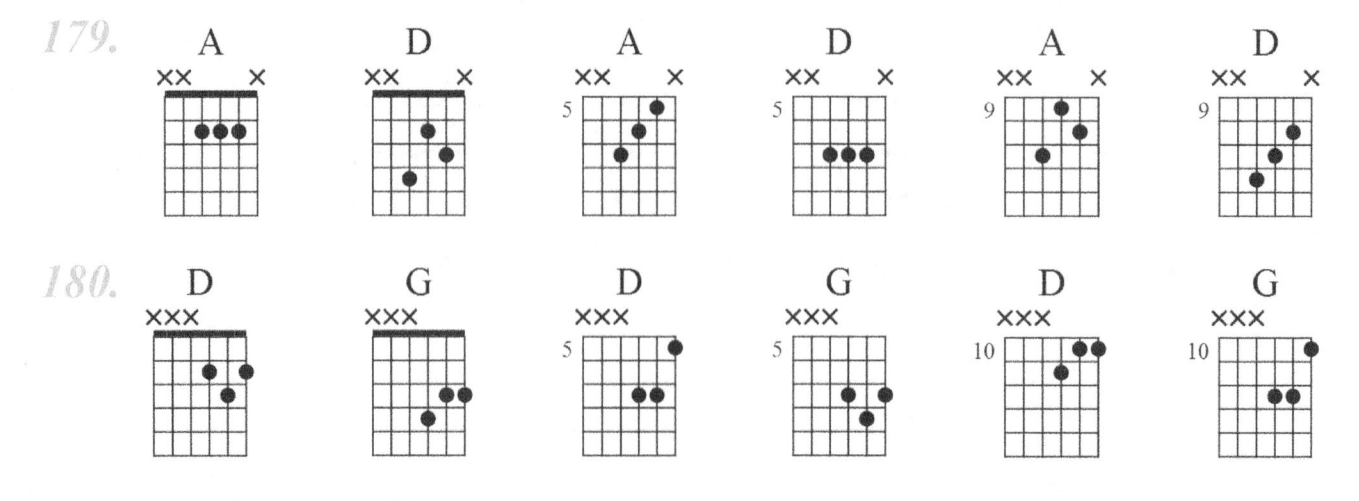

179. A — D — A — D — A — D

180. D — G — D — G — D — G

Chord Systems 40th Anniversary Edition - by Leon White

Triads in the Major Scale

Shown below are the triads made from each note in a major scale. The top row is from C, the second row from G, and the last two rows from the root A. Play across each row to play up the scale on one stringset.

The first row has the *third* of the chord on the high E string. The second row has the *root* on the high E string.

The fourth line shows the same triads from the A major scale as the third line, but *crossing stringsets*.

Play the examples across each row. The examples show two different inversions being used as chord-scales. Play each line ascending and descending to remember the sound.

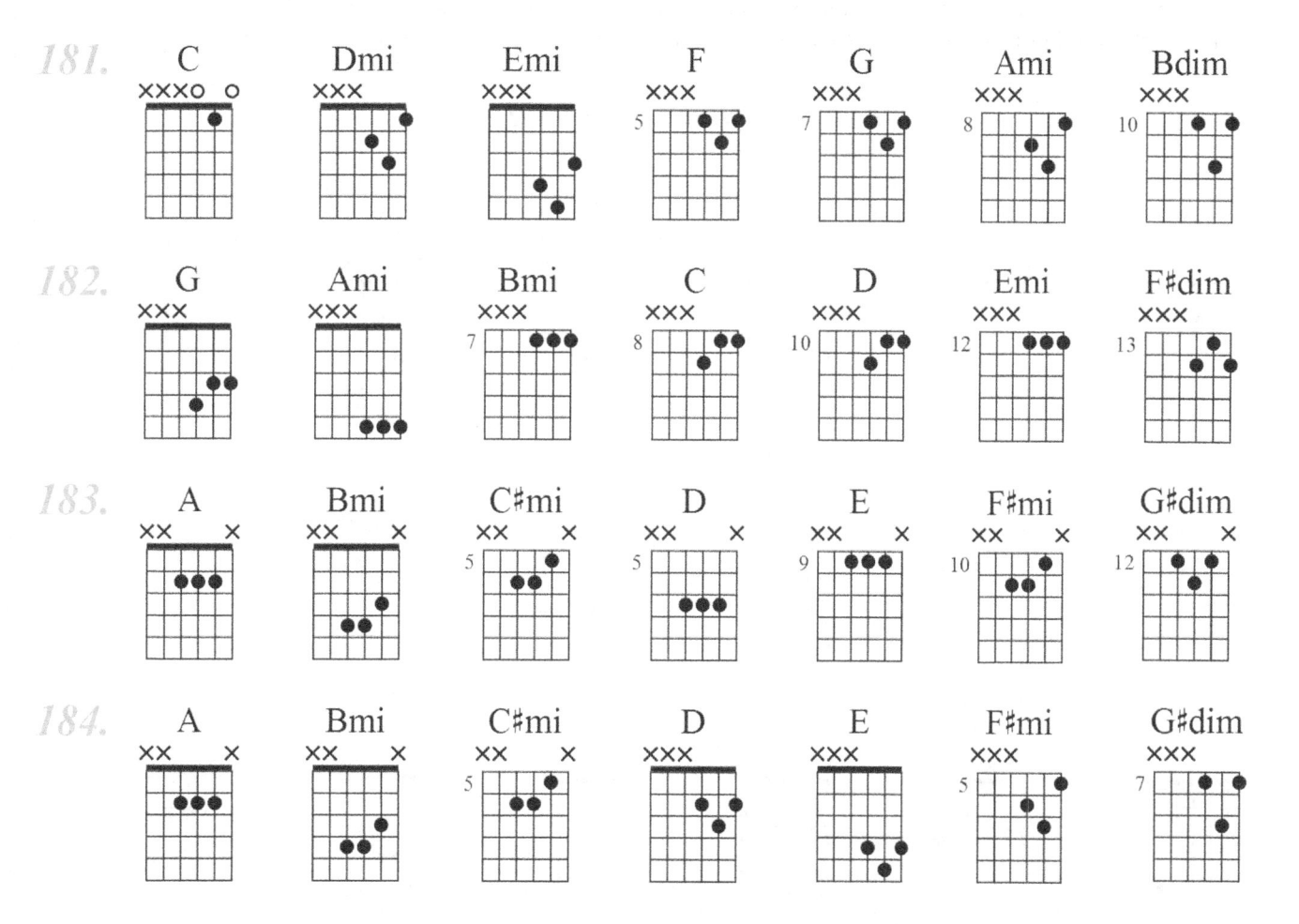

181. C Dmi Emi F G Ami Bdim

182. G Ami Bmi C D Emi F#dim

183. A Bmi C#mi D E F#mi G#dim

184. A Bmi C#mi D E F#mi G#dim

You may hear some triads suggesting other chords then their own. The Bdim chord at the end of the first row may feel like a G7 chord. Bdim is B D F. G7 is G *B D F*. That's OK, but try to remember which root you are playing from in the chord scale. It is not uncommon to play part of the scale and then mistakenly grab a triad that feels right, but is actually in another key. That is sometimes called "song writing."

*Once you're comfortable on several stringsets, you can start playing triads *across* the fingerboard. You may try to play it by thinking about the triad spelling, but I suggest you write out some examples in chord boxes. You'll definitely want to do that if you're just playing by ear. It is much faster! (If I get time, I may try to write them all out in a separate guide.)

The chords below can be treated as short licks, or an entire progression in the key of A. When I wrote this I added a droning bass note on the open A string. I played the bass notes as quarter notes and then used syncopation of various kinds to play the chords shown. This uses the classic "up a fourth" kinds of licks along with ambiguous triad sounds. (In certain fingerings Asus4 = Esus4 = Dsus2.)

I play this fingerstyle so I can have the low A note in one rhythm separate from the chords, but it can be played with or without the A bass note as well as with a flat pick.

The key to fingering success for playing these sounds at a fast tempo is to anchor your left hand index finger on the A chord on the second fret. You can then hammer-on and pull-off most of the other chords.

Each row can also be used as its own little chord lick. I think I counted a dozen variations on this one page (the G chord on the bottom row is one variation). Is the G really acting as a G or is it functioning as something else? Some players love to analyze the harmony involved, but the most important thing is to find ways to remember and use the various sounds you discover. One way to explore is to transpose these kinds of licks to other keys, or . . . to other stringsets. For now, just get the sounds down and experiment.

Excerpt from Etude #101

185.

A	$D^6/_9$	A	A9	D	A
//	//	////	//	//	////

A7	D	A9	D	A
//	//	/	/	//

A7	A7sus4	D	C	D6	A
//	/	/	/	/	//

G6	A	G	Dsus4	Asus4	A
////	////	//	/	/	////

There is an old recording by a band called Canned Heat. The title is "On the Road Again," and the feel of that song started me off when I was writing the etude from which this example is taken.

Section 5 - Chord Substitution

The phrase "Chord Substitution" is commonly associated with jazz music. For guitar we often think of substitution as replacing some standard chords with some newer hipper sounding chords. That's only one small part of what guitar players do when playing chords.

In all forms of popular music, guitarists are always making choices of which voicings, fingerings, and even octaves to use. You've already seen rock and country chord licks where you can add a chord up a 4th from the original chord. (Playing A to D to A instead of just A). While not traditionally thought of as "chord substitution," it is exactly that. When we made little fills out of A7 to A7#5 for an A7 chord, that was the same process again.

My point is that our discussion *in this section* is really an extension of what we've already been doing.

We will discuss the kinds of substitutions found in jazz and solo guitar arrangements, but it's just part of what guitarists always do - personalize, customize, compose, and improvise with chords. That's one of the great joys of playing a chordal instrument.

Diatonic vs. Chromatic

"Enrichment" can add chord tones found in the tonal center of the chord, or from outside the tonal center. "Chromatic" refers to notes added from outside the tonal center. If you're trying for a small change, stay diatonic. If you're looking for something more noticeable, try chromatic notes.

Tone center (or tonal center) means roughly, "where it sounds like you're based" harmonically.

Overview of This Approach

We're going to break down the discussion of chord substitution into three levels:

1. Enrichment
2. Common Tone Substitution
3. Cycles

The levels above become progressively more reliant on harmony knowledge. You can still learn each section, but some of the explanation may be lost on you. (Learn to spell the major scales, and learn how to spell chords using the formulas - like 1, 3, 5 -which refer to the scale tones. That will help.)

In each of the three levels there are two sub-categories - Diatonic and Chromatic.

The other important thing to remember is that this subject can be confusing when discussed out loud. One person may say "add a Cma7 chord," while another person will say "replace the C chord with Cma7," or "substitute Cma7 for C." There are levels of changes:

186.

Original Chords	C	C	C	C
	////	////	////	////
Embellishment	C	Cma7	C6	Cma7
Replacement	Cma9	Cma7	Cma9	Cma7

There are those players who would say both examples are replacement (or substitution) or embellishment. However you choose to think about it, make sure you're consistent, and know what the other person means.

Enrichment Examples

This level is typically done by "fattening up" a chord we've been given. Let's assume we've been given a C major chord for four measures. We can add other chords from the same chord family - major. So we can put Cma7, C6, Cadd9, Cma9, Csus, and so on into the space originally given for the plain C major chord. Which of the new chords you select, the fingerings, and the order you place them in is up to you.

If we were given a C minor chord. We could add/replace it with Cmi7, Cmi9, Cmi6, Cmi13 and so on from the minor chord family.

When given a C7 chord, we can try any chord from the dominant chord family (C11, C9, C13, C13, etc.). With so much modern music in our ears we could also introduce chromatic dominant chords. I've thrown a few in early here to emphasize certain ideas.

In Chord Enrichment . . . .
1. The root of the new chord will be the same as the root of the old chord.
2. The family of the new chord will be the same as that of the old chord.
3. You will be adding or swapping one or more notes to the old chord to create the new chord.

187. Original Chord Progression   C   C
     //// ////
    Enrichment   C   Cma7
     //// ////
    Enrichment   C6   Cma7
     //// ////

188. Original Chord Progression   A7   A7
     //// ////
    Enrichment   A7#9   A7
     //// ////
    Enrichment   A7#9#5 A9#5
     //// ////

189. Original Chord Progression   Dmi7 Dmi7
     //// ////
    Enrichment   Dmi9 Dmi7
     //// ////

Play the examples above and listen to them carefully. You should be able to hear that the fundamental flavor of the chord remains the same. When you feel comfortable with those, play the next example.

Note: For this section of the book we're going to place suspended chords in the major family, so you *may* be able to replace a C major chord with a Csus.

190. Original Chord Progression   C   C

                                        / / / / / / / /

    Enrichment   C   Csus

                                          / / / / / / / /

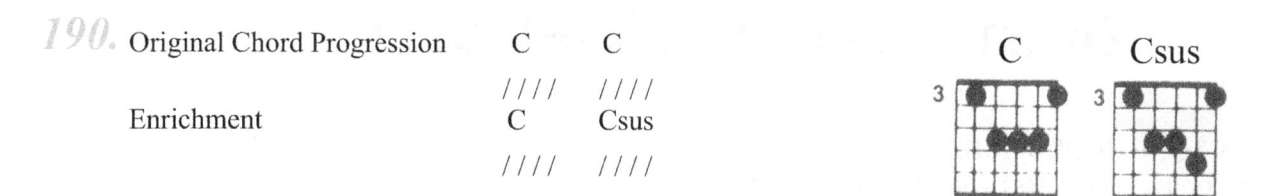

The Csus chord is not an expansion on a C major chord! C major is spelled C E G. Csus is spelled C F G. We have changed the notes in the chord, not added to them. However, this does not cause a complication. In using the concept of enrichment you'll find that, for the most part, a chord can become any other chord in its family, whether or not the new chord is a strict enlargement of the original. To see this concept graphically, look at the chords as they are listed in the family charts, and play the following to "hear" it.

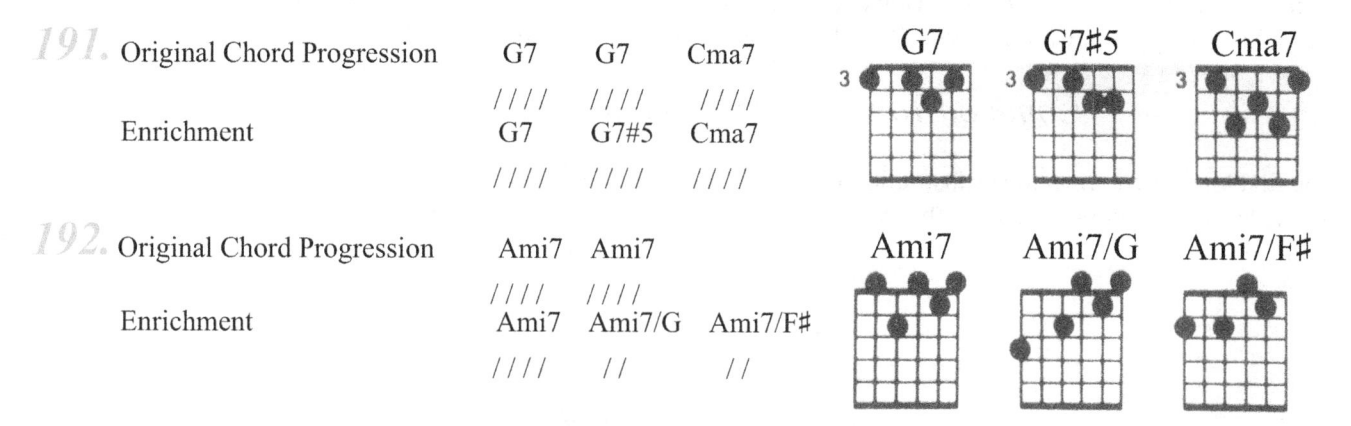

191. Original Chord Progression   G7   G7   Cma7

                                        / / / / / / / / / / / /

    Enrichment   G7   G7#5 Cma7

                                        / / / / / / / / / / / /

192. Original Chord Progression   Ami7 Ami7

                                        / / / / / / / /

    Enrichment   Ami7 Ami7/G Ami7/F#

                                        / / / / / /   / /

Chromatic Enrichment

In the previous examples we introduced a G7#5 and an Ami7/F#. Technically, if G7 is dominant chord in the key of C, the #5, D#, doesn't occur within the C major scale. And the F# in the bass of Ami7 may or may not have been "chromatic" depending on the surrounding chords.

Both chords are candidates to be used in enrichment because, as their sound suggests, they do sound similar to the original chord. They both have three notes in common with the original, and have the same root as the original.

To make the distinction clearer I refer to those kinds of sounds as "chromatic" enrichment. You may choose to do so, or to lump all chords with the same root and family as enrichment. Let your ear guide you as to which sounds are far enough away from the original to be called "chromatic."

Common Tone Chord Substitution

COMMON TONE CHORD SUBSTITUTION is a phrase that generally refers to using a new chord that has several of the same notes as the original. It's that simple.

Some musicians ignore the concept of enrichment and just call everything "common tone substitution" because, after all, there are usually quite a few notes common to the new and original chord in either case.

I don't do that. I prefer to make the distinction because it makes it easier to teach, and the level of harmony knowledge needed is quite different.

In this explanation I will spell out the chords, names, and fingerings so that anyone can see the ideas in action and hear the various sounds. However, if you're not strong on scale and chord spelling, you may find it hard to apply in various keys. The reference sections can be used to improve that area.

Common Tone Chords from the Same Scale

The first kind of common tone substitution is one you've probably heard already. The original chord and the replacement chord(s) are from the same scale. The example below shows that three out of four notes are identical.

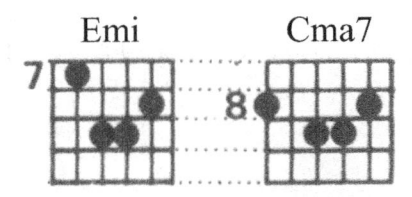

That's the whole explanation. Emi7 is the iii chord of C major. The two chords are from the same major scale and a third apart (C up to E is the interval of a major third).

Key of C major

C major Scale	C	D	E	F	G	A	B	C
Diatonic Chords	Cma7	Dmi7	Emi7	Fma7	G7	Ami7	Bmi7b5	

The basic rule is that up or down 3 notes from the original chord root is a chord similar to the original. Let's say our original chord was Cma7.

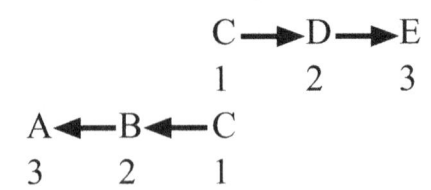

```
         C→D→E
         1  2  3
   A←B←C
   3  2  1
```

To find a chord that can replace the C major, we can count up or down three notes of the C major scale and find chords with common tones.

Three notes above C is E. The chord found in the C major scale on the root E is Emi7.

Three notes down from the note C is the note A. The chord found in the C major scale on the note A is Ami7.

On the following page is a table showing the chords that are related by the interval of a third in the scale.

This can be referred to as *diatonic* common tone chord substitution.

Chord Comparisons in the Major Scale

Original	Replacement
Cma7	Emi7 or Ami7
Dmi7	Fma7, Bmi7♭5 occasionally
Emi7	G7, Cma7 occasionally
Fma7	Dmi7, Ami7
G7	Bmi7♭5, Emi7 occasionally
Ami7	Cma7, Fma7 occasionally
Bmi7♭5	G7, Dmi6

A B C D E F G A B C D

```
A ← C → E
    D
B ← D → F
    E
C ← E → G
    F
D ← F → A
    G
E ← G → B
    A
F ← A → C
    B
G ← B → D
```

Chord Spellings   Similar Chords

Original Chord	**Dmi7**		D	F	A	C		**Dmi6**	D	F	A	B
Up a Third	Fma7			F	A	C	E	**F6**	F	A	C	D
Down a Third	Bmi7♭5	B	D	F	A			**Bdim**	B	D	F	
Original Chord	**Emi7**		E	G	B	D		**G6**	G	B	D	E
Up a Third	G7			G	B	D	F	**G7/6**	G	B	D	F	E
Down a Third	Cma7	C	E	G	B			**Cma9**	C	E	G	B	D
Original Chord	**Fma7**		F	A	C	E		**F6**	F	A	C	D
Up a Third	Ami7			A	C	E	G	**Ami7#5**	A	C	F	G
Down a Third	Dmi7	D	F	A	C			**Dmi9**	D	F	A	C	E
Original Chord	**G7**		G	B	D	F		**G9**	G	B	D	F	A
Up a Third	Bmi7♭5		B	D	F	A		**Bdim**	B	D	F	
Down a Third	Emi7	E	G	B	D			**G6**	G	B	D	E
Original Chord	**Ami7**		A	C	E	G						
Up a Third	Cma7		C	E	G	B		**Ami9**	A	C	E	G	B
Down a Third	Fma7	F	A	C	E			**Fma9**	F	A	C	E	G
Original Chord	**Bmi7♭5**	B	D	F	A			**Bdim**	B	D	F	
Up a Third	Dmi7		D	F	A	C		**Dmi6**	D	F	A	B
Down a Third	G7	G	B	D	F			**G9**	G	B	D	F	A

Common Tone Fingering Examples - Diatonic

Look at the pairs of fingerings below to see the physical similarities between each set of chords.

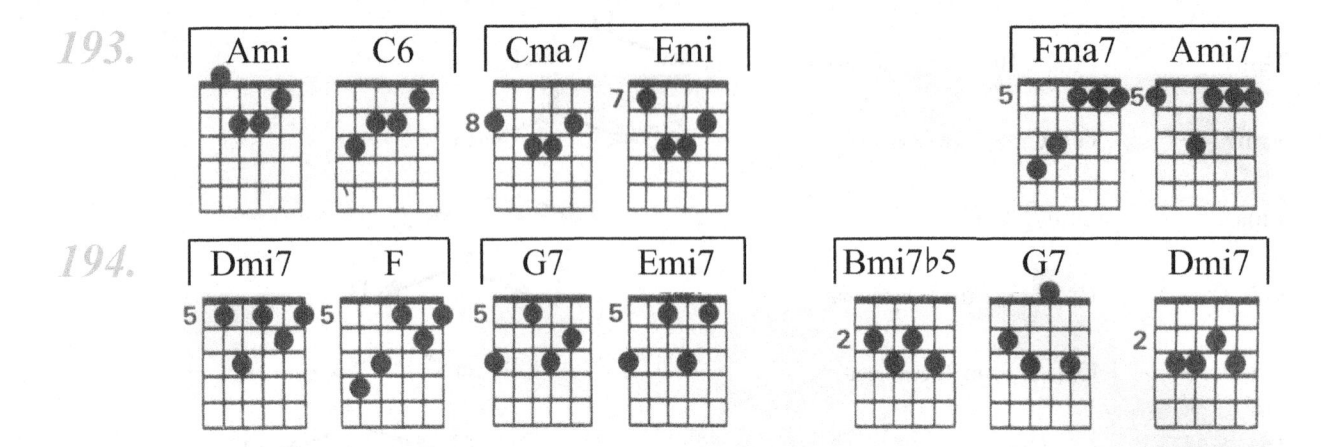

193. [Ami C6]   [Cma7 Emi]   [Fma7 Ami7]

194. [Dmi7 F]   [G7 Emi7]   [Bmi7♭5 G7 Dmi7]

You can see that in DIATONIC common tone chord substitution the replacement chord has a different *root* from the original chord and often a different "color." Since enrichment typically keeps the same root, common tone chord substitution takes the new sound a little farther away from the original sound.

A broader view of these chords separated by a third yields some other interesting common tones:

```
C E G B          Cma7
  E G B D        Emi7/Cma9 - C E G B D
    G B D F      G7/Cma11 - C E G B D F (or G7/C)
```

The example above looks a bit like "the third of the third" kind of jumping. But there is a limit to how useful extending this thinking can go. One dividing line is whether the common tone chord moves the root too far away from the original chord. A fifth, like C to G, is already dealt with in back cycling, so hold your theorizing until we're through this entire section on substitution.

Diatonic Extensions in the Major Scale

The table below is a recap of the common diatonic chords found in the major scale on each degree of the scale. You'll see not all chords occur everywhere in the scale. Emi and Ami have 7#5 chords, but Dmi does not.

195.

I	ii	iii	IV	V	vi	vii
Cma7	Dmi7	Emi7	Fma7	G7	Ami7	Bmi7♭5
C6	Dmi6		F6	G6		Bdim
Cma9	Dmi9		Fma9	G9	Ami9	
C6/9			F6/9	G6/9		
Cma11	Dmi11	Emi11		G11	Ami11	
Cma13	Dmi13	Emi7#5	Fma13	G13	Ami7#5	Bmi7#5

Common Tone Chord Substitution in Minor Scales

The previous examples used the major scale. We can also make the same kind of substitution in other scales. Let's examine the C harmonic minor scale, which is spelled C D Eb F G Ab B C

Original Chord	**Cmi/ma7**		C	Eb	G	B						
Up a Third	Ebma7			Eb	G	B	D	Cmi/ma9	C	Eb	G	B	D
Down a Third	Abma7	Ab	C	Eb	G							
Original Chord	**Dmi7b5**		D	F	Ab	C		Ddim	D	F	Ab	
Up a Third	Fmi7			F	Ab	C	Eb					
Down a Third	Bdim7	B	D	F	Ab			Bdim	B	D	F	
Original Chord	**Ebma7#5**		Eb	G	B	D		Ebaug	Eb	G	B	
Up a Third	G7			G	B	D	F	G7b9	G	B	D	F	Ab
Down a Third	Cmi/ma7	C	Eb	G	B							
Original Chord	**Fmi7**		F	Ab	C	Eb		Fmi9	F	Ab	C	Eb	G
Up a Third	Abma7			Ab	C	Eb	G					
Down a Third	Dmi7b5	D	F	Ab	C			Fmi6	F	Ab	C	D
Original Chord	**G7**		G	B	D	F		G7b9	G	B	D	F	Ab
Up a Third	Bdim7			B	D	F	Ab	G11b9	G	B	D	F	Ab	C
Down a Third	Ebma7#5	Eb	G	B	D			G13b9	G	B	D	F	Ab	E
Original Chord	**Abma7**		Ab	C	Eb	G		Ab6	Ab	C	Eb	F
Up a Third	Cmi/ma7			C	Eb	G	B					
Down a Third	Fmi7	F	A	C	E			Fmi9	F	Ab	C	Eb	G
Original Chord	**Bdim7**		B	D	F	Ab		Ddim7	D	F	Ab	B
Up a Third	Dmi7b5			D	F	Ab	C	G7b9	G	B	D	F	Ab
Down a Third	G7	G	B	D	F							

Common tone chord substitution in minor keys is used in the same way as major keys. One progression frequently appearing in South American arrangements is the ii - V - i;   Dmi7b5 to G13b9 to Cmi.

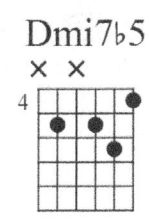

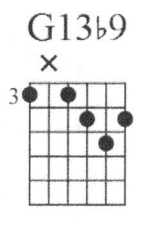

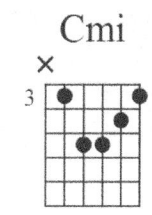

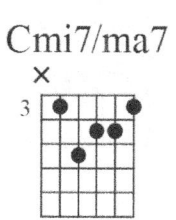

196.

Dmi7b5   G13b9   Cmi   Cmi7/ma7

Diminished 7 and 7♭9 Chord Review

If we compare the findings of our chart to what we have already learned from the major scale chart, we'll see that one of the new correspondences are Bdim7 = G7♭9 and Bdim7 = Ddim7.

The diminished seventh chord and 7♭9 chord were discussed earlier, but as a review, let's look at the fingerings.

Compare each pair of chords. The first chord will be a basic dominant seventh chord.

197. G7   G7♭9   B7   Bdim7   D7   Ddim7

G7♭9 seems to have the same fingering as Bdim7 and Ddim7.

◊ indicates a note that did NOT change to make a diminished chord. Look carefully, name the notes, and see how the fingerings ended up being the same.

Play the progressions below and listen to how the new chords sound. Is it similar enough to you to be useful? Typically the answer is "yes." However, you're in charge so it is your opinion that matters.

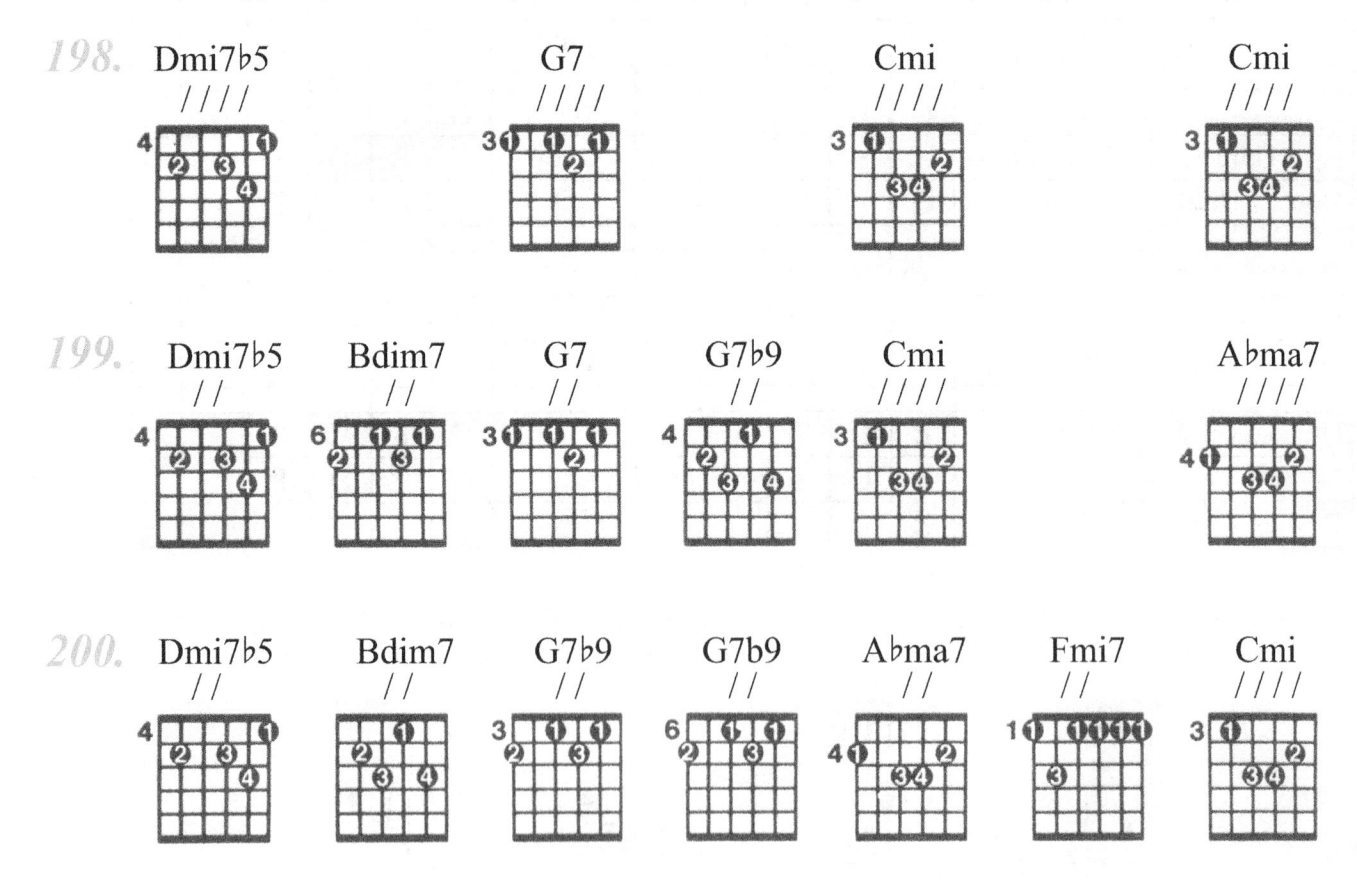

198. Dmi7♭5 | G7 | Cmi | Cmi

199. Dmi7♭5 Bdim7 | G7 G7♭9 | Cmi | A♭ma7

200. Dmi7♭5 Bdim7 | G7♭9 G7♭9 | A♭ma7 | Fmi7 | Cmi

The Melodic Minor Scale Common Tone Chords

The C melodic minor scale is spelled   C D E♭ F G A B C.

It can be thought of as a C major scale with a flatted third (E♭).

Several of the chords and their substitutes are the same as those found in the harmonic minor scale. This is because there is only one note difference between the harmonic and melodic minor scales. (There's an A♭, or ♭6 in the harmonic minor scale - root C.) Review the chart and make sure you understand the chord *names*.

Original Chord	**Cmi/ma7**		**C**	**E♭**	**G**	**B**		E♭aug	E♭	G	B	
Up a Third	E♭ma7#5			E♭	G	B	D	Cmi/ma9	C	E♭	G	B	D
Down a Third	Ami7♭5	A	C	E♭	G			Adim	A	C	E♭	
Original Chord	**Dmi7**		**D**	**F**	**A**	**C**		Dmi6	D	F	A	B
Up a Third	F7			F	A	C	E♭					
Down a Third	Bmi7♭5	B	D	F	A			Bdim	B	D	F	
Original Chord	**E♭ma7#5**		**E♭**	**G**	**B**	**D**		E♭aug	E♭	G	B	
Up a Third	G7			G	B	D	F	G7♭9	G	B	D	F	A♭
Down a Third	Cmi/ma7	C	E♭	G	B							
Original Chord	**F7**		**F**	**A**	**C**	**E♭**						
Up a Third	Ami7♭5			A	C	E♭	G	F9	F	A	C	E♭	G
Down a Third	Dmi7	D	F	A	C							
Original Chord	**G7**		**G**	**B**	**D**	**F**						
Up a Third	Bdim7			B	D	F	A♭	G7♭9	G	B	D	F	A♭
Down a Third	E♭ma7#5	E♭	G	B	D							
Original Chord	**Ami7♭5**		**A**	**C**	**E♭**	**G**						
Up a Third	Cmi/ma7			C	E♭	G	B					
Down a Third	F7	F	A	C	E♭			F9	F	A	C	E♭	G
Original Chord	**Bmi7♭5**		**B**	**D**	**F**	**A**		Dmi6	D	F	A	B
Up a Third	Dmi7			D	F	A	C					
Down a Third	G7	G	B	D	F			G9	G	B	D	F	A

These charts are reference pages, and are a bit advanced for harmony study. However, you'll recognize some of these harmonies in an upcoming jazz blues example. If harmony isn't easy for you, then just remember that there are substitutions based upon scales other then the major scale.

Chromatic Common Tone Chord Substitution

Throughout the book so far you've seen dozens of examples of short chord progressions with one voice moving through the progression - usually descending, but sometimes ascending. Often one note in the first chord moves down one fret to make the second chord:

201.

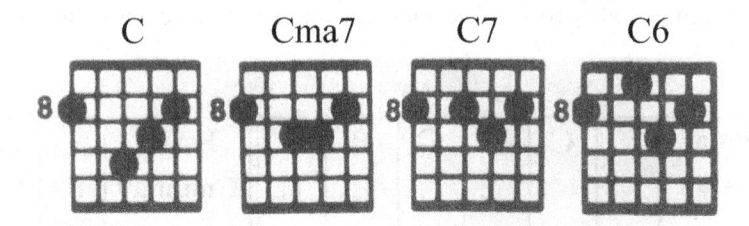

C   Cma7   C7   C6

If this sounds familiar, it may be because it can be found in the song "Something" by the Beatles.

The half step movement includes notes not found in the scale, and so this kind of substitution is referred to as "chromatic." However, the chords have three notes in common. Thus we get a group of chord substitutions referred to as "Chromatic Common Tone."

202.

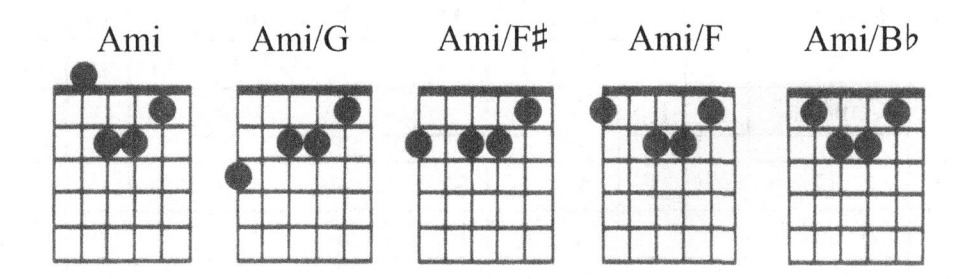

Ami   Ami/G   Ami/F#   Ami/F   Ami/B♭

Often many of us play a progression like this and think of it as a "fingerpicking pattern" or a "moving bass line." And those names are OK. I just want to point out that "chromatic" doesn't have to mean *jazz*. When given an Ami chord, some or all of the example above might be incorporated. Either the F or the F# note is chromatic, depending on what the original tonal center was.

And while we often think of descending bass lines, this could be an *ascending* bass line movement too.

Common Tone Minor Seventh Flat Five Chords

Having looked at the melodic minor scale and the diatonic seventh chords and substitutions, we begin to see some unexpected common tone chords. This first appeared in the major scale, but I just let it go by.

203.
$$G9 = Bmi7♭5 = Dmi6$$

Remember we're using four note chord fingerings. That helps us create synonym chords because we can drop one of the notes in five note chords. Look at how the fingerings are connected:

204. G7   G9   Bmi7   Bmi7♭5   Dmi7   Dmi6

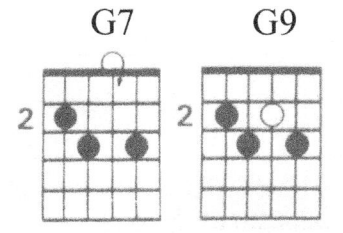

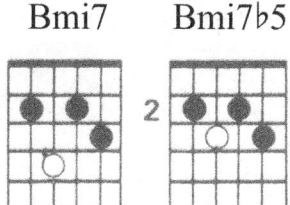

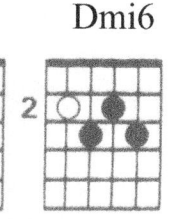

Play each of the four examples below and listen to the substitution of similar chords.

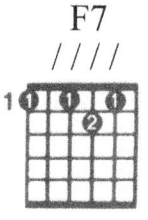

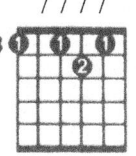

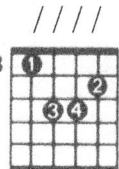

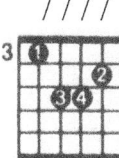

205. F7 / / / /   G7 / / / /   Cmi / / / /   Cmi / / / /

206. F7 / /   Ami7♭5 / /   G7 / /   Bmi7♭5 / /   Cmi / / / /   Ami7♭5 / / / /

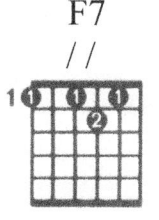

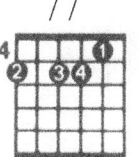

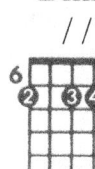

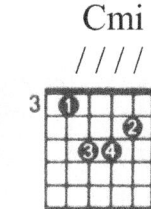

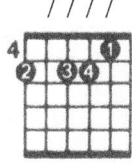

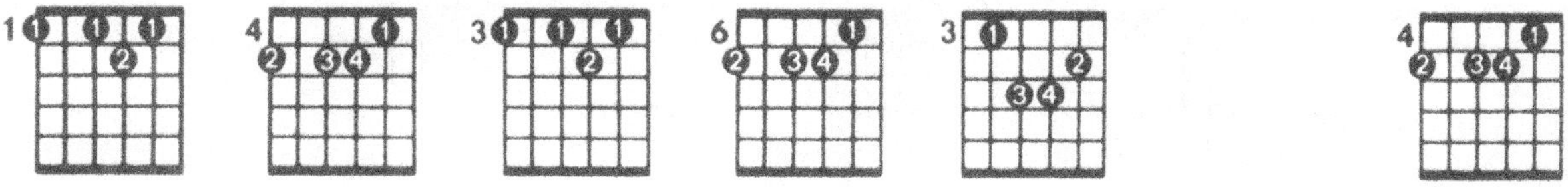

207. F7 / /   Ami7♭5 / /   G7#5 / /   B7♭5 / /   Cmi / / / /   Cmi / / / /

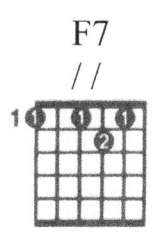

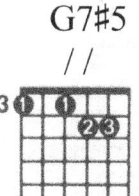

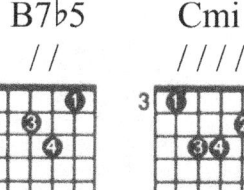

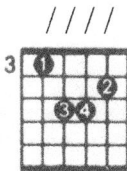

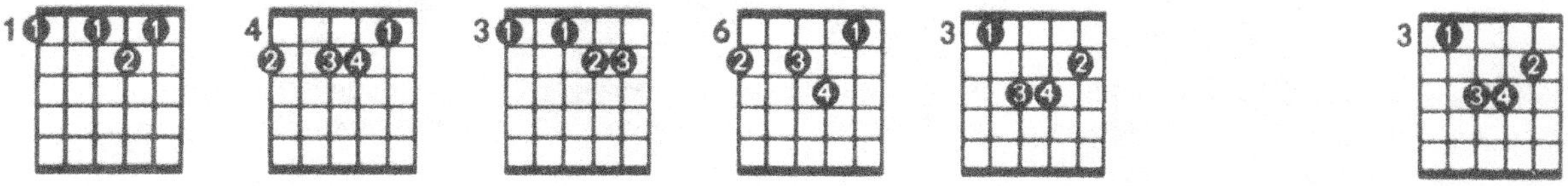

208. F7 / / / /   G7 / /   E♭ma7#5 / /   Cmi / / / /

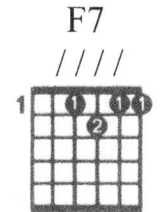

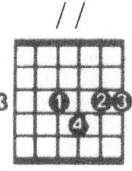

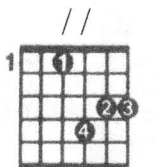

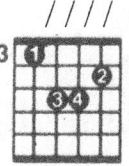

Note the fingering changes from F7 to G7. That's to get ready for the 3rd chord. That's optional.

♭5 Chromatic Common Tone Substitution

One of the most common substitutions is used with dominant family chords whose roots are a flatted fifth apart.

C7♭5 = G♭7♭5 exactly.

```
C  D  E  F  G♭  G
1  2  3  4  ♭5  5
```

Examine the notes in each chord below. Flatting the fifth of two different chords results in the same fingering (and the same chord).

209. C7   C7♭5   G♭7   G♭7♭5

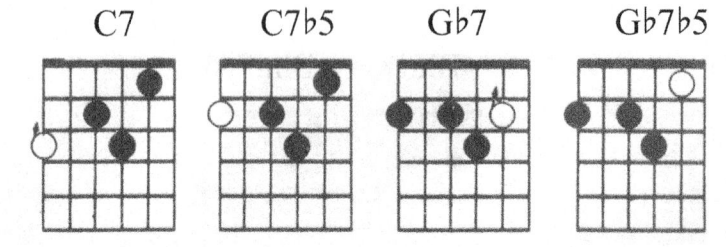

You should remember that a G♭ chord can also be called an F♯ chord. Play each chord below for two beats.

210. C(/G)   C7♭5   Fma7   Fma7

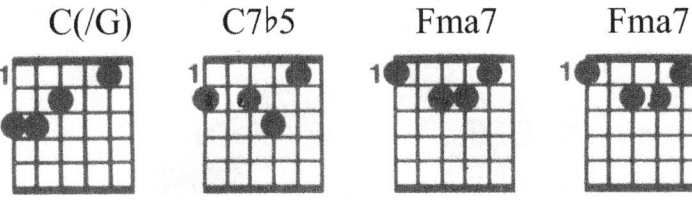

211. Gmi7   C7♭5   Fma7   Fma7

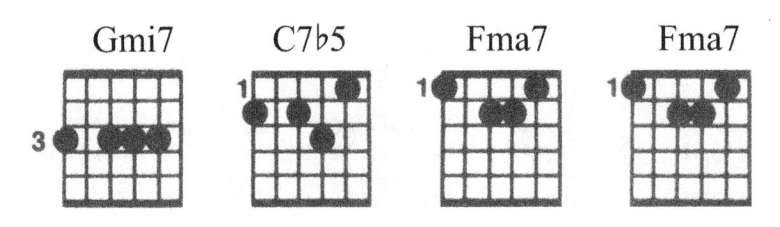

212. Gmi7   F♯7♭5   Fma7   Fma7

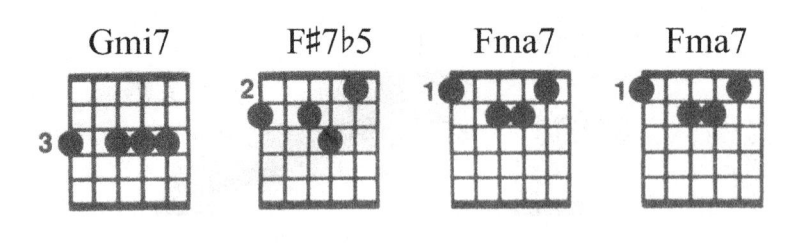

213. Gmi7   F♯7♭5   F♯7   Bma7

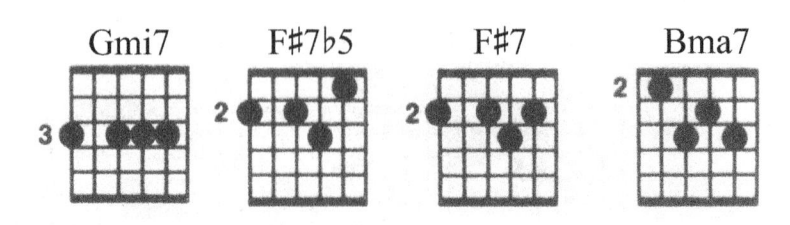

Diminished Sevenths and the 7♭9 Chord

As noted earlier, the diminished seventh chord is an equal interval chord. That is, the interval between each note and its neighbor is a minor third.

$$\text{Cdim7} \quad C \overset{\vee}{} E\flat \overset{\vee}{} G\flat \overset{\vee}{} A$$
$$\text{mi3} \quad \text{mi3} \quad \text{mi3}$$

The notes of the Cdim7 chord are also found in another chord whose root is only a half step away. To see this more clearly, let's first rename the notes in our Cdim7 chord. (We'll change the notes to their enharmonic equivalents.)

Now look at Cdim7	C	E♭ G♭ A	C
Change to	C	D♯ F♯ A	C
B7♭9 is spelled	B	D♯ F♯ A	C

If we eliminate the Root of the B7♭9 chord when we play it, we're playing the same notes found in a Cdim7 chord. And since we often play four note chords, one of the notes is dropped. Compare the following fingerings:

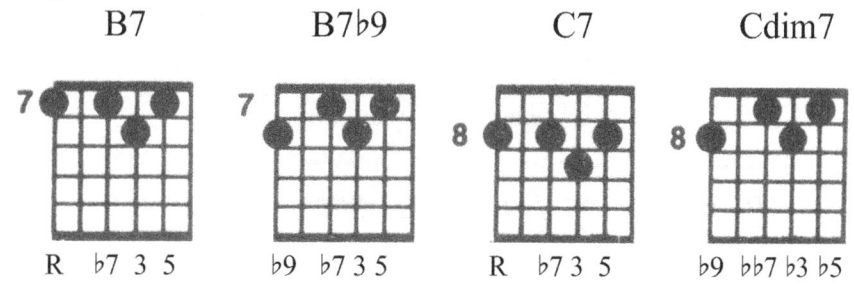

214.

B7 — R ♭7 3 5
B7♭9 — ♭9 ♭7 3 5
C7 — R ♭7 3 5
Cdim7 — ♭9 ♭♭7 ♭3 ♭5

So what?! Cdim7 = B7♭9 (no root). Watch . . .

$$\text{Cdim7} = \quad C \quad E\flat \quad G\flat \quad A$$

$$\text{B7}\flat\text{9} = \quad B \quad C \quad D\sharp \quad F\sharp \quad A$$
$$\text{D7}\flat\text{9} = \quad D \quad C \quad E\flat \quad G\flat \quad A$$
$$\text{F7}\flat\text{9} = \quad F \quad C \quad E\flat \quad G\flat \quad A$$
$$\text{A}\flat\text{7}\flat\text{9} = \quad A\flat \quad C \quad E\flat \quad G\flat \quad A$$

In effect, for common tone chord substitution, we can use the following corresponding chords:

$$\text{B7}\flat\text{9} = \text{D7}\flat\text{9} = \text{F7}\flat\text{9} = \text{A}\flat\text{7}\flat\text{9}$$

The take away from all this is that most diminished named chords are functioning as dominant chords, and there are some common tone substitutions available.

Interestingly, B D F A♭ spells a B diminished 7 chord, and all these roots are a minor third apart.

Now if we could only figure out where Amelia Earhart is . . .

215.

Cdim7

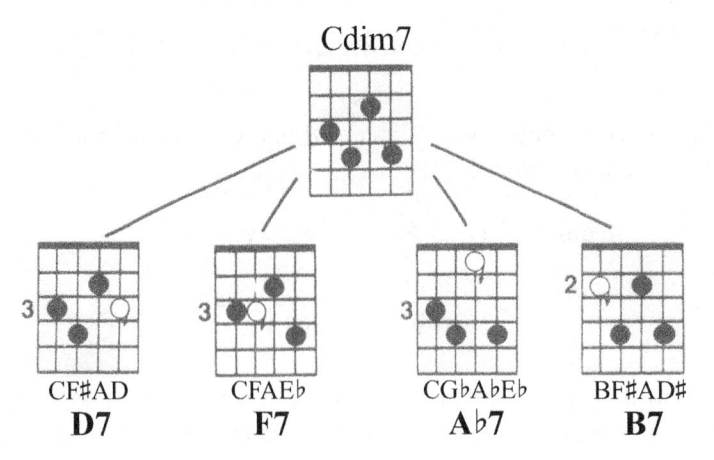

In this row of fingerings notice how the open circle note moves up a half step to make Cdim7.

CF#AD	CFAEb	CGbAbEb	BF#AD#
D7	**F7**	**Ab7**	**B7**

Play the following examples and then analyze them carefully. Each row is one example. These are tricky!

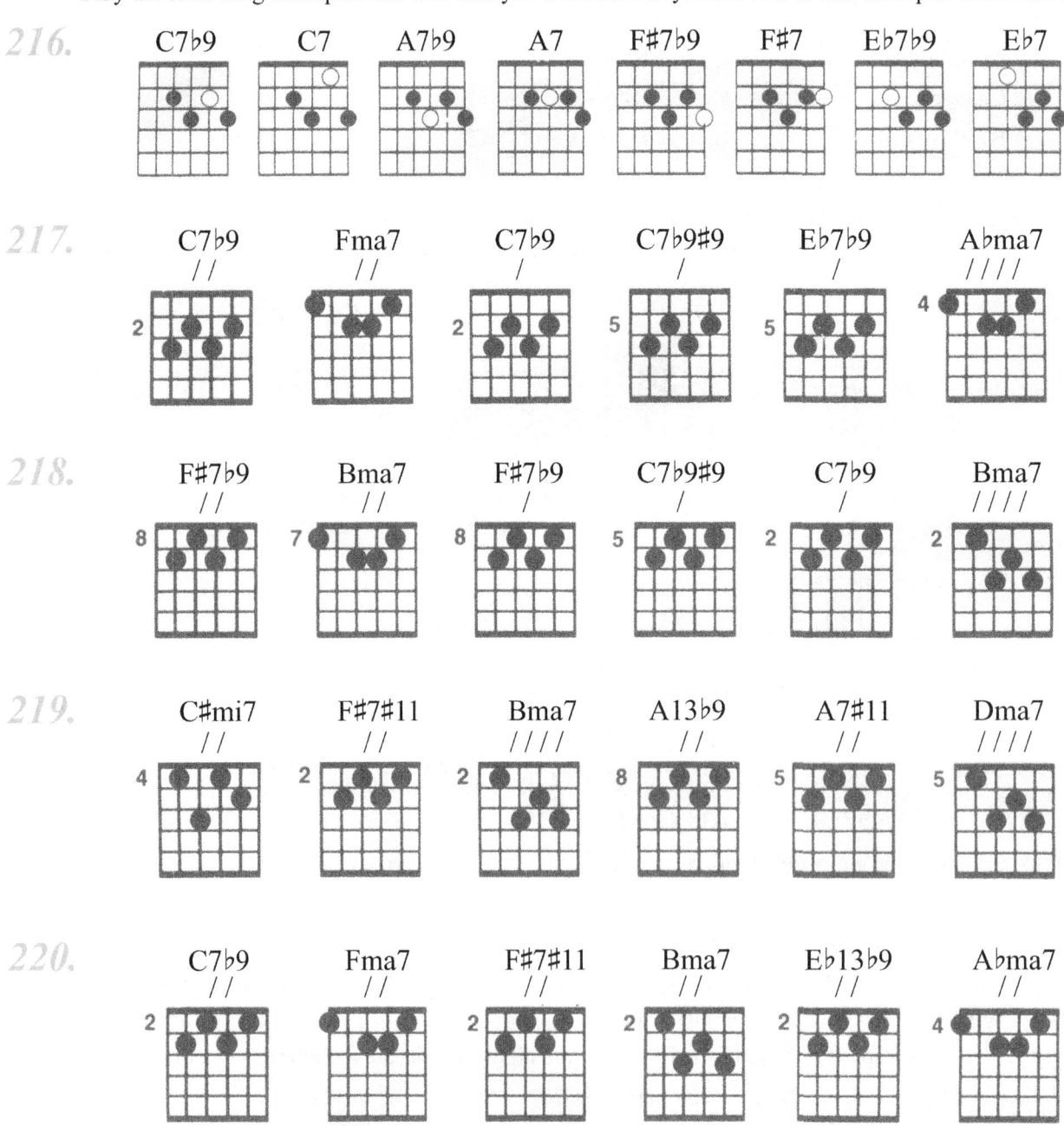

216.   C7b9   C7   A7b9   A7   F#7b9   F#7   Eb7b9   Eb7

217.   C7b9 / /   Fma7 / /   C7b9 /   C7b9#9 /   Eb7b9 /   Abma7 / / / /

218.   F#7b9 / /   Bma7 / /   F#7b9 /   C7b9#9 /   C7b9 /   Bma7 / / / /

219.   C#mi7 / /   F#7#11 / /   Bma7 / / / /   A13b9 / /   A7#11 / /   Dma7 / / / /

220.   C7b9 / /   Fma7 / /   F#7#11 / /   Bma7 / /   Eb13b9 / /   Abma7 / /

Augmented Chord Substitution

As noted earlier, the augmented chord is another equal interval chord. The interval is a *major* third:

$$C \quad E \quad G\# \quad C$$

Like the diminished chord, any note in the chord can be the root of an augmented chord with the same notes.

```
                                C    E    G#    C
                                     E    G#    C
                                          G#    C    E
```

Caug = C E G#   Eaug = E G# C   G#aug = G# C E
C7#5 = C E G# B♭   E7#5 = E G# C D   G#7#5 = G# C E F#
                                                        (A♭7#5 = A♭ C E G♭)

E7#5 =   E G# C D
C9#5 = C E G# B♭ D
E7♭5 =   E G# B♭ D

If this is true then: E7#5 (and Eaug) are both inside a C9#5 chord.

and C7#5 (and Caug) are both inside an A♭9#5 chord (G#9#5)

and G#7#5 (and G#aug) are both inside an E9#5 chord;

And it turns out that E7♭5 is inside a C9#5 chord. The C whole tone scale shows why.

$$C \quad D \quad E \quad F\# \quad G\# \quad B\flat \quad C$$

Perform your own analysis, if you're harmony oriented, and see the other synonyms that are possible.

Play the following examples and analyze them if you're comfortable with that. If not, compare the fingering shapes to see the similarities.

221.   C9#5   E7♭5

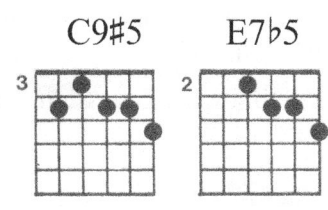

222.   Gmi9   C9#5   Fma7   Fma7

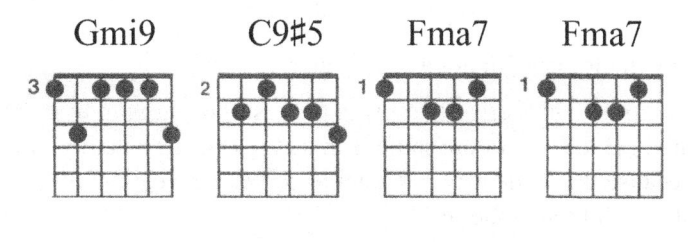

223.   Bmi7   E7♭5   Ama7   Ama7

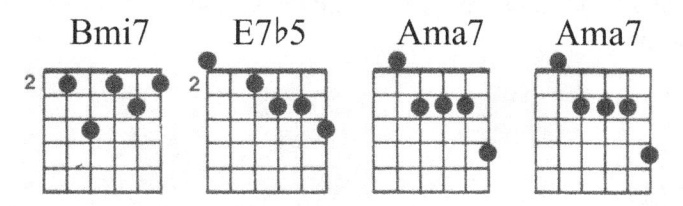

Cycles in Chord Substitution

Introduction

As listeners who have grown up around western European music, we like the sound of a melody or chord moving the interval of a fifth.   C D E F G

                                  1 2 3 4 5   C up to G is the interval of a fifth.

This is no accident. A single musical note is actually composed of a *group* of frequencies. These frequencies are called "partials" or sometimes "harmonics."

Every individual note contains the same set of partials. The loudest frequency is the root. For the note C, the C note frequency is the loudest. The second loudest is a frequency up one octave - a second C note. The next loudest partial is a frequency up a fifth from the octave C partial. The partials continue up for several octaves (and down as well). Thus, whenever we've heard one note, we've been exposed to these partials, and in particular, to the fifth. That seems to be why we like sound of a fifth.

"Back Cycling" is a term used to describe the motion of chords in a particular progression. "Back" means moving backwards, while "Cycle" refers to a favored path of chords that occurs often in progressions. With our natural preference for intervals of a fifth, we've embraced the sound of chords whose roots move a fifth when we change chords. Back cycling refers to *preceding a given chord* with a chord a fifth above (or a fourth below) it. That is, if we're given a C chord of some kind, we can place a G chord before the C chord. Seems crazy at first glance, but that's how it works.

SPECIAL NOTE #1: When is a 5th not a 5th? When it's a 4th -   F G A B C D E F G

                                                                                  1 2 3 4 5

                                                                      4 3 2 1

The color of the chords is separate from the root. We are discussing only *root* movement. C7 to Gmi7, Cmi7 to G, and Cmi to Gma7 are all movements of a 5th in the root.

The colors of the chords are important and are part of the following discussion, but be sure you remember that the root movement is independent of the color.

C up to G is a 5th. C *down* to G is a 4th. C up to F is a 4th, but C *down* to F is a 5th.

SPECIAL NOTE #2: When else is a 5th not a 5th? Watch . . .

C to G to D to A to E to B to F - This series of roots is the result of moving through the C major scale in intervals of a 5th. But . . . B to F is not the same fifth as C to G. It's actually one half step smaller (a "flatted fifth"). Why? Because that's the way it occurs *inside the scale*. (We're going to discuss this more in a minute, but check it out and remember it.)

Now let's get into the rules about chord movement and the various ways to build new chord progressions when re-harmonizing a song.

Rule 1) "Any chord may be preceded by its own five chord (V)." This means that any chord you select can be considered a I chord, and can be preceded by the dominant chord of that key. (This could be rephrased; any chord can be preceded by a dominant chord the interval distance of a fifth above it (or a fourth below it).

Watch:

224.
```
Original Progression   C      C      C      C      F
                       ////   ////   ////   ////   ////
```

1. We select F as our target chord. (The chord into which we've decided to build a new progression.)
2. We say "F is the I of F Major, the V of F Major is C7."
3. We say "any I chord can be preceded by its own V, therefore we can precede F by C7."

```
New Progress/on        C      C      C      C7     F
                       ////   ////   ////   ////   ////
```

225. Let's do this again:
1. C7 is our target chord.
2. We pretend it's the I in this situation (even though it isn't the I chord in the key of the *song*, and it's a dominant chord).
3. We can precede any chord by its V; the V of C is G7.
4. We precede C7 with G7.

```
                       C      C      C      G7     C7     F
                       ////   ////   ////   //     //     ////
```

226. Let's try another example:

```
C7     G7
////   ////
```

1. G7 is our target chord, and we pretend it's a I chord.
2. The 5th of G is D. The V chord of G is D7. We get   C7   D7 G7
                                                       //// // //
3. Let's make D7 the target chord.
4. The 5th of D is A; A7 is the V chord of D. We get   C7 **A7** D7 G7
                                                       // // // //

This progression occurs frequently in the key of C at the end of songs as a "turn around."

To keep our discussion simple, I'm ignoring two very important parts of every song - the melody and the style. No matter how many rules we concoct, if the substitution doesn't sound pleasing, it's not useful on that occasion.

Let's look at our next rule; it's very similar to the first.

Rule 2) "Any dominant chord may be preceded by its own two chord(ii)." That is, when you find a dominant chord, you can pretend it is the V of a key, and you can try to put the ii of that key before the V. Watch:

227. Original Progression   C   C   C   C   F
                                 //// //// //// //// ////

Our First Substitution: C   C   C   C **C7**   F
                                 //// //// //// // // ////

Our Next Substitution:

     1.   Our target chord is C7. (A dominant family chord).

     2.   C7 is the V of F major.

     3.   Gmi7 is the ii of F.

     4.   We can precede C7 by Gmi7.

228. New Progression   C   C   C   **Gmi7 C7**   F
                             //// //// //// // // ////

Here it doesn't matter whether or not if the C7 is really the V chord of the *song*, as long as it's a dominant chord. *Notice that in the Gmi7 to C7 the root G is a fifth in front of the C.* Hmmm . . .

The first two additions occur so often, and ii - V is such a strong progression that we can combine the two moves into a single rule -

Rule 3) "Any chord may be preceded by its own ii-V."

     Let's start with this progression:

     1.   Our target chord is F   C   C   C   F

     2.   ii-V of F is Gmi7 C7   //// //// //// ////

     3.   New progression.   C   C   **Gmi7 C7**   F
                                      //// //// // // ////

Notice in this progression that we replaced C with Gmi7 C7. The Gmi7 - C7 are only there only because later there's an F chord. Watch:

229.   Original Progression   C   C   Ami   F
                                      //// //// //// ////

                      New   C   C   **Gmi7 C7**   F
                                      //// //// // // ////

We can build the same substitution regardless of the chord before the F (subject to it sounding OK).

230. Another Example: C   C   C   **C7**   F
                            //// //// //// //// ////

     1.   C7 is our target chord.

     2.   We call it the I of its key even though it's dominant!!! The chord color doesn't matter.

     3.   ii - V of C is Dmi7 G7 We precede the C7 with these chords-

                               C   C   **Dmi7 G7**   C7   F
                               //// //// // // //// ////
                                           ii   V

231. Let's try this progression:

```
               C     C     C     Gmi7 C7   F
               ////  ////  ////  //   //   ////
```

1. Our target chord is Gmi7.
2. We assume the root is the I chord in its own key (even though it's a minor 7th chord).
3. The ii - V of G is **Ami7 D7.**
4. Our new progression:

```
   C     C     Ami7 D7  Gmi7 C7   F
   ////  ////  //   //   //   //   ////
```

Back Cycling Within a Major Key

So far we've been back cycling using the *interval of a perfect 5th.*

Rule 4) Another approach is to back cycle through chords from a *single key.* If a C major chord were our target chord, we'd get a complete back cycle that looks like this:

```
         Fma7  Bmi7b5  Emi7  Ami7  Dmi7  G7   Cma7
         IV    vii     iii   vi    ii    V    I
Root     F     B       E     A     D     G    C
                                   GFEDC
                                   5 4 3 2 1
                             DCBAG
                             5 4 3 2 1
                       AGFED
                       5 4 3 2 1
                 EDCBA
                 5 4 3 2 1
           BAGFE
           5 4 3 2 1
     FEDCB
     5 4 3 2 1
```

Read the chart above from *right to left* starting with the C. You'll find that the roots of the chords are 5 *scale tones* away from each other in each instance. This is the cycle of 5th's in a major key. It's called "back cycling" because we started with the last chord (Cma7, our "target chord") and worked BACKWARDS. Notice the color of each chord:

232.
```
     Em   Am   Dm   G7   C
     //   //   //   //   ////
```

The color of each chord is chosen because the chords are all in the Cmajor scale.

Let's look at some examples:

233.

Original Progression	C ////	C ////	C ////	C ////	F ////	F ////
1. V of C	C ////	C ////	C **G7** // //	C ////	F ////	F ////
2. ii - V of C	C ////	C ////	**Dm G7** // //	C ////	F ////	F ////
3. vi - ii - V of C	C ////	C **Am** // //	**Dm G7** // //	C ////	F ////	F ////
4. iii - vi - ii - V of C then ii - V of **F**	C ////	**Em Am** // //	**Dm G7** // //	**Gm C7** // //	F ////	F ////

♭5 Substitution and Half Steps

Rule 5) As you recall, the ♭5 substitution provided us with many new chord sounds, and we found that we could add the *7♭5 chord* as well. This sound can be generalized beyond this one level.

234.

Original Progression	C7		Fma7
Direct Substitution	C7♭5 ////		Fma7 ////
Direct Substitution Renamed	C7♭5 ///	F#7♭5 /	Fma7 ////
"Looser" Substitution	C7	F#7♭5	Fma7

If we focus our attention on the F#7♭5 moving to Fma7 we see that the ROOT movement is a half step.

In another area . . . Have you ever played Blues or Rock where you slid down into each chord from a chord one fret above?

235.
```
     C   F# |  F   C# |  C    C    Etc.
    ///  /  | ///  /  | //// ////
```

All of this leads us to two more rules regarding chord substitution:

- Any chord may be preceded by a *dominant* chord a half step above.

236.
```
  Cma7 F#7 |  F7   | Cma7 Am  E♭7 | Dmi7  G7
   ///  /  | ////  |  //  /   /   |  //   //
```

- Any chord can be preceded by its *own color* of a chord from a half step above.

237.
```
  Cma7   | Ami  E♭mi | Dmi7  G♭7 | G7
  ////   | ///   /   |  ///   /  | ////
```

The following example combines half step (♭5) concept and back cycling.

♭5 and Back Cycling Examples

Analyze the examples below, but remember these examples ignore MELODY. The purpose is to illustrate what the various rules look and sound like.

238.

Original Progression	C / / / /	C / / / /	C / / / /	F / / / /
1. ii - V of F	C / / / /	C / / / /	**Gmi7 C7** / / / /	F / / / /
2. ii - ♭V of F	C / / / /	C / / / /	**Gmi7 C7♭5** / / / /	F / / / /
3. ii *of* ♭V (renamed) of F (C#mi7 is the ii of F#)	C / / / /	C / / / /	**C#mi7 F#7♭5** / / / /	F / / / /

239.

Original Progression	C / / / /	C / / / /	Gmi7 C7 / / / /	F / / / /
1. V of Gmi	C / / / /	C **D7** / / / /	Gmi7 C7 / / / /	F / / / /
2. ♭V replaces D7 using a 7♭5 chord too	C / / / /	C **A♭7♭5** / / / /	Gmi7 C7 / / / /	F / / / /
3. ii of ♭V (A♭7)	C / / / /	**D♭mi7 A♭7♭5** / / / /	Gmi7 C7 / / / /	F / / / /
4. Replace C7 with C7♭5	C / / / /	**D♭mi7 A♭7♭5** / / / /	Gm **C7♭5** / / / /	F / / / /

240.

Original Progression	Bmi / / / /	E7 / / / /	Ami / / / /	D7 / / / /
1. Precede any chord by its own V (B7 is V of E7)	**Bmi B7** / / / /	E7 / / / /	Ami / / / /	D7 / / / /
2. ♭V replaces B7 (F for B)	Bmi **F7♭5** / / / /	E7 / / / /	Ami / / / /	D7 / / / /
3. Replace Dominant with ♭5	Bmi F7♭5 / / / /	**B♭7♭5** / / / /	Ami / / / /	**A♭7♭5** / / / /
4. Precede ♭V by its ii (F is ii of B♭ as a V)	**Fmi** / / / /	B♭7♭5 / / / /	**E♭mi** / / / /	A♭7♭5 / / / /

Back Cycling Substitution Review

The following table is a master reference listing the various rules we have covered so far. Study the table carefully and then play each example. To show how easily re-harmonizations work, the chords in the examples have been fingered wherever possible to include an *E note as the top melody note*.

This is the kind of situation you'll be dealing with when you use re-harmonization. The E note is included as a little "problem melody" (and this is also a useful chord melody exercise).

241. Original Progression   C   C   C   C   Fma7
/ / / /   / / / /   / / / /   / / / /   / / / /

1. Place V before 1 (F here)   C   C   C   C   **C7**   Fma7
/ / / /   / / / /   / / / /   / /   / /   / / / /

2. ii - V of 1 (F here)   C   C   C   **Gmi7**   **C7**   Fma7
/ / / /   / / / /   / / / /   / /   / /   / / / /

3. ♭5 of V (here C7 which becomes F#7♭5)   C   C   C   C   **F#7♭5**   Fma7
/ / / /   / / / /   / / / /   / /   / /   / / / /

4. ii - V and ♭V   C   C   C   Gmi7   C7   F#7♭5   Fma7
/ / / /   / / / /   / / / /   / /   /   /   / / / /

242. Original Progression   C   C   C   Gmi7   **C7**   Fma7
/ / / /   / / / /   / / / /   / /   / /   / / / /

5. ii - V of I where G(mi7) is I   C   C   **Ami7**   **D7**   Gmi7   C7   Fma7
/ / / /   / / / /   / /   / /   / /   / /   / / / /

The example from the prior page had   Ami7   D7
                                         / /   / /

243. 6. b5 substitution   C   C   Ami7   D7   **Ab7b5**   Gmi7   **C7**   Fma7
     of Ab7b5/D7b5   / / / /   / / / /   / /   /   /   / /   / /   / / / /

244. 7. b5 substitution   C   C   Ami7   Ab7b5   Gmi7   **Gb7b5**   Fma7
                                 / / / /   / / / /   / /   / /   / /   / /   / / / /

245. 8. Precede I by V7   C   C   C   D7   G7   C7   Fma7
     D7 - G7 - C7 - Fma7   / / / /   / / / /   / /   / /   / /   / /   / / / /

246. 9. Precede I by V7   C   C   A7   D7   G7   C7   Fma7
     A7 before D7   / / / /   / / / /   / /   / /   / /   / /   / / / /

247. 10. b5 substitute   C   C   A7   Ab7b5   G7   Gb7b5   Fma7
     for D7 and C7   / / / /   / / / /   / /   / /   / /   / /   / / / /

As mentioned earlier, the b5 substitutions often place chords a half-step in front of the next chord. You should consider the half-step approach to a chord as a separate but connected idea to the b5 substitution rule.

Let's walk through the F major scale chords, in fifths, and starting from the IV chord - Bbma7.

248.
IV	vii	iii	vi	ii	V	I
Bbma7	Emi7b5	Ami7	Dmi7	Gmi7	C7	Fma7

The example below steps through the F major scale from the vii chord.

249. b5 substitute

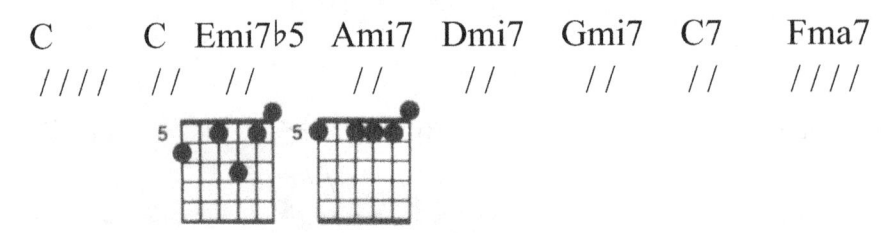

C	C	Emi7b5	Ami7	Dmi7	Gmi7	C7	Fma7
/ / / /	/ /	/ /	/ /	/ /	/ /	/ /	/ / / /

Notice how the Emi7b5 fingering, with a b5 in the bass, suggests a half-step or b5 substitution.

Now consider the progression below, which is a simple jazz twelve bar blues in C major.

250.

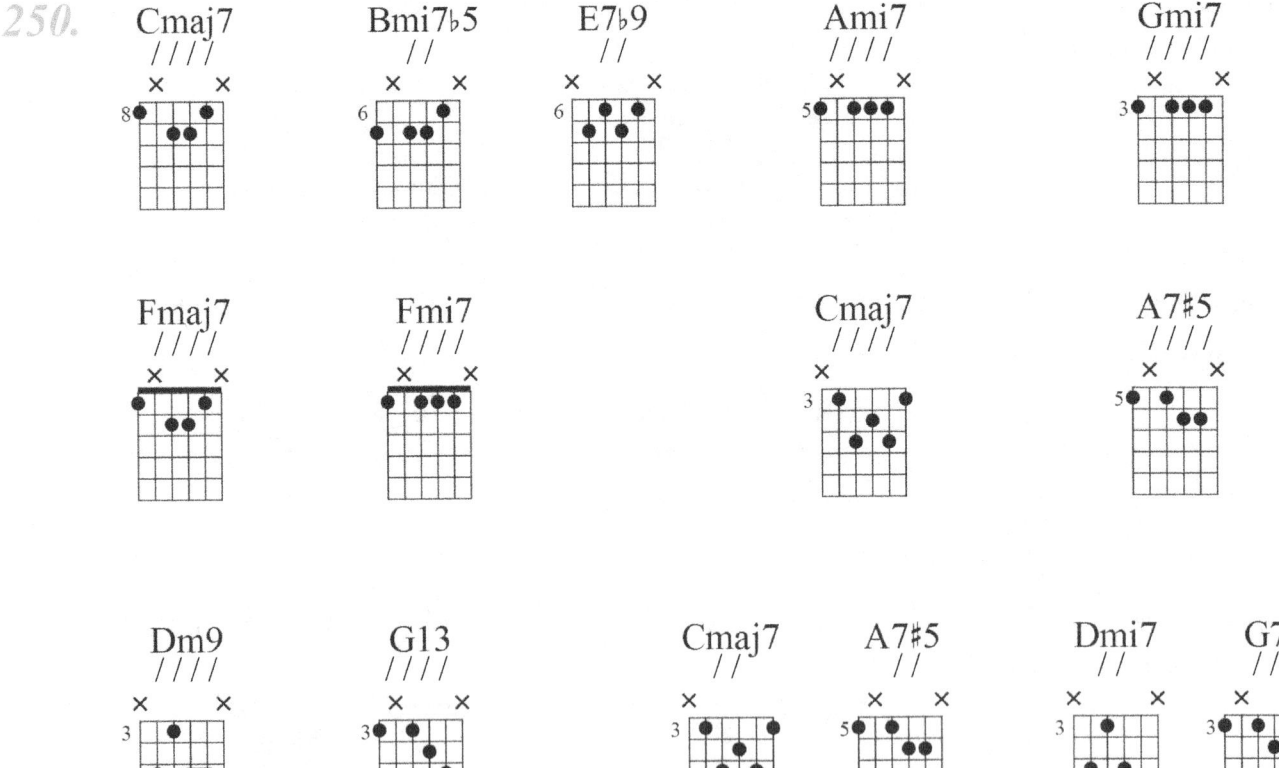

Cmaj7	Bmi7b5	E7b9	Ami7	Gmi7
/ / / /	/ /	/ /	/ / / /	/ / / /

Fmaj7	Fmi7	Cmaj7	A7#5
/ / / /	/ / / /	/ / / /	/ / / /

Dm9	G13	Cmaj7	A7#5	Dmi7	G7
/ / / /	/ / / /	/ /	/ /	/ /	/ /

The example above uses 6432 and 5432 stringsets. Can you move the progression to the 5321 and 4321 stringsets? Or move it all to the 4321 stringset?

Here's the prior example with additional chord substitutions. The third and fourth measures have ♭5 or half-step substitutions. Measure six has an embellishment of the mi7 chord.

251. | Cmaj7 | Bmi7♭5 | E7♭9 | Ami7 | A♭7♭5 | Gmi7 | G♭7♭5 |

| Fmaj7 | Fmi7 | Fmi6 | Cmaj7 | A7♯5 |

| Dmi9 | G13 | Cmaj7 | A7♯5 | Dmi7 | G7 |

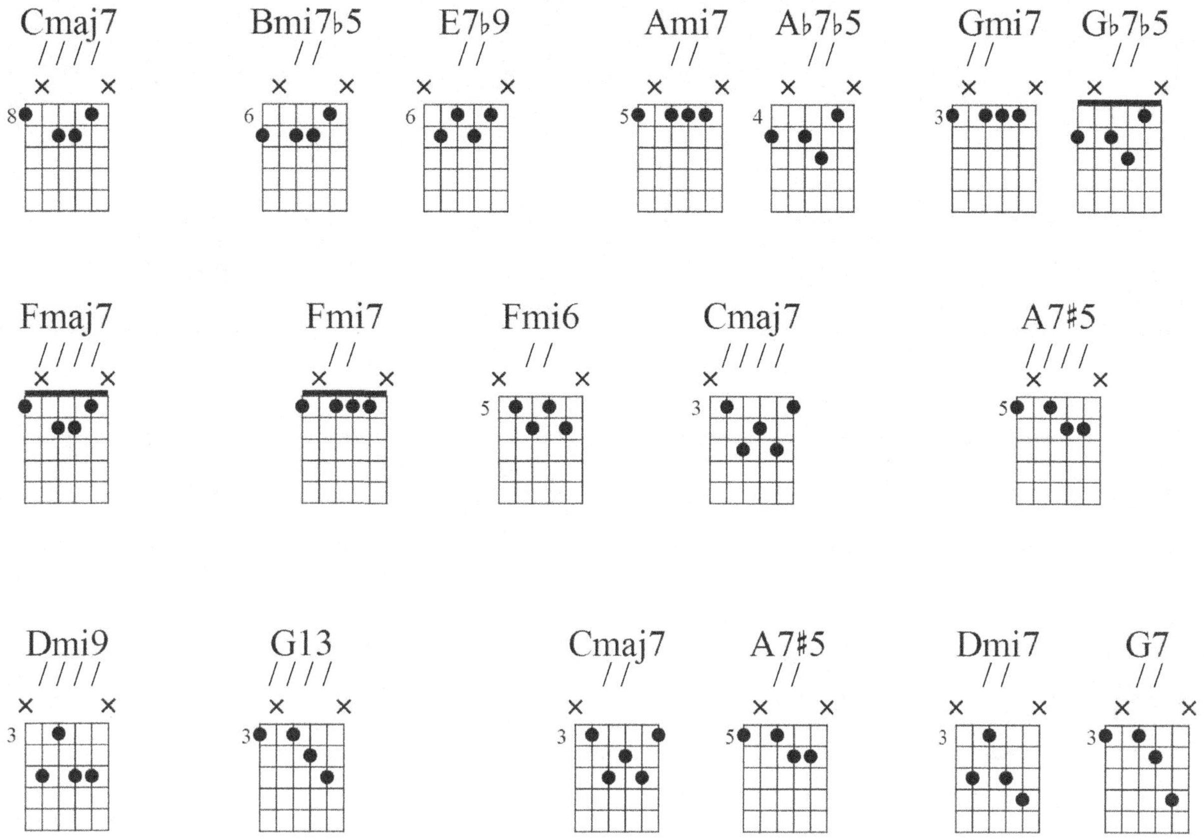

The traditional song "Dixie" is a good vehicle for experimenting with some of the concepts shown so far. Let's look at it in both stock and custom versions. The following example is showing accompaniment only. It is NOT a chord melody example.

252.

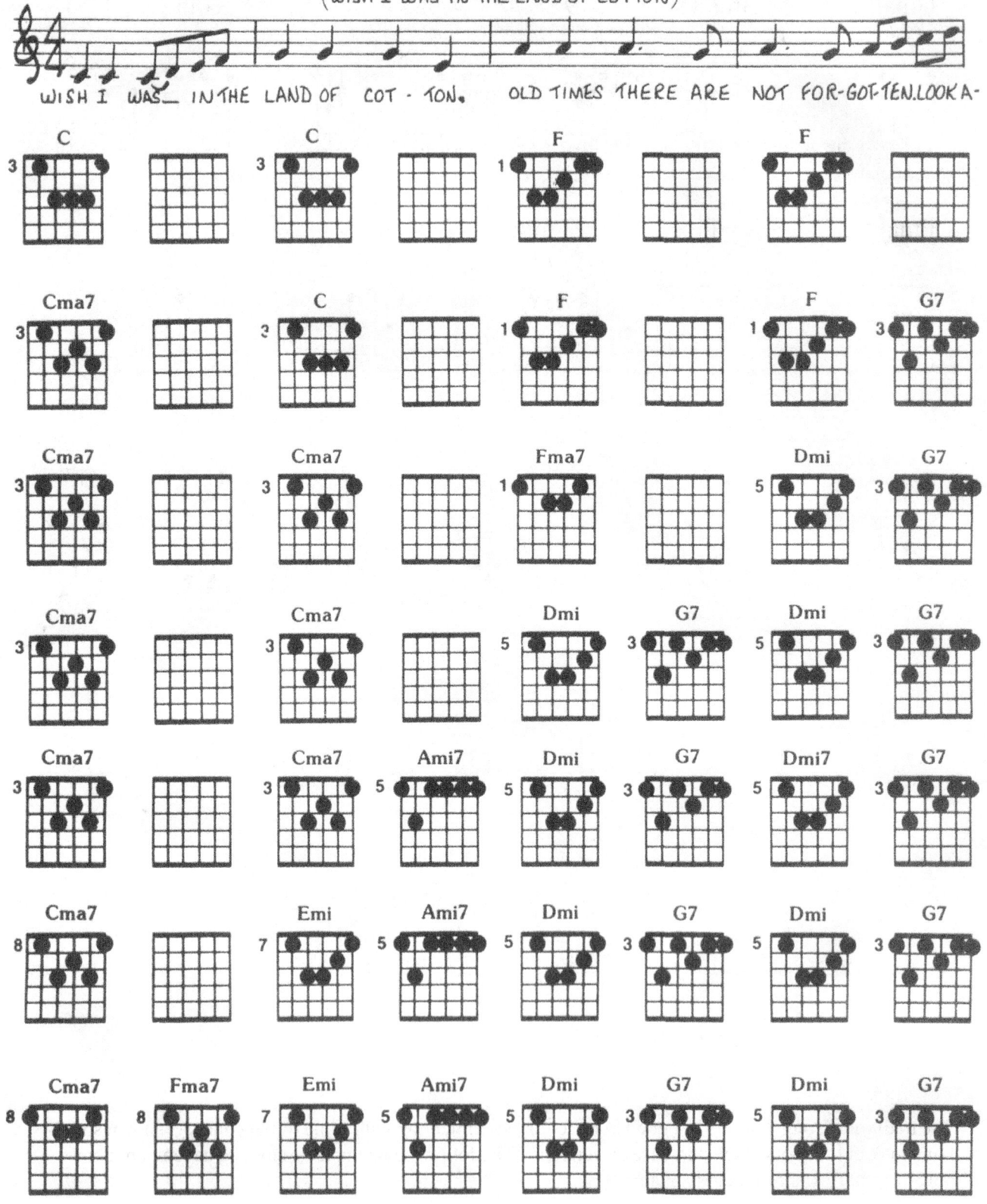

DIXIE
(WISH I WAS IN THE LAND OF COTTON)

WISH I WAS IN THE LAND OF COT-TON. OLD TIMES THERE ARE NOT FOR-GOT-TEN. LOOK A-

C		C		F		F	
Cma7		C		F		F	G7
Cma7		Cma7		Fma7		Dmi	G7
Cma7		Cma7		Dmi	G7	Dmi	G7
Cma7		Cma7	Ami7	Dmi	G7	Dmi7	G7
Cma7		Emi	Ami7	Dmi	G7	Dmi	G7
Cma7	Fma7	Emi	Ami7	Dmi	G7	Dmi	G7

253.

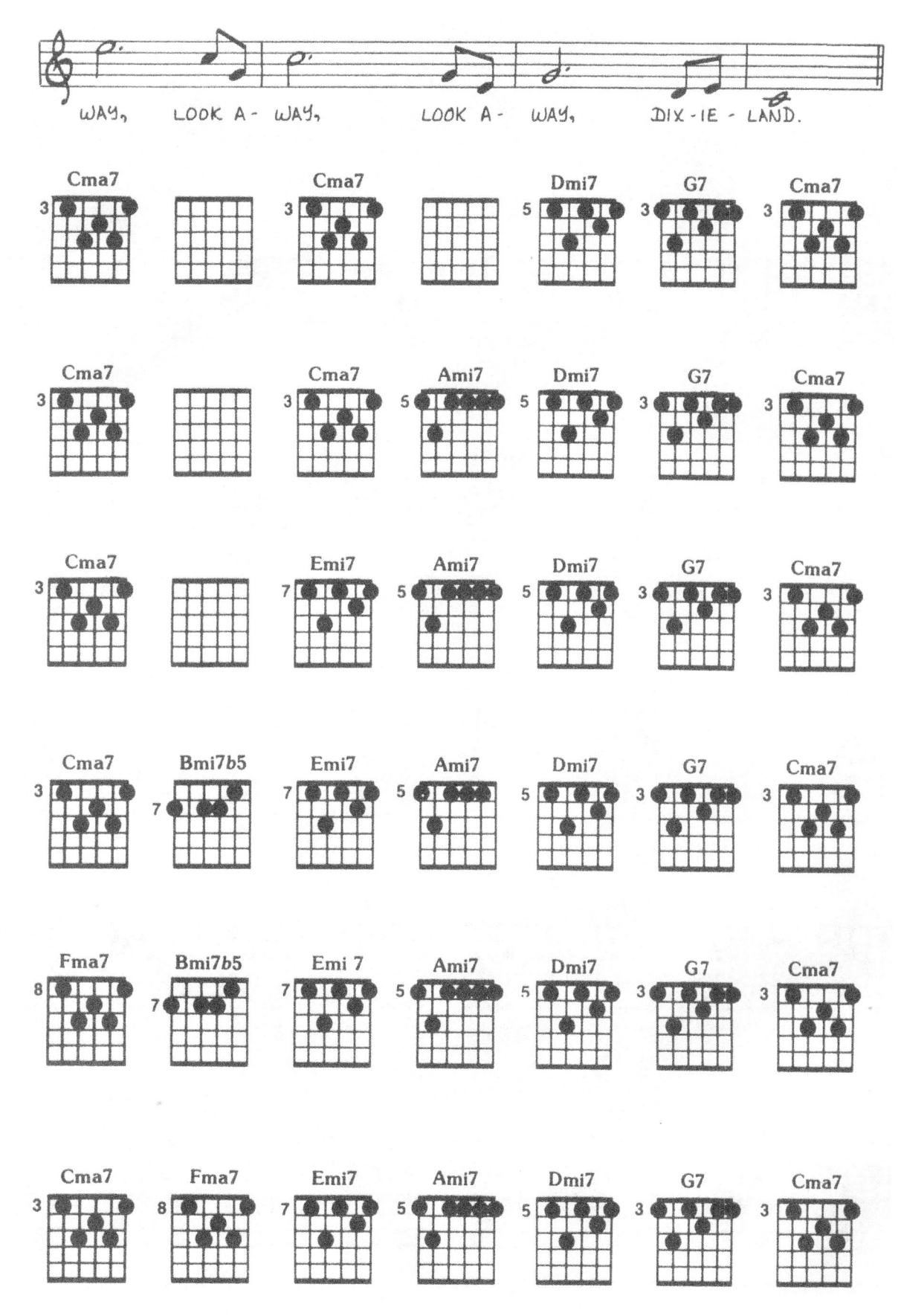

way, look a- way, look a- way, Dix-ie- land.

Cma7		Cma7		Dmi7	G7	Cma7

Cma7		Cma7	Ami7	Dmi7	G7	Cma7

Cma7		Emi7	Ami7	Dmi7	G7	Cma7

Cma7	Bmi7b5	Emi7	Ami7	Dmi7	G7	Cma7

Fma7	Bmi7b5	Emi 7	Ami7	Dmi7	G7	Cma7

Cma7	Fma7	Emi7	Ami7	Dmi7	G7	Cma7

DIXIE
(WISH I WAS IN THE LAND OF COTTON)

WISH I WAS— IN THE LAND OF COT-TON. OLD TIMES THERE ARE NOT FOR-GOT-TEN. LOOK A-

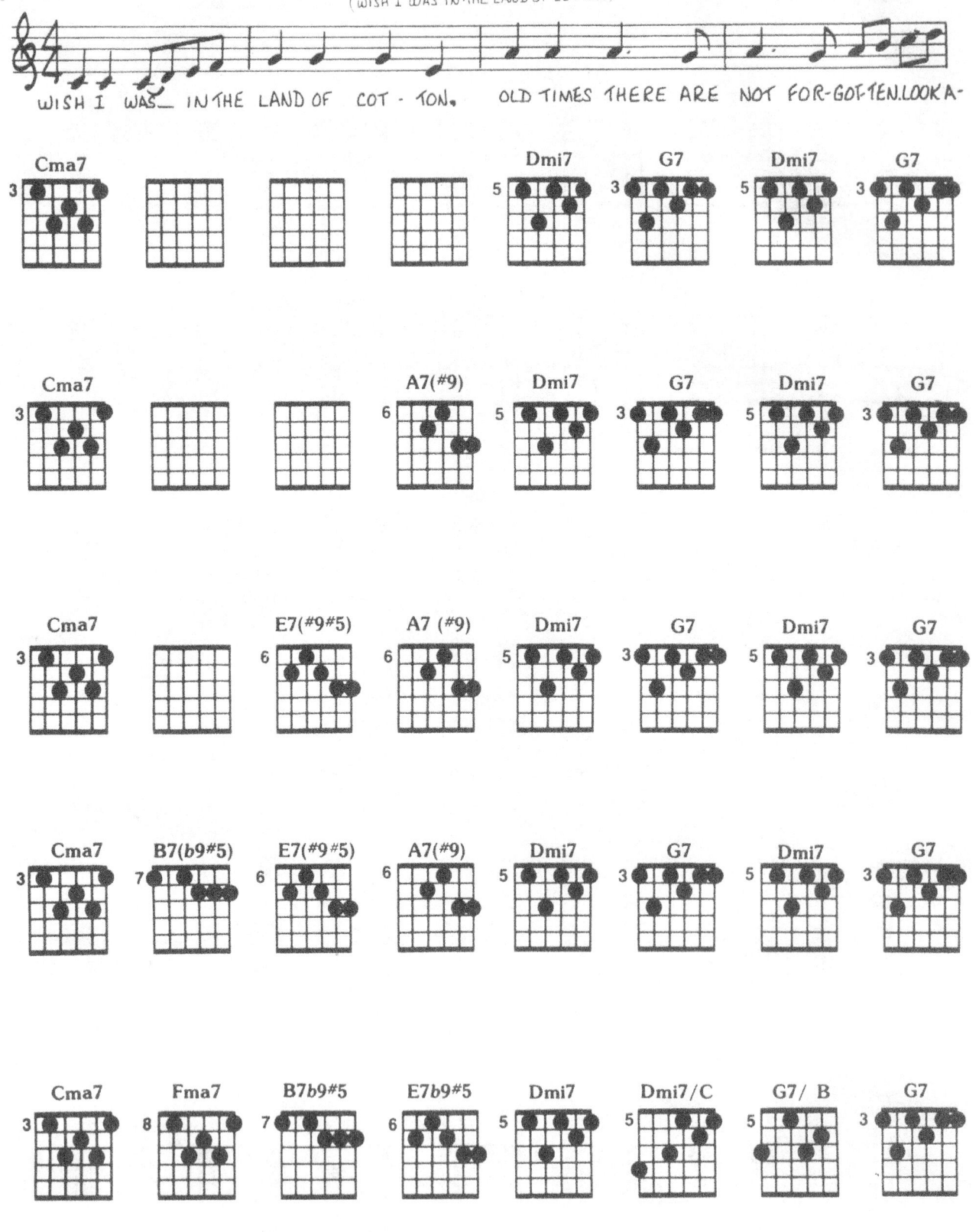

| Cma7 | | | | Dmi7 | G7 | Dmi7 | G7 |

| Cma7 | | | A7(#9) | Dmi7 | G7 | Dmi7 | G7 |

| Cma7 | | E7(#9#5) | A7(#9) | Dmi7 | G7 | Dmi7 | G7 |

| Cma7 | B7(b9#5) | E7(#9#5) | A7(#9) | Dmi7 | G7 | Dmi7 | G7 |

| Cma7 | Fma7 | B7b9#5 | E7b9#5 | Dmi7 | Dmi7/C | G7/B | G7 |

255.

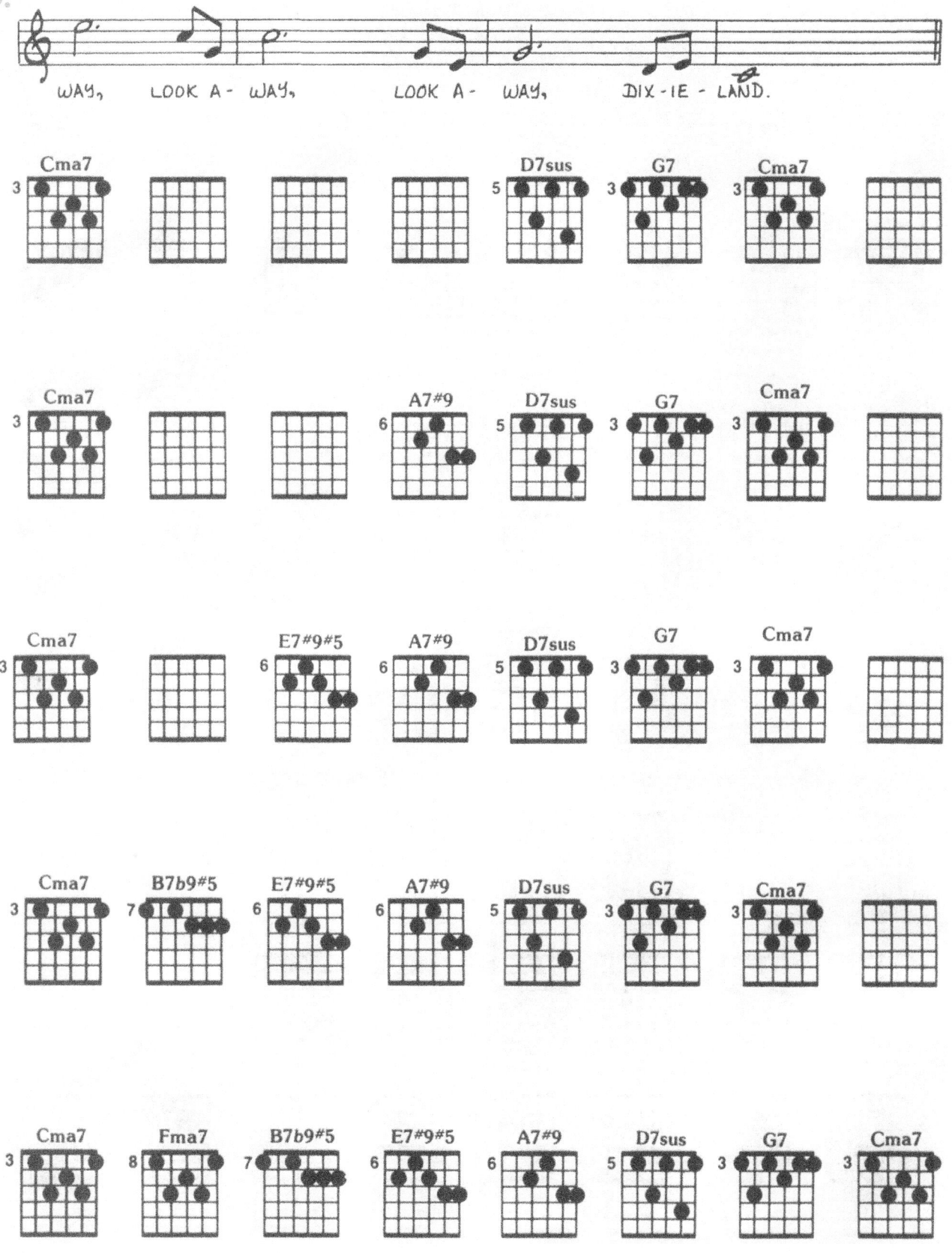

WAY, LOOK A- WAY, LOOK A- WAY, DIX-IE-LAND.

256. DIXIE
(WISH I WAS IN THE LAND OF COTTON)

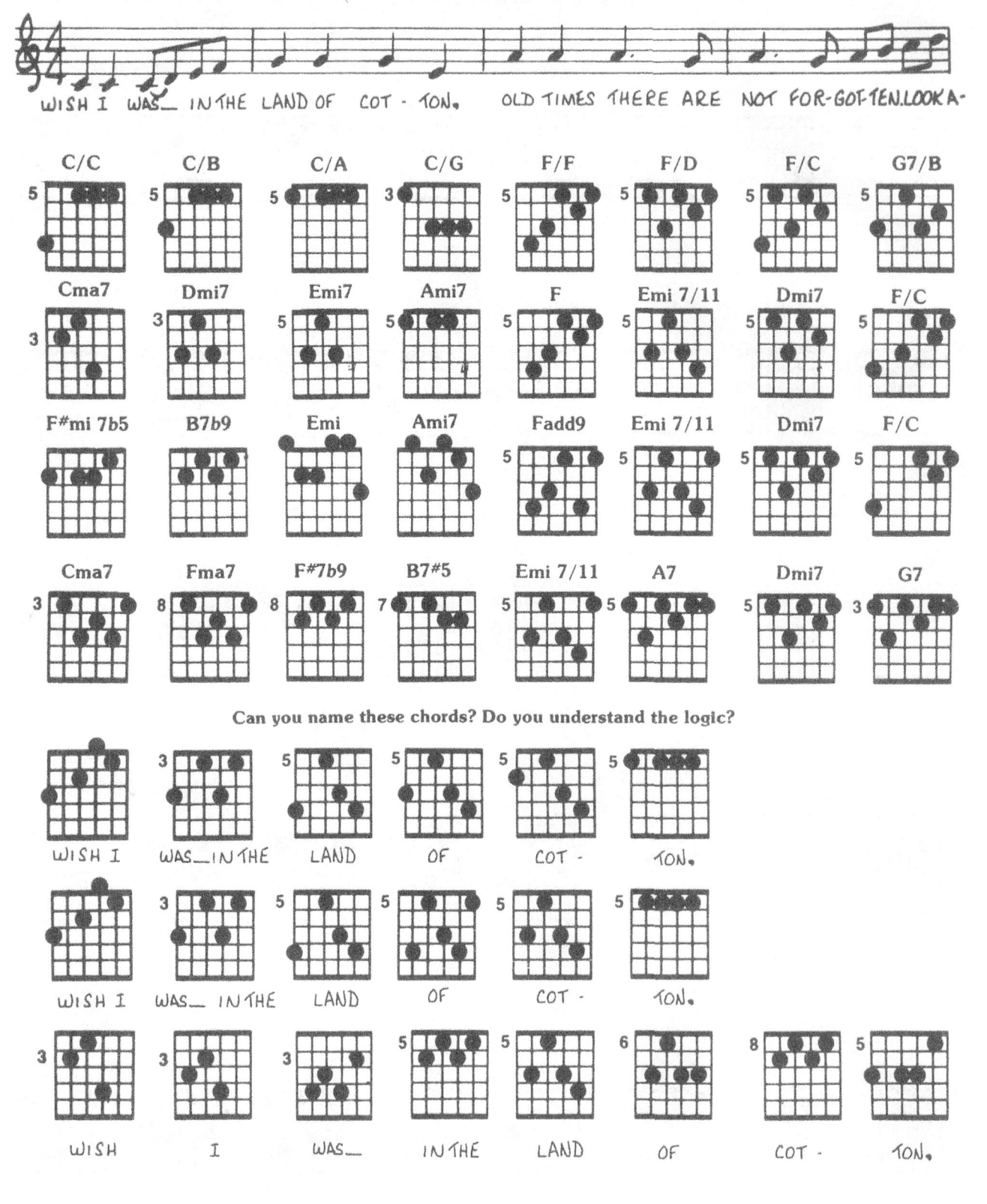

WISH I WAS_ IN THE LAND OF COT - TON. OLD TIMES THERE ARE NOT FOR-GOT-TEN. LOOK A-

C/C	C/B	C/A	C/G	F/F	F/D	F/C	G7/B
Cma7	Dmi7	Emi7	Ami7	F	Emi 7/11	Dmi7	F/C
F#mi 7b5	B7b9	Emi	Ami7	Fadd9	Emi 7/11	Dmi7	F/C
Cma7	Fma7	F#7b9	B7#5	Emi 7/11	A7	Dmi7	G7

Can you name these chords? Do you understand the logic?

WISH I WAS_ IN THE LAND OF COT - TON.

WISH I WAS_ IN THE LAND OF COT - TON.

WISH I WAS_ IN THE LAND OF COT - TON.

Changing Tonality

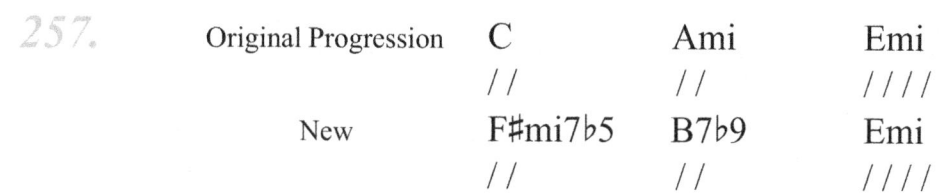

257.

Original Progression	C	Ami	Emi
	/ /	/ /	/ / / /
New	F#mi7b5	B7b9	Emi
	/ /	/ /	/ / / /

In the example above the original progression was moving along in the key of C major. The tonality of C major was changed to minor. In fact, because of the Emi chord, a ii (F#mi7b5) and a V (B7b9) were used to precede the Emi. Those two chords come from the E harmonic minor scale.

As it happens the changes were made by pianist Oscar Peterson on the verse of the song "Somewhere Over the Rainbow." Here's one version of it to try:

258.

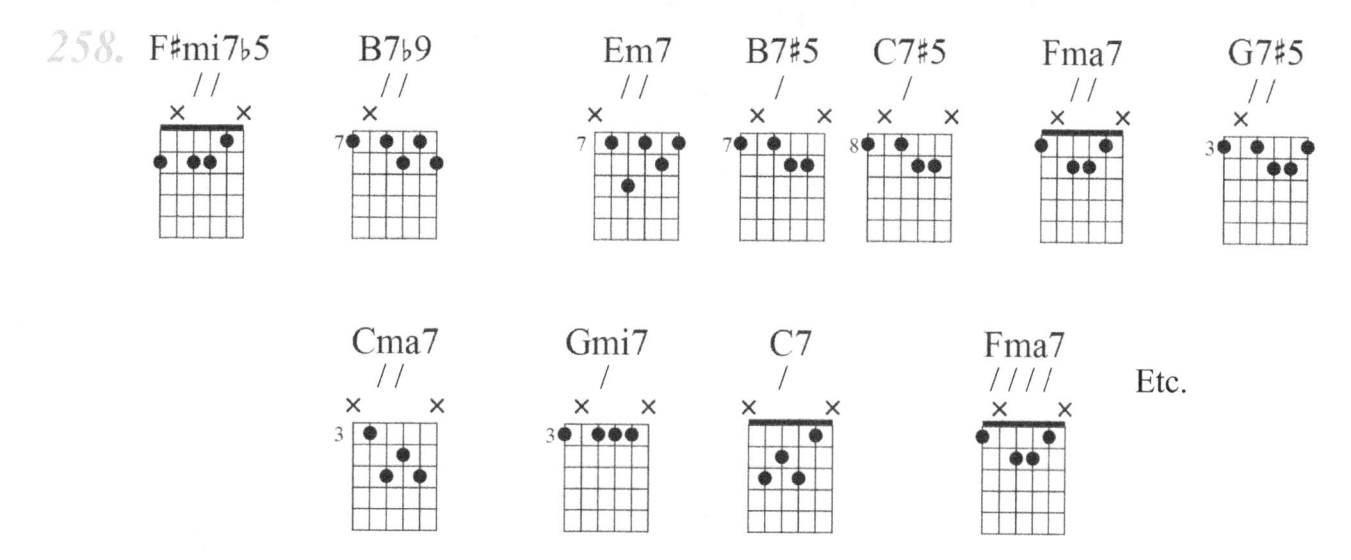

F#mi7b5   B7b9   Em7   B7#5   C7#5   Fma7   G7#5
 / /   / /   / /   /   / /   / /   / /

Cma7   Gmi7   C7   Fma7
 / /   /   /   / / / /   Etc.

We've been working with individual chords in enrichment, common tone substitution, and in back cycling. The change above relates to the *tonal center of the original song* and not to individual chords.

We can go a step further, and actually change the melody to conform to the new tonal center. While this might sound far-fetched, you've heard it in film scores and symphonic pieces (like Beethoven's Fifth Symphony) numerous times. It is an advanced concept, but in the examples that follow I've placed one obvious tonality change. While this kind of study is outside the scope of this book, see how it works, and try it yourself. My example goes from major to minor, but you can change to any tonal center that you like.

Your experimenting is taking you into the world of master guitarist Ted Greene. His recordings show these sounds in action.

To illustrate how tonality changes can be used to support a melody, here's the song "Oh, Susannah" arranged in three different tonalities: major scale, melodic minor and harmonic minor. Play it and analyze each example carefully, (remember, to fit the complete song into a new tonality the melody may also have to move).

259. OH, SUSANAH!

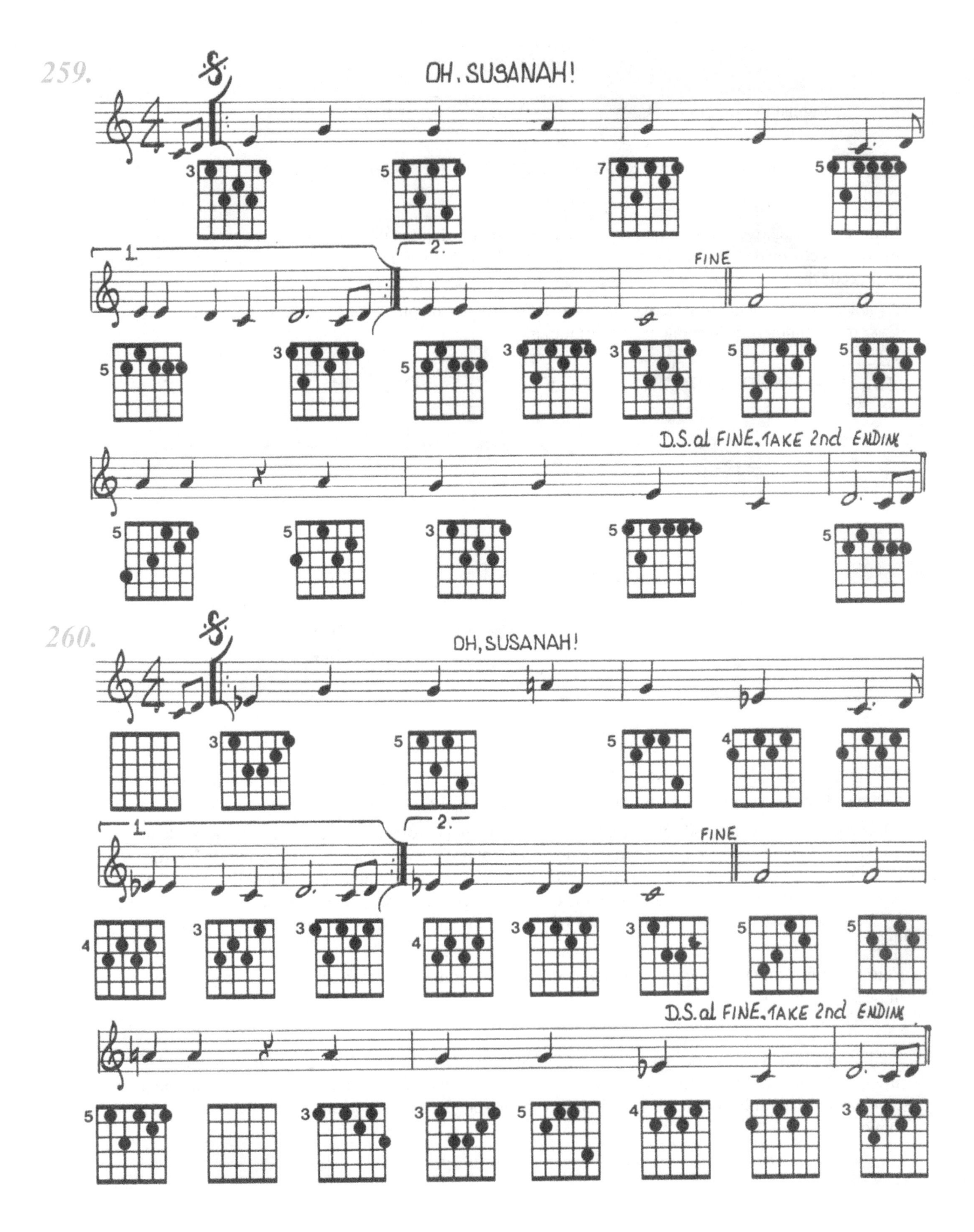

260. OH, SUSANAH!

261. OH SUSANAH !

Section 6 - References
Technique

Left Hand Techniques

Throughout the book I've pointed out the value of using barres and double stops to help with chord fingerings. And I've also discussed the value of being able to use different fingers for the same fingering.

262.

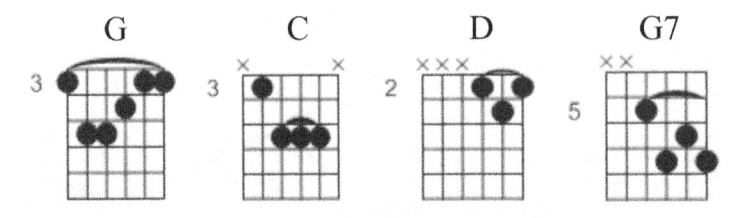

Left Hand Mute

There is an additional technique for controlling the sound of chords - the left hand mute.

While it is simple to perform, if you've never used it you may need some repetition to incorporate it.

Essentially you mute the chord by lifting the left hand fingers *up*, but not *off* the fretted notes. Good rhythm guitar playing requires that you both start and stop the chord sound when needed. Without the left hand mute you'll have sustaining notes and other noises creeping into your sound. The use of silence in between chord sounds is critical, and I cannot over emphasize your need to master this.

1. Press down on the fingerboard
2. Sound the chord
3. Lift up from the fingerboard while still keeping light pressure on the strings so they don't sound.

Left Hand "Lean Over"

Open chords, or fingerings with at least one open string both require that you find a way to mute the chord when necessary. One way is the right hand mute (see below). Another way is to use the left hand to stop the open string. There are a number of ways to do so, but the easiest is to just lift the left hand, as before, *and* lean one or more of your left hand fingers over against the higher neighboring string.

Vibrato

"Vibrato" is a term that refers to moving a pitch up and down in a controlled manner. You've may have seen guitarists holding a chord fingering down and seeming to rock their left hand back and forth. The entire chord will move very slightly in pitch - up as you move one way, and then back down when you return your hand to the starting point.

Right Hand Techniques

Right Hand Mute

The right hand mute is also fairly easy to perform, but may need repetition if you haven't used it. The idea is to mute the strings by placing the fatter part of your palm against the strings. Fingerstyle players may also use their right hand *fingers* to rest on the strings and stop the sound. The danger with using the palm movement is that it may alter the way you play with your right hand. My personal preference is the left hand mute, but on occasion I find myself covering all the strings with my right hand palm (for me it appears to be when playing acoustic guitar). Experiment and see what works for you.

Arpeggiating Chords

As noted earlier, "arpeggiating" a chord means to play the chord one note at a time. You can use this right hand technique to create a lot of different sounds, and get yourself out of some tight spots when changing chords.

This technique is often described as "fingerpicking," but many of the examples can also be played with a flat pick. However, I strongly recommend you learn to fingerpick if you currently play *only* with a flat pick. The emphasis in our discussion will be on ways to make more music out of chords, and not fingerpicking patterns for "This" or That" style of music.

The example below uses a version of TAB, but right hand tab. The chord box gives you the left hand fingering and the TAB gives you the right hand fingers, the strings to play, and the order in which the notes are played.

263.

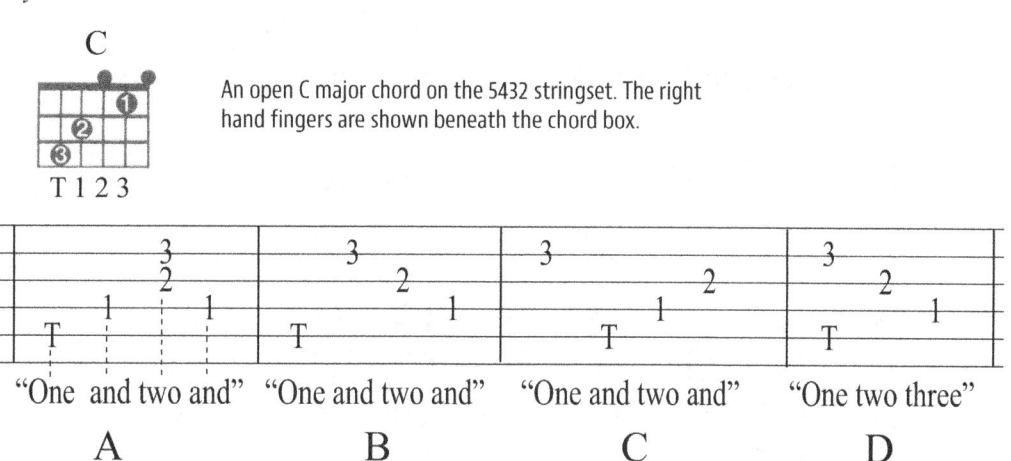

C

An open C major chord on the 5432 stringset. The right hand fingers are shown beneath the chord box.

T 1 2 3

```
"One and two and"    "One and two and"    "One and two and"    "One two three"
       A                    B                    C                    D
```

Each of the patterns above (A through D) are on the 5432 stringset, like the C chord. Since you know that stringset, you can play any pattern without having to look at your right hand.

- Ex. A is the most basic pattern and places the bass note first. To play the pattern for four beats, play it twice in a row.
- Ex. B has a more open sound as each note is sounded separately. The bass note is still first to anchor the sound.
- Ex. C starts with the highest chord tone. When changing chords quickly, this pattern may help you make the change if the highest note is the first left hand finger you get down on the second chord.
- Ex. D is a three beat pattern as the counting underneath indicates. ("Waltz anyone?")

If you're playing "hybrid" style, your thumb and index finger will hold the pick and you'll have to use your 2nd, 3rd, and 4th fingers to play these patterns. The weaker pinky will take a bit more practice, but the patterns are still easily learned.

To switch to chords to the 6432 stringset (like several of the examples in the 6432 section), keep your right hand fingers where they are and just move your thumb to get the 6th string.

All the examples in the book can be played using patterns like these, and you can make up your own, of course, and alter the rhythm. To get started however, basic patterns like these are all you'll need.

As you practice you'll feel the thumb as one part of the pattern and the group of three fingers as the second part of the pattern. You'll be able to feel where your right hand should be without looking. Part of the reason is the logic of the stringsets in the book - there are always at least three strings next to each other. Often you can just leave the three fingers in one spot and move the thumb around to get bass notes.

Harmony Quick Reference

The Chromatic Scale

The Notes

	C#		D#			F#		G#		A#	
C	|	D	|	E	F	|	G	|	A	|	B	C
	Db		Eb			Gb		Ab		Bb	

Scale Degrees:
Root, 2, 3, 4, 5, 6, 7
9, 11, 13

Major Scale Spellings and Seventh Chords

	I	ii	iii	IV	V	vi	vii	VIII	(I - Root)	Key Signatures
	Maj7	mi7	mi7	Maj7	Dom7	mi7	mi7b5	Maj7		
	C	D	E	F	G	A	B	C	C	No Accidentals
The 'Sharp' Keys	G	A	B	C	D	E	F#	G	G	1 #
	D	E	F#	G	A	B	C#	D	D	2 #
	A	B	C#	D	E	F#	G#	A	A	3 #
	E	F#	G#	A	B	C#	D#	E	E	4 #
	B	C#	D#	E	F#	G#	A#	B	B	5 #
The 'Flat' Keys	F	G	A	Bb	C	D	E	F	F	1 b
	Bb	C	D	Eb	F	G	A	Bb	Bb	2 b
	Eb	F	G	Ab	Bb	C	D	Eb	Eb	3 b
	Ab	Bb	C	Db	Eb	F	G	Ab	Ab	4 b
	Db	Eb	F	Gb	Ab	Bb	C	Db	Db	5 b
The SAME Keys	Gb	Ab	Bb	Cb	Db	Eb	F	Gb	Gb	6 b
	F#	G#	A#	B	C#	D#	E#	F#	F#	6 #
A Really Ugly Key	Cb	Db	Eb	Fb	Gb	Ab	Bb	Cb	Cb	7 b

Using the Table

The major scales are spelled from left to right. The Roman numerals are the degrees of the scale. Under each degree is the type of diatonic seventh chord found on that degree. To answer "What is the iii chord of D major?" Look on the left to root D. Look across to the third degree (F#) and look up to see the chord type - minor seventh.

Key signatures are on the right with the number of accidentals used. "Which key is two sharps?" The answer is D major (or possibly B minor, but that is outside our discussion here. Sorry. B is the vi chord of D major.)

Spelling Triads and Seventh Chords

Below are shown the basic triad spellings and the *seventh* chord spellings.

Root	Major Triad			7th	Minor Triad			7th	Dominant 7th Triad (major)			7th
C	C	E	G	B	C	E♭	G	B♭	C	E	G	B♭
F	F	A	C	E	F	A♭	C	E♭	F	A	C	E♭
G	G	B	D	F.	G	B♭	D	F	G	B	D	F
D	D	F#	A	C#	D	F	A	C	D	F#	A	C
A	A	C#	E	G#	A	C	E	G	A	C#	E	G
E	E	G#	B	D#	E	G	B	D	E	G#	B	D
B	B	D#	F#	A#	B	D	F#	A	B	D#	F#	A
B♭	B♭	D	F	A	B♭	D♭	F	A♭	B♭	D	F	A♭
E♭	E♭	G	B♭	D	E♭	G♭	B♭	D♭	E♭	G	B♭	D♭
A♭	A♭	C	E♭	G	A♭	C♭	E♭	G♭	A♭	C	E♭	G♭
D♭	D♭	F	A♭	C	D♭	F♭	A♭	C♭	D♭	F	A♭	C♭
F#	F#	A#	C#	E#	F#	A	C	E	F#	A.#	C#	E
G♭	G♭	B♭	D♭	F	G♭	B♭♭	D♭	F♭	G♭	B♭	D♭	F♭

To use the table look at the examples below.

C major triad is spelled C E G.

A C major seventh chord is spelled C E G B.

A C minor triad is spelled C E♭ G.

A C minor seventh chord is spelled C E♭ G B♭.

A C dominant seventh chord is composed of a C major Triad (C E G) and B♭.

A G minor seventh chord is spelled G B♭ D F.

To learning to spell triads (and then larger chords) you might try this trick:

Memorize this string of notes for sharp keys: **F C G D A E B**

Group the triads according to their accidentals:

F A C	**D** F# A	**B** D# F#
C E G	**A** C# E	**F#** A# C#
G B D	**E** G# B	**C#** E# G#
No accidentals	One accidental In the middle	Two accidentals on B, three on the rest

For flat keys, memorize the same string, but backwards:

<u>B E A D G C F</u>   The triads are grouped like this:

B♭ D F	E♭ G B♭	G♭ B♭ D♭
	A♭ C E♭	C♭ E♭ G♭
	D♭ F A♭	F♭ A♭ C♭
One accidental	Two accidentals on outside	Three accidentals

Interval Names

Diatonic Intervals	Non-Diatonic Intervals	Enharmonic Equivalents of Non-Diatonic Intervals
C-C Unison or Prime	C-D♭ Minor 2nd	C-C♯ Augmented Prime
C-D Major 2nd	C-E♭ Minor 3rd	C-D♯ Augmented 2nd
C-E Major 3rd	C-F♭ Diminished 4th	C-E♯ Augmented 3rd
C-F *Perfect 4th	C-G♭ Diminished 5th	C-F♯ Augmented 4th
C-G *Perfect 5th	C-A♭ Minor 6th	C-G♯ Augmented 5th
C-A Major 6th	C-B♭♭ (A) Diminished 7th C-B♭ Minor 7th	C-A♯ Augmented 6th
C-B Major 7th	C-C♭ Diminished Octave	
C up to C Octave or 'Perfect Octave'		C-B♯ Augmented 7th

The rules for naming intervals:

1. If any MAJOR interval is made *smaller* by one half step, the new resulting interval shall be called "MINOR." C to E is a major third. C to E♭ is a minor third.

2. If any PERFECT interval is made *smaller* by one half step, the new resulting interval shall be known as "DIMINISHED." C to G is a Perfect fifth. C to G♭ is a diminished fifth.

3. If any MINOR interval is made one half step smaller, the new resulting interval is also known as "DIMINISHED." The lone "C-B♭♭" interval in the middle of the table shows the diminished 7th - as would be found in the C diminished 7th chord. It was made by lowering the B♭ one half step.

4. If a MAJOR, OR PERFECT interval, is made one half step *larger*, the new resulting interval is called "AUGMENTED." C to A is a major sixth. C to A♯ is an augmented sixth.

5. C to F♯ is an augmented fourth. C to G♭ is a diminished fifth. These two intervals sound the same. Why the two different names? (This is an old hang-up but still in existence.) The ♯ implies that you RAISED the F to F♯ (Augmented) while the ♭ implies that you LOWERED the G to G♭ (Diminished). It is still considered bad manners, and incorrect, to call C to F♯ a diminished fifth.

Other Stringsets

This book has focused on four stringsets, but there are many more. Their distribution of strings makes most of them useful only in fingerstyle playing however. While there are quite a few other possible stringsets, I'd like to show you a couple that illustrate the sound of multiple large intervals.

The first example uses triads on the 431 stringset (and ends on the 542 stringset - one string over). The large interval between the top voice and the next voice gives a very unique sound.

264.

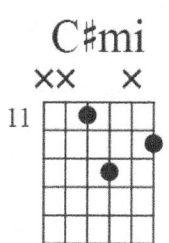

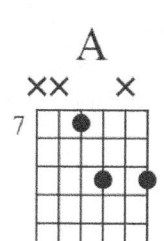

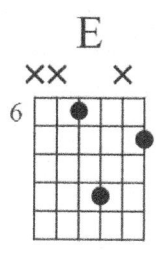

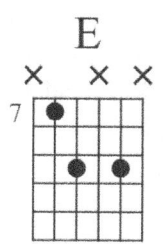

C#mi   A   E   E

Each chord receives two beats. After playing this, try adding melody notes on the highest string to connect the fingerings.

The next example uses four notes on the 5421 stringset (one empty string in between two pairs). The frets are high but that makes the stretches more manageable. The range is also better for this kind of figure. Use two beats for each chord.

265.

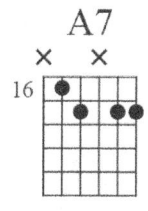

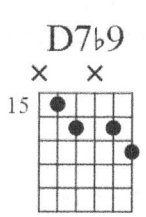

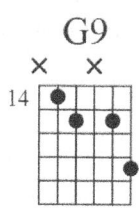

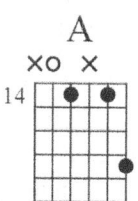

A7   D7b9   G9   A

The example above started out as part of a Ted Greene example that I heard someone else play. I've extended it in the final example below. Like the example at the top of the page, these voicings have the larger intervals. Here they suggest horn parts or other instruments than guitar. Each fingering should receive two beats.

266.

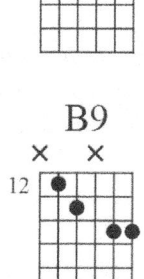

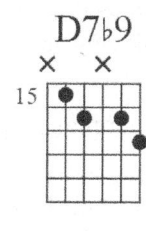

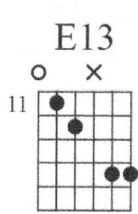

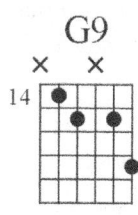

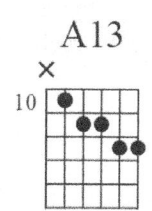

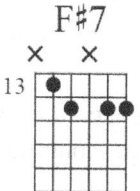

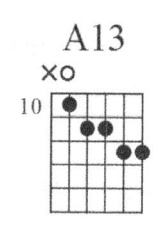

A7   D7b9   G9   F#7

B9   E13   A13   A13

The last A13 here shows an optional open string. Try it.

Other Reference Materials

For chords I recommend Ted Greene's book *Modern Chord Progressions Vol 1*. There are many short chord progressions that are beautiful. You'll need to apply your stringset logic and search for the stringsets you can play, but there are many adjacent string fingerings that are stunning.

For intermediate and advanced players, Ted's *Chord Chemistry* (with my PDF "A Trail Guide to Chord Chemistry") will show you chord melody and other great sounds and ideas.

Lastly, if you're looking for help with rock-country-blues-pop soloing, I hope you'll try my book "Styles for the Studio - 40th Anniversary Edition." It includes scales, arpeggios and how they all fit together much like Chord Systems. There are also over 100 backing tracks for the examples in the book available as a separate download. (It is a very large download!) There's more information on our website.

Epilogue

First, I'd like to say "thank you" for taking the time and effort in using my books. It means a lot to me.

Chord Systems is a book that has been in progress for 40 years and I think that this version is by far the best. In some respects it may also be the most important because it breaks down the subject of chords on the guitar in a variety of ways. Doing so should help make chords more accessible to guitarists of all levels and interests.

A few additional thoughts:

All music is connected. I can't emphasize that too much, and Chord Systems is designed to show you the connections by sounds, fingerings, musical style, and harmony. If you've filled in some holes in your chord knowledge, or had some "ah-ha" moments when using the book, I'll feel I've done my job.

There is a great deal of information in the book, and it can be overwhelming to some players at first glance. Taking topics piecemeal can help you manage ideas and examples bit-by-bit without having to have worked in the entire book.

The book does not emphasize musical styles (it isn't 'country rock chords' or 'jazz chords'). The styles you've heard should pop out at you. More importantly, I hope you find chords you like and use them wherever you wish. Style can be a constraint, and there is no reason for that. As a guitarist, you should be confident enough to know when you *must* play in a certain style in one situation, but feel free to play whatever you feel the rest of the time. That kind of playing seems to be the most fun and the most satisfying to me.

One of the most useful techniques is listening. Listen to other players playing rhythm guitar. Listen to their tone, voicings, control, and intonation.

If you have questions or comments I hope you'll contact me and share them. Have fun, and don't be intimidated by other players or musical subjects. You can learn and play the way you wish. The teacher owes you the explanation and you owe yourself a good effort. That's all it takes. Good luck!

Leon White
lwhite@sixstringlogic.com